Subjugated Voices and Religion

Subjugated Voices and Religion

Edited by

Souad T. Ali and Emily Leah Silverman

SHEFFIELD UK   BRISTOL CT

Published by Equinox Publishing Ltd.
UK: Office 415, The Workstation, 15 Paternoster Row, Sheffield, South Yorkshire S1 2BX
USA: ISD, 70 Enterprise Drive, Bristol, CT 06010

www.equinoxpub.com

First published 2025

© Souad T. Ali, Emily Leah Silverman and contributors 2025

All rights reserved. No part of this publication may be reproduced or transmitted in any form or by any means, electronic or mechanical, including photocopying, recording or any information storage or retrieval system, without prior permission in writing from the publishers.

British Library Cataloguing-in-Publication Data

A catalogue record for this book is available from the British Library.

ISBN-13	978 1 80050 671 8	(hardback)
	978 1 80050 672 5	(paperback)
	978 1 80050 673 2	(ePDF)
	978 1 80050 711 1	(ePub)

Library of Congress Cataloging-in-Publication Data

Names: Ali, Souad T. editor | Silverman, Emily Leah editor
Title: Subjugated voices and religion / edited by Souad T. Ali and Emily Leah Silverman.
Description: Sheffield : Equinox Publishing Ltd, 2025. | Includes bibliographical references and index. | Summary: "This volume brings marginalized voices to the center of religious studies, theological and spirituality discourses"-- Provided by publisher.
Identifiers: LCCN 2025020342 (print) | LCCN 2025020343 (ebook) | ISBN 9781800506718 hardback | ISBN 9781800506725 paperback | ISBN 9781800506732 pdf | ISBN 9781800507111 epub
Subjects: LCSH: Women in Islam | Feminism--Religious aspects--Islam | Women in Judaism | Feminism--Religious aspects--Judaism | Feminist theology
Classification: LCC BP173.4 .S83 2025 (print) | LCC BP173.4 (ebook) | DDC 200.82--dc23/eng/20250716
LC record available at https://lccn.loc.gov/2025020342
LC ebook record available at https://lccn.loc.gov/2025020343

Typeset by Sparks Publishing Services Ltd—www.sparkspublishing.com

Contents

Introduction   1
Souad T. Ali and Emily Leah Silverman

Part I: Feminism, Spirituality, and Connection   11

1. Honoring "Our Mothers' Gardens": The Integration of Spirituality and Social Justice   13
   Arisika Razak

2. Shekhinah: Transgendered or Transvestite? A comparison of the *Zohar* and *Sha'are Orah*   33
   Emily Leah Silverman

3. Aspects of Old and New Approaches to Feminism in Islam: A Focus on the Middle East   52
   Souad T. Ali

4. Of Strange Strangers: Interconnected Others in Religion and Ecology   77
   Kimberly Carfore

Part II: Centering Marginalized Voices   89

5. Sufism, the *Shatahat*, and a New Examination of Al-Ghazali's Writings   91
   Souad T. Ali

6. Surprise! Four Jewish Thinkers' Views of the "Other"   108
   Emily Leah Silverman

7. Religion, Values and the Claims of Value Free Education: An Examination of My Teaching and Publications over Fifty Years   143
   Rosemary Radford Ruether

Part III: Solidarity and Activism — 155

8 Intersectionality, Solidarity, and Ultimately Flourishing — 157
Sarah E. Robinson

9 #OrlandoStrong: Yes, Baby, the Gay Bar is Still Our Church—Still Our Religion — 170
Marie Cartier

10 Bodies of Evidence and Why Thanxgrieving? — 177
Ibrahim Abdurrahman Farajajé

11 Moayyad — 195
Shiraz Abdullahi Gallab

Index — 197

Introduction

Souad T. Ali and Emily Leah Silverman

This anthology originated from the American Academy of Religion Western Region Conference in 2014, held at Loyola Marymount University with the theme "Subjugated Voices and Religion." We, Professors Souad T. Ali and Emily Leah Silverman, decided to work together as authors and co-editors to bring this volume to fruition.

We have a deep personal friendship and thought it would be exciting to co-edit this volume as a Feminist Muslim and Jewish Feminist. Souad T. Ali is a professor of Middle Eastern and Islamic Studies at Arizona State University. She is Sudanese-American and grew up in a Sufi family. She has lived and studied in London and the United States, and has been working on several issues related to subjugated voices including Sufism, Arab and Muslim women and feminists. An internationally acclaimed scholar, Souad has published extensively on gender, women's movements, politics, Sudanese studies, and secularism in Islam, often highlighting notable contributors to these areas. Her research and publications include three books, over thirty-five articles, and over one hundred conference presentations in her areas of expertise of Middle Eastern and Islamic Studies. Souad has also been a freedom fighter for peace, democracy, and justice in Sudan and the Middle East. Emily Leah Silverman is a visiting scholar at Graduate Theological Union and an ordained Konenet Hebrew Priestess. She has taught at GTU and San Jose State University, published two books and a number of research articles. Emily is an Ashkenazi Jew who was brought up in a Reform Jewish family and was sent to an Orthodox Day School. She works on retrieving the subjugated feminine in Judaism, with the understanding that, while in the USA Ashkenazi Jews are perceived as white people, in Europe Jews are viewed as the "other," a strange minority. Emily has published work on reclaiming the theology of spiritual resistance of the Catholic Jewish nun Edith Stein and the first woman Rabbi Regina Jonas, both of whom died in Auschwitz.

We feel our work together fosters dialogue between ourselves and our colleagues and role models the power of inter-faith dialogue and conversations which bring forth the voices of the other. Both Souad and Emily are former presidents of the American Academy of Religion/Western Region. When Emily came up with the conference theme, she pondered the methodologies used by religious studies scholars and how to create space for the voices of the marginalized, colonized, and displaced. This volume offers voices from different locations and disciplines bringing them into conversation with one another.

As this work progressed, American and world politics have regressed. We feel we are losing our democracy and that the Trump administration invited white supremacists to marginalize and murder non-whites. That administration enacted a war on immigrants and refugees by instituting the Muslim ban, expanding the border wall, and separating children from parents and subjecting them to deplorable conditions. Hate crimes have increased dramatically and many people of faith no longer feel in their houses of worship, especially since the Charleston church shooting, the shooting rampage at the Pittsburgh synagogue, and the massacre at the New Zealand mosques. Souad herself has been the victim of hate crimes. Black people are openly and increasingly murdered by police. Indigenous voices are repressed and their lands are used to destroy the earth, as with the creation of the Dakota Access Pipeline. Sadly, Roe v. Wade has been overturned since we started this project. That means women in a number of states have lost control of their bodies and are condemned to suffering and possible death. War is being waged on the environment when our highest priority needs to be slowing down climate change to prevent the extinction of our own species and that of others. There are no safe spaces; children can no longer go to school without worrying about being killed, people can no longer feel safe congregating in their houses of worship, and people cannot go to movie theatres or shopping centers without the possibility of death. There is a war on reversing legislative rights for LGBTQIA+.

In 2019, there was a revolution in Sudan. The Sudanese people were attempting to remove their oppressive government through acts of non-violence by staging sit-ins and going on general strikes, but they were met with violence and massacres. Through this popular revolution, the Sudanese people were successful in removing dictator Omar Al-Bashir. Prior to that, the Sudan was on the verge of a civil war and the military dictatorship of the Bashir regime was conscripting child soldiers to fight Saudi Arabia's proxy war in Yemen. Although the Bashir regime was removed from power, the Sudanese people are still suffering under the current transitional government controlled by the military. The Sudanese Armed Forces (SAF) and Rapid Support Forces (RSF), which both inaccurately claimed their allegiance to the Sudanese people, want absolute control of the Sudan. Most recently, since April 15, 2023, war has broken out in the Sudan between the Sudanese Armed Forces (SAF) and the Rapid Support Forces (RSF). Businesses have been closed, a famine declared, and, as of today, millions of Sudanese people have fled from the country and have been displaced in neighboring countries or internally. It is a humanitarian crisis that has received very little attention from the world at large. However, the real story isn't the armed conflict. It is the deliberate campaign of ethnic and racial cleansing that is being systemically carried out in Darfur, a continuation of the brutal violence and genocide that started there in 2003. This has now spread into the Kurdufan and Nuba Mountain regions of the country. Non-Arab women and girls are being targeted, terrorized, raped and killed. Major cities in Southern Darfur, Nyala and Geneina, have been decimated. To date, the international community has focused on humanitarian responses and a flawed peace process which relies on the "good" faith of those very warlords responsible for this catastrophe. It is indeed a story of millions of subjugated voices of marginalized and displaced human beings.

In the interim of that 2014 AAR/WR conference to now, two of our plenary speakers and contributors have suffered greatly. We sadly lost Ibrahim Abdurrahman Farajajé to a massive heart attack in 2016. He was skeptical of the mainstream medical system for their systemic racism and negligence of Black people. Rosemary Radford Ruether suffered a massive stroke that left her with aphasia. Because of a dysfunctional medical system, she was not able to receive rehabilitation. Rosemary passed away on May 21, 2022. These acts of scholarship that comprise this collection are a form activism in response to the harsh political climate.

Chapter Outlines

The following chapters are organized into three parts thematically. The first part centers on feminism, spirituality and activism. Part two highlights particular marginalized voices. The third part offers examples of solidarity and activism.

In her essay, "Honoring 'Our Mothers' Gardens': The Integration of Spirituality and Social Justice" Arisika Razak discusses the important, yet often overlooked, intersection between spirituality and social justice. She starts her essay by discussing Western society's depiction of the "divine feminine," an idealized goddess woman who displays abilities and standards of beauty that are both unachievable and unrepresentative of every woman. Instead,

Razak advocates for the "divine feminist," calling on the reader to recognize the divinity of every woman in every feminist. This divine feminist accepts, acknowledges, and integrates secular feminism, religious studies, and ethnic/indigenous studies. To elaborate on the concept of the divine feminist, Razak draws on artists, activists, teachers, and scholars, some widely known and some unknown, from the African, Native, Queer, Latinx, and Islamic communities. For the divine feminist, drawing on spirituality and secularism when pursuing social justice is empowering.

Emily Leah Silverman's "Shekhinah: Transgendered or Transvestite? A comparison of the *Zohar* and *Sha'are Orah*," examines the views of Shekhinah from two thirteenth-century kabbalistic texts, the *Zohar* (*Book of Splendor*) and *Sha'are Orah* (*Gates of Lights*). Shekhinah, also known as Malchut (kingdom), is an attribute of God and is considered to be the feminine sphere or the feminine face of God. While interest in her has grown amongst Jewish feminists, further analysis of a scholarly nature is lacking. Silverman examines if it is possible to redeem Shekhinah from the texts and investigates if kabbalistic sources are valid for Jewish feminist theologies. The focus of Emily's discussion is how each text portrays Shekhinah's mutable gender qualities. In this preliminary investigation of a complex subject, Silverman examines the verbs and some of the symbols that each text uses to describe Shekhinah's dynamic and transformative nature.

Souad T. Ali's "Aspects of Old and New Approaches to Feminism in Islam: A Focus on the Middle East" identifies and discusses what she posits as three significant approaches to feminism within Middle Eastern societies with a particular focus on Egypt. There have been several reactions to feminism in the region. Some argue that feminism in Egypt emerged as a response to the British occupation in 1882 and feminist movements in the country date back to the 1890s, thus establishing feminism as a traditionally Arab concept. Others argue that the word feminism should not be used at all. Similarly, women differ in how they view the Arab world's interaction with "Western" feminism. These arguments have evolved throughout time, leading to three major groups of feminist thought in the Middle East: Islamic feminism, secular feminism, and Islamist feminism. One common theme found throughout the groups is that female subjugation is not inherent in the Qur'an. That being said, each group differs on where they believe patriarchal tendencies come from. This chapter examines each argument and discusses the merits and criticisms relating to each school of thought, effectively analyzing old and new approaches to feminist issues in Egypt within the context of the Middle East.

Kimberly Carfore's chapter is entitled "Of Strange Strangers: Interconnected Others in Religion & Ecology." While many theorists have done much to represent the voices of subjugated others (gendered, post-colonial, racial, and ethnic otherness), in this piece Carfore extends these theories of alterity by applying them to the field of religion and ecology. While an ethics of alterity can be inclusive to humans, she offers nuance and complexities involved when developing a non-anthropocentric ethics of alterity. Building off insights from ecophilosophy (Timothy Morton), ecofeminism (Val Plumwood and Karen Warren), eco-phenomenology (Ed Casey), and eco-deconstruction (Jacques Derrida), Carfore's contributions highlight religious dimensions of the ethics of Earth Others.

In Souad T. Ali's second chapter, "Sufism, the *Shatahat*, and a New Examination of Al-Ghazali's writings," she delves into al-Ghazali's contributions to Sufi literature. Focusing on al-Ghazali's discussions regarding the Sufi understanding of union with God and the temporary state of intoxication experienced by Sufis, this chapter contends that al-Ghazali's body of work sought to right many of the injustices levied against other Sufi scholars. It argues that al-Ghazali provides vital insight into re-examining the violence committed against such Sufi figures as Mansur Ibn al-Hallaj (d. 922) and Bayazid Bistami (d. 874). Using historical and textual analysis, this study elucidates that, contrary to widely held beliefs, al-Ghazali provided justification that the Shatahat, or exotic utterances of the classical Sufis, were not as they were perceived and that the speech of God's lovers should not be revealed but concealed and "not spread out." Furthermore, this chapter examines the legacy of al-Ghazali as evidenced through the extensive literature written about him in the last century.

In Emily Leah Silverman's second chapter, "Surprise! Four Jewish Thinkers' Views of the 'Other,'" she contends that Franz Rosenzweig, Martin Buber, Emmanuel Levinas, and Hannah Arendt all describe the moment of surprise when one is truly present with and encounters the Other. The major ideas of these Jewish philosophers took shape during the darkest times of the twentieth century with the principal texts of Rosenzweig and Buber emerging in response to World War I and those of Levinas and Arendt to World War II. In this light, we can appreciate poet Karl Wolfskehl's description of his encounter with a paralyzed, disease-stricken Franz Rosenzweig. The poet's encounter with Rosenzweig was nothing like what he had imagined. It was a type of "surprise," which is the primary concept to be examined in this essay. The life narratives of all four philosophers had an impact on how they approached and recognized the Other and realized this moment. Each describes the encounter from a different perspective, which can be demarcated by a notion of time and a structure of language. Yet, they are getting at the same paradoxical moment of experiencing and living in the present, the only moment in which we can truly engage with the Other. This paper chronologically analyzes these four philosophers' views of the Other and how they all lead to a sense of wonder and surprise

Rosemary Radford Ruether's plenary address for the 2014 American Academy of Religion Western Region is the basis for the chapter entitled "Religion, Values, and the Claims of Value Free Education: An Examination of My Teaching and Publications over Fifty Years." Ruether seeks to examine the relationship between the role of values in education, especially religious studies, and in particular the objective of value-free education. This leads to a retrospective of Ruether's teaching, research, and writing over a career spanning more than fifty years. Through these academic pursuits, she sought to locate women's voices in religious movements throughout history. Ruether notes that her interests have always been driven by her values and that this relationship serves the goal of addressing the injustices of the erasure of women's contributions and perspectives.

Sarah E. Robinson's essay, "Intersectionality, Solidarity, and Ultimately Flourishing," describes the importance of intersectionality and solidarity. She writes about these subjects in the context of her academic background in religious studies, and the current political climate since the 2016 Presidential election in the United States. Robinson draws upon Kimberlé Crenshaw's original definition of intersectionality, stating that race, religion, gender, class, sexuality, and age cannot be considered separately when examining social issues. Academics should dissect the socialized nature of many of these categories and how they function within society's power structures to better their research and communities. Solidarity, Robinson describes, is as crucial as intersectionality because solidarity provides voices to the voiceless. It is the obligation of those with privilege to support movements for liberation from oppression. Using the example of Rosemary Radford Ruether, a theologian and prominent figure in religious studies during the late 20th and early 21st century, Robinson highlights the need for the privileged to directly engage with the oppressed to gain perspective and increase the impact and effectiveness of their activism. By combining intersectionality and solidarity, individuals and communities will flourish.

Marie Cartier's chapter, "#OrlandoStrong: Yes, Baby, the Gay Bar is Still Our Church—Still Our Religion," is a memorial to the members of the LGBTQ+ community who were tragically murdered in a gun massacre at the Pulse nightclub in Orlando, Florida in 2016. Social media platforms enabled a rapid response with memorials and vigils held nationwide. The massacre underscored the significance of gay bars as sanctuaries for the LGBTQ+ community. Cartier further describes gay bars as sacred spaces, indeed the first spaces historically to offer solidarity, empowerment, and self-discovery to LGTBQ+ people. In remembering the forty-nine victims of the Pulse nightclub massacre, Cartier highlights the ongoing struggle for acceptance and the vital role these spaces play in the lives of queer individuals. This chapter celebrates the place gay bars hold in LGBTQ+ history, the author's personal experiences, and the vital role they continue to play for so many.

The late Ibrahim Abdurrahman Farajajé was a guerilla scholar; he viewed social media as a forum for subaltern voices to use to express themselves. His chapter is composed of two pieces: "Bodies of Evidence," an address for the 1998 AIDS and Religion in America Conference held in Atlanta, and an essay written for social media entitled "Why Thanxgrieving?" In the first, Farajajé introduces the terms HIV the@logies, innovative theologies derived from experiences and movements that seek to address and serve those with HIV in areas where traditional theology has fallen short, and HIV-in-intersection, which encourages people to acknowledge the intersecting issues and oppressions that are part of the HIV/AIDS crisis in an effort to liberate the self. The second piece, "Why Thanxgrieving?," dedicated to the late Jon Paul Hammond, shares the origin story of a yearly celebration within Farajajé's circle meant to take the place of traditional Thanksgiving and the historical baggage that accompanies that holiday. These writings continue Farajajé's legacy of love, solidarity, and resistance.

This volume closes with a brief but poignant reflection from Shiraz Abdullahi Gallab entitled "Moayyad" which memorializes her late cousin who tragically died on the Sudanese-Egyptian border in the midst of the current conflict in Sudan.

Taken as a whole, this volume strives to bring voices which are often left unheard into greater view, elevating stories of strength and resistance in the face of marginalization and oppression. These writings are an act of resistance. They speak truth to distortions and stereotyping. The act of scholarship and the retrieval of subjugated knowledge is a rebuke to repression. Contributors include prominent professors such as Rosemary Radford Ruether and emerging scholars in the fields of Religious Studies, Theology, Feminist Theology, Jewish Studies, Holocaust Studies, Muslim Studies, Latinx Studies, Women and Gender Studies, Women's History, Disability Studies, Feminist Studies, Religion and Ecology, Queer Studies, and Womanist Studies.

About the Authors

Professor Souad T. Ali is head of Classics and Middle Eastern studies, founding chair of the Arizona State University Council for Arabic and Islamic Studies, coordinator of Arabic Studies, associate professor of Arabic literature and Middle Eastern/Islamic studies in the School of International Letters and Cultures (SILC). She is simultaneously an affiliate graduate faculty member in English, women and gender studies, religious studies, and justice and social inquiry; as well as an affiliate faculty member in the Center for the Study of Religion and Conflict, African and African-American studies, Center for the Study of Race and Democracy, Institute for Humanities Research, and Arizona Center for Medieval and Renaissance Studies. A scholar with international recognition, Professor Ali is a recipient of several awards including, the ASU Faculty Women's Association Outstanding Graduate Mentor Award (2017); the ASU Outstanding Advisor of the Year (2019), among others. A Fulbright Scholar, Professor Ali is the author of *A Religion, Not A State: Ali 'Abd al-Raziq's Islamic Justification of Political Secularism* (University of Utah Press 2009). *The Road to Two Sudans*, an edited volume of which she is the lead editor, has been published internationally by Cambridge Scholars Publishing (2014). Ali's third book is *Perspectives of Five Kuwaiti Women in Leadership Roles: Feminism, Islam and Politics* (CSP, 2019). Professor Ali's impressive scholarship also includes over 30 scholarly articles in several languages, and more than 100 scholarly conference presentations. With degrees from prestigious institutions such as the University of Utah and Brigham Young University, as well as the University of Khartoum and the Polytechnic of North London, Professor Ali brings a wealth of knowledge and expertise to her work. She has held several key leadership roles, including serving as the past president of the American Academy of Religion/Western Region (AAR/WR), president of the Sudan(s) Studies Association of North America, and executive committee member of the International Association of Intercultural Studies (IAIS) in Cairo, Egypt and Bremen, Germany.

Kohenet, Dr. Emily Leah Silverman is a visiting scholar at the Graduate Theological Union, Berkeley, CA. She received Smicha (ordination) from the Hebrew Priestess Institute and is a recent Past President of the American Academy of Religion/Western Region. Silverman has developed the field study of Feminist Theology of Spiritual Resistance. Her current research is on the Feminist theology of Spiritual Resilience and Resistance of Jewish Women during the Nazi Holocaust. She most recently was an invited lecturer at the University of Wales and was formerly a lecturer at San Jose State University and taught at the Graduate Theological Union. Dr. Silverman also investigates the reclaiming and retrieval of Hebrew Priestess lineage, their 12 spiritual pathways and practice. Dr. Silverman was the organizer of Rosemary Radford Ruether Frestschrift and co-edited with Dirk Von der Horst and Whitney Bauman *Voices of Feminist Liberation: Writing in Celebrations of Rosemary Ruether*. Silverman has also published *Edith Stein and Regina Jonas: Religious Visionaries of the Death Camps*. Silverman is a sought after invited speaker. She holds a Master of Divinity from Harvard Divinity School and a Ph.D. from the Graduate Theological Union.

PART I

Feminism, Spirituality, and Connection

1 Honoring "Our Mothers' Gardens": The Integration of Spirituality and Social Justice[1]

Arisika Razak

I want to begin this piece by honoring "our mothers' gardens," a phrase taken from the essay, "In Search of Our Mothers' Gardens," published in 1983 by Alice Walker.[2] In this essay, Walker honored the many poor and working class Black women who were denied the time and leisure to create what the Western world deems as "art"—but whose work in designing quilts, making songs, or growing large, "ambitious (flower) gardens"[3] reflected their need to create beauty and art *regardless* of their circumstances. Her loving tribute to those who came before her reflects Indigenous protocols of respect which are embedded in many traditional spiritual practices of Africa and the Americas.

In these traditions, before any ceremony begins, the human community must acknowledge those who came before us, on whose shoulders we stand. In many holistic, embodied Indigenous religions, those who the West designates as "human beings" include the dead, the living, and the yet to be born. They include the recently dead, the elder, yet still remembered ancestors, and those ancestors born so long ago that they are seen as spiritual entities who stand as intermediaries between human life and the primal powers of the universe. These primal forces include the elemental powers of wind, water, earth, fire, metal and air; they include the life-giving and life-guiding presences of the sun, the moon, the mountains, and the stars. They include rivers, deserts, oceans and streams as well as herbs, plants, and forests. Finally, they include the spirit/s that animate all our human and non-human kin and the deities who preside over the entire web of life—those who have guided the life and work of our ancestors in the past, who continue to inform the life and work of our kin today, and who will, Spirit willing, continue to inform the lives of our children, grandchildren, and great-grandchildren.

Following this tradition, I begin by acknowledging the many artists, activists, teachers, and scholars who have not only contributed to my thinking, but who have made the world a better place through their thinking, their courage, their generosity, and their work. Some of the women I wish to acknowledge are established scholars whose written works are published and well known. Others, less well known, are community activists, healers, and religious practitioners. Some, nameless, and unknown, are mothers, community mothers, other-mothers[4] and elders, including the unknown ancestors who endured the unspeakable, in hopes that life would be better for their children. I am their descendant—and I would like to honor them with a poem by Luisah Teish[5] called "Mother of the Night:"

> I am the Mother of the Night.
> The Great Dark Depth, the Bringer of Light.
> All that was, that is, that ever shall be,
> All that could or should can only come from me.
>
> High above and far below.
> I am the ebb, I am the flow.
> The stars in the sky, the fish in the sea.
> Every seed, every stone, every critter is me.
>
> I am the Center, the Beginning, the End.
> I am without and I am within.
> I am the lair, the nest and the den.
> I am the Earth, the Water and Wind.
>
> The Horned Cow, the many-teated Sow, the Queen bee,
> the Mother tree, the Pregnant Womb, the Grain-seed broom, the candle's wick, the Matrix, and woman, you are my daughter.
>
> Praise and Love to the Mothers of the World. Praise and Love to the Sisters of the World. Praise and Love to the Women of the World. Praise and Love to my daughters.
>
> To the women in the fields, who plow and plant and turn mill wheels. To those who spin and weave at looms who make the mats, the cloth and brooms. To those who sew the royal robes, to those who pierce the child's earlobes. To those who rub and oil and braid. To all the Queens and all the Maids.
>
> Praise and Love to my daughters.
>
> To those who nurse babes on their breasts, who carry on without due rest. Then rise up early as the dawn to mend the fence and mow the lawn. To those who mix and stir the pot, to those who bake and clean and mop, to those who have and who have not.

Praise and Love to my daughters.

Praise and Love to those who seek, to those who know, and those who speak. To those who smile with tender eyes, whose wisdom penetrates the lies. To those who sing and those who cry. For those who fight for right and die! To those who live to ripe old age, to great-grandma the family sage.

Praise and Love to my daughters.

To those unborn and yet to come, we bid you on with song and hum. From other worlds and through birth-water. Come forth child, beloved daughter.

Praise and Love to the Mothers of the World. Praise and Love to the Sisters of the World. Praise and Love to the Women of the World.
Praise and Love to my daughters.[6]

In this poem, Luisah Teish, who is an initiated elder, an *Iyanifa*,[7] and a woman-chief, offers honor and praise not only to the Goddess and her daughters of the natural world, but to the many ordinary and extraordinary human women who are Her living embodiments.[8] The common tasks that she names are works that sustain, heal and enrich the world, making life possible and enjoyable for millions of people locally and globally. Even today, this work is carried out by millions of women throughout the world.

I know that, for some, the term "Divine Feminist"[9] is quite confusing. I want to acknowledge Dr. Alka Arora, Program Chair of the CIIS Women's Spirituality Program, for creating this term. In what is commonly called the Western worldview—and I do want to acknowledge that there are currently a variety of "Western" worldviews—the sacred and secular realms, if not opposed, are at least separate. "Divine feminist," therefore, is an attempt to bridge two very conflicting world views.

However, if we explore the work of borderlands/*nepantlera*[10] theorist, Gloria Anzaldua, we find that many of us live in the contested areas of conflict and convergence that frame the diverse and opposing paradigms in which we live. In an essay titled "La conciencia de la mestiza/Towards a New Consciousness,"[11] Anzaldua writes about the theorizing of Mexican philosopher Jose Vasconcelos in regards to *La Raza*, the multi-ethnic, bicultural people who emerged after forced encounters between the Spanish conquistadores and the Indigenous inhabitants of Latin America:

> Opposite to the theory of the pure Aryan, and to the politics of racial purity that white America practices, his theory is one of inclusivity. At the confluence of two or more genetic streams…this mixture of races rather than resulting in an inferior being, provides hybrid progeny, a mutable…species with a rich

gene pool. From this racial, ideological, cultural and biological cross-pollination, an "alien" consciousness is presently in the making – a new *mestiza* consciousness, *una conciencia de mujer*. It is a consciousness of the Borderlands.[12]

Developing this theory further, Anzaldua continues:

> Cradled in one culture, sandwiched between two cultures, straddling all three cultures and their value systems, la mestiza undergoes a struggle of flesh, a struggle of borders, an inner war. Like all people, we perceive the version of reality that our culture communicates. Like others having or living in more than one culture, we get multiple, often opposing messages. The coming together of two self-consistent but habitually incompatible frames of reference causes *un choque*, a cultural collision.[13]

While all of us do not (and should not) claim a *mestiza* identity, I would argue that many of us straddle traditional, non-traditional, and modern worldviews. We are trying to walk a path of integrity that honors and integrates older, more holistic practices with the more limited frameworks of the modern techno-industrial West in which we have been raised.

A *divine feminist* is one who walks the contested borderlands that have arisen between secular feminisms, religious studies, and ethnic/Indigenous studies. Standing at the crossroads where goddess studies, feminist studies in religion, and newer spiritual frameworks elaborated by people of color and others involved in the reclamation and renewal of women's and other oppressed genders' ancient and contemporary roles, rights, and powers meet. She, he, or they weave together Euro-centric perspectives on philosophy and religion with older frameworks drawn from goddess studies, ethnic/Indigenous studies and new paradigms arising in women, gender, and disability studies, to name a few of the transdisciplinary areas that women's spirituality touches upon. We are claiming and reclaiming ancestral traditions; we are using that knowledge to inform our activism; we are uncovering the original women-honoring traditions in frameworks labelled patriarchal; we are making alliances across difference and continually interrogating and challenging our work and the work of others.

While the terrain that the Divine Feminist walks is contradictory and perplexing, its breadth allows it to be more fully inclusive of our human lives and our human struggles. For example, the term itself is related to, but not synonymous with, the term "Divine Feminine." The Divine Feminine is a term which is often used to describe female divinities. However, as someone embedded in Western traditions who is still seeking to decolonize her mind, I believe that when we imagine female divinity, we all too often imagine a "Divine

Feminine" that is viewed as perfect: healthy, able-bodied, and *perfectly* beautiful—even though our standards may differ. All too often, we fall into a trap in which we choose the unattainable "ideal," rather than the material, the real, and the mundane in order to represent what is spiritual and "beautiful."

I have studied women's visionary art for a long time—and I finally understand what some of my students who reject the term "Divine Feminine" have been telling me. If we talk about a "Divine Feminine"; surely, she is different from the fat, imperfect, female body that sweats beside us at the gym, or who squats, ragged, and homeless on the street. The slender, full-breasted, long-haired, narrow-waisted, full-hipped "Divine Feminine" that is celebrated in contemporary artistic depictions of female divinity all too often looks like a white, brown, or golden-skinned Barbie doll, or even worse, a Playboy pinup.[14]

Even in women's goddess circles, we rarely see or imagine the Divine Feminine as being embodied by the genderqueer youth or the middle-aged butch; she is not the disabled woman with cerebral palsy or an elderly woman of color living with dementia in a nursing home. In the dominant culture's worldview that places us into binary boxes of good and evil, beautiful and ugly, white and non-white, young and old, able-bodied and disabled, and cisgender male and cis-gender female, we only count if we are able to successfully impersonate the values and embodiments deemed most worthy by the dominant culture. In addition, dominant culture values may be as embedded in the alternative movements we create as they are in the systems we struggle against. All too often, the Goddess—who in some traditions is a primary spiritual icon of liberation—is embodied by images reflecting the values of the dominant culture, rather than images that reflect our actual bodies.

Fortunately, all of us have roots in Indigenous traditions that valorized the "real" or material world as well as the spiritual realm. In many "traditional" Indigenous world views, everything is part of Creation—and everything is sacred. In a poem written by Native American (Mvskoke Nation) Joy Harjo titled "Remember," the poet states:

> Remember the sky that you were born under,
> know each of the star's stories.
> Remember the moon, know who she is. I met her
> in a bar once in Iowa City.
> Remember the sun's birth at dawn, that is the
> strongest point of time. Remember sundown
> and the giving away to night.
> Remember your birth, how your mother struggled

> to give you form and breath. You are evidence of
> her life, and her mother's, and hers.
> Remember your father. He is your life, also.
> Remember the earth whose skin you are:
> red earth, black earth, yellow earth, white earth,
> brown earth, we are earth.
> Remember the plants, trees, animal life who all have their
> tribes, their families, their histories, too. Talk to them,
> listen to them. They are alive poems.
> Remember the wind. Remember her voice. She knows the
> origin of the universe. I heard her singing Kiowa war
> dance songs at the corner of Fourth and Central once.
> Remember that you are all people and that all people
> are you.
> Remember that you are this universe and that this
> universe is you.
> Remember that all is motion, is growing, is you.
> Remember that language comes from this.
> Remember the dance that language is, that life is.
> Remember.[15]

This poem reminds us that in the Indigenous world, *everything* is sacred. I had intellectually been aware of this for decades, but its true meaning eluded me for many years. The good, the bad, the human, the non-human—all are part of the circle of life. As my friend, teacher, and colleague, Angelita Borbon, states, Indigenous thought is based on the three R's: respect, relationship and reciprocity. We live, she says, in an embodied universe in which there are numerous living entities, many of whom are not human. Our life is conducted in *relationship* to these entities, which include—but are not limited to—the elements of earth, air, fire, water, metal and rock; the plants, animals, birds, insects, microbes, and fish which share the earth with us; and sacred sites represented by mountains, rivers, forests, caves, trees and oceans.

According to San Francisco elder, healer, and Indigenous spiritual teacher, Dr. Concha Saucedo-Martinez, co-founder of Instituto De La Raza in San Francisco, we owe these powers *respect*, since they are the forces that make life possible. The Four Directions are not compass directions, metaphors, or psychological archetypes—they are the spiritual powers and sacred entities that enable human beings to live on this planet. Reciprocity, according to Borbon, means that what we do as humans, comes back to us. It is no surprise to Indigenous peoples that if we pollute the land and the waters, it will affect our lives—and the lives of our children and grandchildren. All things are connected and the acts we take or do not take have very real repercussions in the world.

In this world of sacred sentient life, we are all sacred because that is how we were born. We are not less sacred because we are disabled or different; the drunken woman who has abandoned her child has lost her way, but she is still a sacred being. She needs help and healing—and if she persists in following a particular road, certain consequences will occur. But she is still a child of the Creator. She is still a manifestation of the Divine. And, in some Indigenous traditions, which understand and accept the many roads that humans travel, there may be a special deity for the thief or the prostitute or the one who has lost their way. All are part of the circle of life.

The idealized Divine Feminine may not live in this realm, but the divine feminist transverses it. She knows that roads can change; she knows that light follows darkness and that darkness follows light. Braided together like life and death, suffering and ease, the divine feminist is the common woman that Judy Grahn writes about:

> She's a copper headed waitress,
> tired and sharp-worded, she hides
> her bad brown tooth behind a wicked
> smile, and flicks her ass
> out of habit, to fend off the pass
> that passes for affection.
> She keeps her mind the way men
> keep a knife—keen to strip the game
> down to her size. She has a thin spine,
> swallows her eggs cold, and tells lies.
> She slaps a wet rag at the truck drivers
> if they should complain. She understands
> the necessity for pain, turns away
> the smaller tips, out of pride, and
> keeps a flask under the counter. Once,
> she shot a lover who misused her child.
> Before she got out of jail, the courts had pounced
> and given the child away. Like some isolated lake,
> her flat blue eyes take care of their own stark
> bottoms. Her hands are nervous, curled, ready
> to scrape.
> The common woman is as common
> as a rattlesnake.[16]

She is all of it—the resistance, the survivor, the teacher, the healer. She is the abused woman leading other women out of brothels; the acid burned woman who walks with her scars publicly and tells others to resist. She is Lora Jo Foo,[17] the daughter of a Chinatown sweatshop worker—and a garment worker, herself at 11—who grew up to become a labor organizer and attorney and who broke the silence about her family's life in a memoir of photographs that document her healing. She is Dorothy Allison, the lesbian organizer of battered women's shelters who was kicked out of the feminist movement because of her alternative sexual practices.[18] She is Amina Wadud, an African-American Qur'anic theologian who proudly asserts:

> As a descendant of African slave women, I have carried the awareness that my ancestors were not given any choice to determine how much of their bodies would be exposed at the auction block or in their living conditions. So, I chose intentionally to cover my body as a means of reflecting my historical identity, personal dignity and sexual integrity.[19]

She is Doris Davis, an orthodox Jewish teacher from Long Island whose husband refused to grant her a divorce—effectively preventing her from being able to remarry within her community. With help from the Organization for the Resolution of Agunot,[20] she led rallies outside of her husband's home and posted his photo in synagogues in Brooklyn—protests which eventually led to his granting her a divorce.[21] She is you and me and women we will never see—and yes, she is divine because what is more spiritual than our liberty and freedom? What is more spiritual than struggling to stay alive and making a better world for those who you love—your family, your children, your community?

Moreover, the issue of spirituality can be problematic. The linkage of social oppression with dominant culture religious traditions has a long and multicultural history—and that legacy is very much alive today. Many feminist scholars are very aware of how women and other genders are affected by fundamentalist religious traditions both here and abroad. The Christianity taught to enslaved Africans by their Euro-American owners justified slavery and encouraged the slaves to be content with their lot. The ill treatment of Dalit people in India was justified by certain strands of Hindu religion. And, at different points in time, all three Abrahamic religions accepted the fact that female captives could become the sexual slaves of men who owned them. This means, and let me be explicit, that these women could be raped at will.

However, religion has also been used to support resistance. Sometimes, as in the example of *Osa Meji*, which is one of the Yoruba *odu*, or verses in *Odu Ifa*, the compendium of stories, proverbs, divinations and moral and ethical guidelines which form the body of the sacred oral "texts" of traditional Yoruba religion, even when sexism is postulated to exist at the time of Creation, it turns out not to be sanctioned by the Supreme Being. According to *Osa Meji*, when the original (17 in some versions and 401 in others) orishas, or deities, came to the earth to make the world habitable, they excluded Oshun, the only female deity who travelled with them, from their deliberations. Maulana Karenga's modern translation of the Yoruba text reads:

> This is the teaching of Ifa for Odu Obarisa and Ogun,
> When they were coming from heaven to earth.
> Odu asked: "O Olodumare, *Lord of Heaven*, this earth where we are going,
> What will happen when we arrive there?"
> Olodumare said that they were going to make the world
> So that the world will be good.
> He also said that everything that they were going to do there,
> He would give them the ase,[22] power and authority, to accomplish it,
> So that it would be done well.
> Odu said "O Olodumare this earth where we are going,
> Ogun has the power to wage war.
> And Obarisa has the ase to do anything He wishes to do.
> What is my power?
> Olodumare said: "you will be their mother forever.
> And you will also sustain the world."
> Olodumare, then gave her the power
> And when he gave her power, he gave her the *spirit* power of the bird.
> It was then that he gave women the power and authority so that anything men wished to do,
> They could not dare to do it successfully without women.
> Odu said that everything that people would want to do,
> If they do not include women,
> It will not be possible.
> Obrisa said that people should always respect women greatly.
> For if they always respect women greatly, the world will be in right order
> Pay homage; give respect to women.
> Indeed, it is woman who brought us into being
> Before we became recognized as human beings.
> The wisdom of the world belongs to women.
> Give respect to women then.
> Indeed it was a woman who brought us into being.
> Before we became recognized as human beings.[23]

Women and other oppressed genders are certainly at the heart of feminism as an activist enterprise—and I hope that this verse, which is as old as the Yoruba creation story—helps us understand how long sexism is postulated to have existed even in (some) non-Western cultures. However, the fact that sexism has existed for millennia, does not mean that it has always existed[24] —nor does it mean that women have always accepted it.

If we review the term "womanist," which was developed by Alice Walker,[25] I believe that we can better understand the term "divine feminist." While Walker had used the term *womanism* before, it is in the book *In Search of Our Mothers' Gardens: Womanist Prose* that she first fully defined the term *womanist*.[26] Walker developed this term to differentiate between the feminist (or liberatory) activism of Black women and the feminist activism of Euro-American women.

According to Karla Simcikova, "This definition…was in many ways a response to the white feminist movement of the time and its agenda, which was not particularly inclusive of or sensitive to black women's issues."[27] Beginning with the statement that a *womanist* was a Black feminist or feminist of color,[28] Walker's four part definition praised Black women's historic and contemporary ability to take leadership in liberation struggles benefiting *all* members of the African-American community.

However, a womanist, for Walker, was not only a social activist. Walker's womanist definition validated Black women's ability to love, support and nurture women and men "sexually and non-sexually";[29] honored the diversity, beauty and *"roundness"*[30] of black women's physical form/s, and proclaimed the importance of rest, healing, and self-care. In her definition of womanism, Walker also listed music, dance, Spirit, and the Folk[31] among the elements loved by womanists. Walker's holistic definition was also inclusive of many colors and ethnicities and, in her enumeration of the varied hues of humanity, she defined a womanist as a "universalist" rather than a separatist, citing as a metaphor both a garden of flowers and a family of many colors.[32]

While some Black women of diverse identities have embraced this term, others have rejected it. Some Black women prefer to be called Black feminists. Some Indigenous women prefer the term *tribalists*.[33] And there are other definers of the term "womanist" that support or reject Walker's definition either in whole or in part.[34] However, the work of supporting, improving, or reclaiming culturally appropriate rights of women and other genders is alive and well in a multitude of Indigenous and African societies. Writing of Africa, Filomina Steady states:

The birthplace of human life must also be the birthplace of human struggles, and feminist consciousness must in some way be related to the earliest divisions of labor according to sex on the continent. But even more significant is the fact that the forms of social organization which approach sexual equality, in addition to matrilineal societies where women are central, can be found on the African continent.... Above all, true feminism is impossible without intensive involvement in production. All over the African diaspora, but in particular on the continent, the black woman's role in this regard is paramount. It can therefore be stated with much justification that the black woman is to a large extent the original feminist.[35]

If we review women's roles in selected areas of West Africa, we see that, even in the patriarchal societies of the Yoruba and the Ibo, women: 1) held social and political roles of authority; 2) worked outside the home; 3) had the right to engage in money-making commercial activities and; 4) held roles of spiritual authority in their culture's religious institutions. The term "mother," which in the west connotes a lack of power in the "outside world" of politics, economics, and religion, is a term of authority and agency within many African societies. The Yoruba even have a term, *iyalode*, "mother of the outside,"[36] which is used as a title for the women who hold authoritative roles in the political, economic, and spiritual realms—e.g., the woman chief of the marketplace, the chief of the women's military organization, or the senior priestess who is involved with politics of the land. According to Oyewumi, kingship was not denied to Yoruba women, and she argues that several of the "kings" in Yoruba history were actually female.[37] Childbirth was neither unimportant nor secular. In a culture where the goal of existence was to be reborn again and again, it reflected spiritual harmony, social balance and *empowerment*.[38]

Rejected by many modern-day feminists as essentialist, the powers of birth giving and/or life making were—and in some cases still are—seen as magical, mysterious and *empowering* in many African socio-spiritual contexts. The figure of a woman kneeling in the traditional (active) stance of giving birth was often depicted in pre-colonial and/or "traditional" Yoruba sculptures. Stripping naked and exposing their vulvas was an act of women's power in many areas of pre-colonial Africa—especially when done by married or elderly women—and this has been repeatedly employed by African women of the 20th century in protests against government taxation, ecological depredations by oil companies, and in support of peacemaking efforts.[39]

Even in patriarchal settings, Nigeria's Ibo women could (collectively) go on sex strikes and "sit on a man"—e.g., go to war against an individual or a group who aroused their anger.

Judith Van Allen writes:

"Sitting on a man" or a woman, boycotts and strikes were the women's main weapons. To "sit on" or "make war on" a man involved gathering at his compound, sometimes late at night, dancing, singing scurrilous songs which detailed the women's grievances against him and often called his manhood into question, banging on his hut with the pestles women used for pounding yams, and perhaps demolishing his hut or plastering it with mud and roughing him up a bit. A man might be sanctioned in this way for mistreating his wife, for violating the women's market rules, or for letting his cows eat the women's crops...In tackling men as a group, women used boycotts and strikes. Harris describes a case in which, after repeated requests by the women for the paths to the market to be cleared (a male responsibility), all the women refused to cook for their husbands until the request was carried out. For this boycott to be effective, all women had to cooperate so that men could not go and eat with their brothers.[40]

I cite these issues because I want to clearly state that women in Africa were not waiting to learn about their oppression from Euro-American feminists. While sexism did exist in Africa prior to contact with Islam, Christianity and European colonialism, many cultures in Africa were not based on a model of gender *equity* but on the principle of *complementarity* in gender relationships. In such cultures, the powers of men were believed to be *balanced* by the power of women, ensuring that social, spiritual, and ecologic harmony prevailed.

Women often had power not as individuals but as part of a collectivity of women. Among the Nnobi of Nigeria, for example, there was a Women's Council that was responsible for the welfare of all Nnobi women: it set rules to regulate or protect women against physical abuse,[41] regulated the market, and independently acted to support the welfare of the town.[42] The *Agba Ekwe*, or most highly titled woman, was considered to be a representative of the Goddess Idemili herself, and only she and the shrine priest could consult with the Goddess directly. However, under Christianity and colonization, the authority and titles of men were readily translated into male norms of the colonial administration, while the authority and responsibilities of powerful women were seen as "pagan" and discontinued.[43]

Most of us understand that the struggle of women for justice and empowerment is a global one. My description of the precolonial power of African women is meant to help us understand that the issue of women's rights and powers in selected patriarchal non-Western societies is more complex than many of us have considered. However, while most of us would support political systems that provide justice and equality for women, many of us do not make the connection between liberation struggles and the practice of spirituality. For many of us, religion has created a divide between social justice and spirituality, for we have been raised entirely in a secular world, or one in which the material and spiritual realms are seen as separate.

I believe that everyone knows that the world needs to change. How we do it, with whom we do it, and with what tools, are some of the important questions we need to ask. And while we often contrast contemplative spiritual traditions with socially engaged or activist ones, I believe that a closer examination of diverse, traditional, contemporary and/or Indigenous spiritual traditions from around the world reveal that the questions we face today were not unknown to peoples of the past, nor to their colonized and oppressed descendants.

In some contemplative religious traditions, the material world, while beautiful, is not divine. Divinity—and sacredness—resides in a realm outside of material reality. If we suffer in our current physical world, it may be because of our transgressions in a previous life. It may be that suffering is the reality of our life on earth, and only after our death and release to a heavenly realm, or our rebirth as a member of a different caste or gender, that our earthly suffering will be reversed or redeemed.

In other traditions, some of which are branches of the same contemplative religions, we are called to take action to relive the suffering of all sentient life. The Bodhisattva Vow of Mahayana Buddhist tradition, which has been interpreted as meaning that we vow to return again and again to the world until all sentient beings have attained enlightenment, and the engaged Buddhism, under which some Buddhist monks burnt themselves to death to protest the Viet Nam war or provided healing to wounded soldiers and civilians on both sides of the war, were both spiritual and secular acts. In many Jewish traditions, one is expected to engage in the concept of *tikkun olam*—or the repair of the world—which has been interpreted by some as meaning that one is obligated to take righteous *social action* to foster the creation of a peaceful and egalitarian world that honors all races, ethnicities, spiritualities, orientations, genders, and abilities.

Many of the Indigenous peoples of the Americas understand that their spirituality is intrinsically linked to liberation from oppression. The ability to practice many Indigenous religions is often linked to particular landscapes which provide access to, and custody of, the sacred sites, plants, and other items that are necessary for the proper spiritual practices of particular First Nations peoples.[44] The right of access to their traditional lands, along with the right to speak the languages in which their spiritual traditions are embedded, and the right to have custody of their children and to train them in their ancestral ways, were rights that were denied to many Indigenous inhabitants of the USA for centuries. The reclamation of these rights—and they have not been granted to all First Nations peoples of the USA—has only come about because of political, spiritual, and activist struggles.

Whether we accept the notion of a spiritual and/or ensouled universe, or whether we find our most profound connection to legacies of human activism on behalf of justice, our human connections to the natural world remain. I would like to close with a poem by Alice Walker that invokes the union of spirituality and social justice—and that reminds us of the natural world's ability not only to sustain our bodies but to feed our souls. It is called "Torture":

> When they torture your mother /Plant a tree
> When they torture your father / Plant a tree
> When they torture your brother/ and your sister
> When they assassinate your leaders/ and lovers/ Plant a tree
> When they torture you/ too bad / to talk/ Plant a tree
> When they begin to torture / The trees / And cut down the forest they have made Start another.[45]

Notes

1. A version of this work originally appeared in *Integral Review* 13, no. 1 (2017). Used with permission.
2. Alice Walker, "In Search of Our Mothers' Gardens," in *In Search of Our Mothers' Gardens: Womanist Prose* (San Diego: Harcourt Brace Jovanovich, 1983), 231–243.
3. Ibid., 241.
4. This term arises out of the African-American notions of extended family and *fictive kin* which recognize biological motherhood as well as extended "family" relatives who take in, care for, and shelter the young of the community when their own parents are unable or unwilling to do so. While they may be called "mother," "aunt," "uncle," "cousin," etc., *fictive kin* may or may not be related by blood; sometimes they are related only by ties of affection. See Collins, Patricia Hill, *Black Feminist Thought: Knowledge, Consciousness, and the Politics of Empowerment,* 2nd ed (New York: Routledge, 2000), 179–183.
5. Luisah Teish, Woman-Chief, initiated elder, and *Iyanifa,* is an internationally known scholar, priestess and healer. Her works include *Jambalaya: The Natural Woman's Book of Personal Charms and Practical Rituals* (New York: HarperCollins, 1985); *Carnival of the Spirit: Seasonal Celebrations and Rites of Passage* (New York: HarperCollins, 1994).
6. Luisah Teish, *Carnival of the Spirit: Seasonal Celebrations and Rites of Passage* (New York: HarperSanFrancisco, 1994), 22–23.

7   *Iyanifa* is a priestly title in the Yoruba religious system that is granted to women who are considered "mothers of wisdom" or full diviners. See Badejo, Diedre, *Osun Seegesi: The Elegant Deity of Wealth, Power, and Femininity* (Trenton, NJ: Africa World Press, 1996), 90–93.

8   While I have no desire to *essentialize* that work women do as mothers and child rearers, or to limit our capacities to work that is pre-industrial in nature (thus denying our intellectual, scientific, and scholarly abilities), the work that Teish names is still done by a majority of working-class women all over the world.

9   This paper was part of a panel at CIIS by Dr. Alka Arora titled "The Divine Feminist."

10 Anzaldua defines *nepantilism* as "an Aztec Word meaning torn between ways." See "La conciencia de las mestiza/Towards a New Consciousness" in Anzaldua, Gloria. *Borderlands/La Frontera: The New Mestiza*, 3rd ed. (San Francisco: Aunt Lute Books, 2007/1987), 100.

11 Gloria Anzaldua, *Borderlands/La Frontera: The New Mestiza* 3rd ed. (San Francisco: Aunt Lute Books, 2007/1987), 99–120.

12 Ibid., 100.

13 Ibid.

14 While some readers may view Barbie dolls and Playboy pinups as positive, I see them as representing unrealistic and/or unattainable templates of female embodiment, since the form they present is rarely seen naturally, and many women and girls experience mental, physical and emotional suffering in their attempts to attain this ideal.

15 Joy Harjo, "Remember," in *Cries of the Spirit: A Celebration of Women's Spirituality*, ed. Marilyn Sewell (Boston: Beacon Press, 1991), 234.

16 Judy Grahn, "Ella, in a square apron, along Highway 80," in *The Judy Grahn Reader* (San Francisco: Aunt Lute Books, 2009), 11–12.

17 Lora Jo Foo, *Earth Passages: Journeys Through Childhood* (Castro Valley: Earth Passages Nature Photography, 2008).

18 Dorothy Allison, *Skin: Talking about Sex, Class and Literature* (Ithaca: Firebrand Books, 1994)

19 Amina Wadud, *Inside the Gender Jihad: Women's Reform in Islam* (Oxford: Oneworld, 2006), 221.

20 The Organization for the Resolution of Agunot is a non-profit organization based in New York whose mission is to "eliminate the infliction of abuse within the Jewish divorce process." www.getora.org/about-us (accessed 6/28/2016).

21 Bernadette Brooten (ed.) *Beyond Slavery: Overcoming its Religious and Sexual Legacies* (New York: Palgrave Macmillan, 2010).

22 *Ase* is an important and multilayered term in Yoruba religion and has no direct English equivalent. A short definition might be "primal life-force energy".

23 Maulana Karenga, *Odu Ifa: The Ethical Teachings* (Los Angeles: University of Sankore Press, 1999), 72–74.

24 A number of Women's Spirituality scholars (Eisler, Riane, *The Chalice and the Blade* (New York: HarperCollins, 1987); *Sacred Pleasure: Sex, Myth, and the Politics of the Body* (New York: HarperSanFrancisco, 1995); Gadon, Elinor. *The Once and Future Goddess: A Sweeping Visual Chronicle of the Sacred Female and Her Reemergence in the Cultural Mythology of Our Time* (San Francisco: HarperOne, 1989); Gimbutas, Marija. *The Civilization of the Goddess: The World of Old Europe* (New York: HarperSanFrancisco, 1991); Stone, Merlin, *When God Was a Woman* (New York: Harvest/Harcourt Brace, 1976) have all challenged the notion of the continuous existence of sexism/patriarchy, arguing that Neolithic/Paleolithic artifacts suggest a veneration of the feminine, resulting in egalitarian/partnership/gynocratic societies. Other Indigenous scholars (Allen, Paula Gunn. *The Sacred Hoop: Recovering the Feminine in American Indian Traditions,* 2nd ed. (Boston: Beacon Press, 1992); Talamantez, Ines, "Images of the Feminine in Apache Religious Tradition" *After Patriarchy: Feminist Transformations of the World Religions,* eds. Paula M. Cooey, William R. Eakin, and Jay B. McDaniel (Maryknoll, NY: Orbis Books, 1991), 131–144) have suggested that some American Indian societies never adopted patriarchal structures and are either matrilineal, matriarchal, or gynocratic.

25 According to Layli Phillips (now Maparyan), the term *womanism*, was independently coined by three separate writers during the 80s: Alice Walker, Chikwenye Ogunyemi, and Clenora Hudson-Weems (who was very specific about using the term *Africana womanism*). See Phillips, Layli. "Introduction. Womanism: On Its Own" in *The Womanist Reader,* ed. Layli Phillips (New York: Routledge, Taylor and Francis Group, 2006), xix–xx.

26 "Womanist: 1. From *womanish*. (Opp. of "girlish," i.e., frivolous, irresponsible, not serious.) A black feminist or feminist of color. From the black folk expression of mothers to female children, "you acting womanish," i.e., like a woman. Usually referring to outrageous, audacious, courageous or *willful* behavior. Wanting to know more and in greater depth than is considered "good" for one. Interested in grown up doings. Acting grown up. Being grown up. Interchangeable with another black folk expression: "You trying to be grown." Responsible. In charge. *Serious.* 2. *Also*: A woman who loves other women, sexually and/or nonsexually. Appreciates and prefers women's culture, women's emotional flexibility (values tears as natural counterbalance of laughter), and women's strength.

Sometimes loves individual men, sexually and/or nonsexually. Committed to survival and wholeness of entire people, male *and* female. Not a separatist, except periodically, for health. Traditionally universalist, as in: "Mama, why are we brown, pink, and yellow, and our cousins are white beige, and black?" Ans.: "Well, you know the colored race is just like a flower garden, with every color flower represented." Traditionally capable, as in: "Mama, I'm walking to Canada and I'm taking you and a bunch of other slaves with me." Reply: "It wouldn't be the first time." 3. Loves music. Loves dance. Loves the moon. *Loves* the Spirit. Loves love and food and roundness. Loves struggle. Loves the Folk. Loves herself. *Regardless.* 4. Womanist is to feminist as purple to lavender" from Walker, *In Search of Our Mothers' Gardens,* xi–xii.

27 Karla Simcikova, *To Live Fully, Here and Now: The Healing Vision in the Works of Alice Walker* (Lanham, MD: Lexington Books, 2007), 11.

28 Walker, *In Search of Our Mothers' Gardens*, xi.
29 Ibid.
30 Ibid., xii
31 Ibid.
32 Ibid., xi
33 See, Mihesuah, Devon Abbott, "Feminists, Tribalists or Activists?" in *Indigenous American Women: Decolonization, Empowerment, Activism* (Lincoln: University of Nebraska Press, 2003), 159–171.
34 See, Phillips, "Introduction. Womanism: On Its Own," xix–xx. See also: Hudson-Weems, Clenora, "Africana Womanism," in *The Womanist Reader*, ed. Layli Phillips, (New York: Routledge, Taylor and Francis Group, 2006), 44–54.
35 Filomina Chioma Steady, "The Black Woman Cross-Culturally: An Overview," in *The Black Woman Cross- Culturally*, ed. Filomina Chioma Steady (Cambridge, MA: Schenkman Publishers, 1981), 35–36.
36 Badejo, *Osun Seegesi*, 8.
37 According to Oyewumi, the list of Yoruba rulers—termed as "kings" after colonial encounters with the West—actually includes several female rulers. See: Oyewumi, Oyeronke, "Making History, Creating Gender: Some Methodological and Interpretive Questions in the Writing of Oyo Oral Traditions," in *African Gender Studies: A Reader*, ed. Oyeronke Oyewumi (New York. Palgrave MacMillan, 2005), 169–205.
38 Badejo, *Osun Seegesi*, 78–86.
39 See Disney, Abigail E. and Gini Reticker, *Pray the Devil Back to Hell*, (New York: Fork Films LLC and RO*CO Films International, 2008). Also: https://www.africanexponent.com/post/the-rise-of-naked-female-protests-in-africa- 3031 (accessed 6/29/2016); http://exhibitions.globalfundforwomen.org/exhibitions/women-power-and- politics/biology/curse-of-nakedness (accessed 6/29/2016); http://www.okayafrica.com/culture-2/naked-protest- and-african-feminism/ (accessed 6/29/2016)
40 Judith Van Allen, "Sitting on a Man: Colonialism and the Lost Political Institutions of Igbo Women," in "The Roles of African Woman: Past, Present and Future," ed. Audrey Wipper, special issue, *Canadian Journal of African Studies / Revue Canadienne des Études Africaines*, 6, no. 2, (1972): 170.
41 Ifi Amadiume, *Male Daughters, Female Husbands: Gender and Sex in an African Society* (New Jersey: Zed Books, 1998/1987), 66.
42 Ibid.
43 Ibid., see "Colonialism and the Erosion of Women's Power," 119–133 and "The Erosion of Women's Power," 134–143.
44 Christopher Mcleod, *In The Light of Reverence* (2001; San Francisco: Bullfrog Films).
45 Alice Walker, *Horses Make a Landscape More Beautiful.* (New York: Harcourt Brace Jovanovich, 1989/1979), 63.

References

Allen, Paula Gunn. *The Sacred Hoop: Recovering the Feminine in American Indian Traditions*, 2nd edition. Boston: Beacon Press, 1992.

Allison, Dorothy. *Skin: Talking about Sex, Class and Literature*. Ithaca: Firebrand Books, 1994.

Amadiume, Ifi. *Male Daughters, Female Husbands: Gender and Sex in an African Society*. New Jersey: Zed Books, 1998/1987.

Anzaldua, Gloria. *Borderlands/La Frontera: The New Mestiza*, 3rd edition. San Francisco: Aunt Lute Books, 2007/1987.

Badejo, Diedre. *Osun Seegesi: The Elegant Deity of Wealth, Power, and Femininity*. Trenton, NJ: Africa World Press, 1996.

Brooten, Bernadette, editor. *Beyond Slavery: Overcoming its Religious and Sexual Legacies*. New York: Palgrave Macmillan, 2010.

Collins, Patricia Hill. *Black Feminist Thought: Knowledge, Consciousness, and the Politics of Empowerment*, 2nd edition. New York: Routledge, 2000.

Disney, Abigail E. and Gini Reticker, dir. *Pray the Devil Back to Hell*. New York: Fork Films LLC and RO*CO Films International, 2008.

Eisler, Riane, *The Chalice and the Blade: Our History, Our Future*. New York: HarperCollins, 1987.

———. *Sacred Pleasure: Sex, Myth, and the Politics of the Body*. New York: HarperOne, 1995.

Foo, Lora Jo. *Earth Passages: Journeys Through Childhood*. Castro Valley: Earth Passages Nature Photography, 2008.

Gadon, Elinor. *The Once and Future Goddess: A Sweeping Visual Chronicle of the Sacred Female and Her Reemergence in the Cultural Mythology of Our Time*. San Francisco: HarperOne, 1989.

Gimbutas, Marija. *The Civilization of the Goddess: The World of Old Europe*. New York: HarperSanFrancisco, 1991.

Grahn, Judy. "Ella, in a square apron, along Highway 80." In *The Judy Grahn Reader*, edited by Lisa Maria Hogeland. San Francisco: Aunt Lute Books, 2009.

Harjo, Joy. "Remember." In *Cries of the Spirit: A Celebration of Women's Spirituality*, edited by Marilyn Sewell. Boston: Beacon Press, 1991.

Karenga, Maulana. *Odu Ifa: The Ethical Teachings*. Los Angeles: University of Sankore Press, 1999.

Hudson-Weems, Clenora, "Africana Womanism." In *The Womanist Reader*, edited by Layli Phillips. New York: Routledge, Taylor and Francis Group, 2006.

Mcleod, Christopher. *In The Light of Reverence*. San Francisco: Bullfrog Films, 2001.

Mihesuah, Devon Abbott, "Feminists, Tribalists or Activists?" In *Indigenous American Women: Decolonization, Empowerment, Activism*. Lincoln: University of Nebraska Press, 2003.

Oyewumi, Oyeronke, "Making History, Creating Gender: Some Methodological and Interpretive Questions in the Writing of Oyo Oral Traditions." In *African Gender Studies: A Reader*, edited by Oyeronke Oyewumi. New York. Palgrave MacMillan, 2005.

Phillips, Layli. "Introduction. Womanism: On Its Own." In *The Womanist Reader*, edited by Layli Phillips. New York: Routledge, 2006.

Simcikova, Karla. *To Live Fully, Here and Now: The Healing Vision in the Works of Alice Walker.* Lanham, MD: Lexington Books, 2007.

Steady, Filomina Chioma. "The Black Woman Cross-Culturally: An Overview." In *The Black Woman Cross-Culturally*, edited by Filomina Chioma Steady. Cambridge, MA: Schenkman Publishers, 1981.

Stone, Merlin. *When God Was a Woman.* New York: Harvest/Harcourt Brace, 1976.

Talamantez, Ines. "Images of the Feminine in Apache Religious Tradition." In *After Patriarchy: Feminist Transformations of the World Religions*, edited by Paula M. Cooey, William R. Eakin, and Jay B. McDaniel. Maryknoll, NY: Orbis Books, 1991.

Teish, Luisah. *Carnival of the Spirit: Seasonal Celebrations and Rites of Passage.* New York: HarperCollins, 1994.

Van Allen, Judith. "Sitting on a Man: Colonialism and the Lost Political Institutions of Igbo Women." In "The Roles of African Woman: Past, Present and Future," edited by Audrey Wipper. Special issue, *Canadian Journal of African Studies / Revue Canadienne des Études Africaines*, 6, no. 2, (1972): 165–181.

Wadud, Amina. *Inside the Gender Jihad: Women's Reform in Islam.* Oxford: Oneworld, 2006.

Walker, Alice. *Horses Make a Landscape More Beautiful.* New York: Harcourt Brace Jovanovich, 1989/1979.

———. "In Search of Our Mothers' Gardens." In *In Search of Our Mothers' Gardens: Womanist Prose.* San Diego: Harcourt Brace Jovanovich 1983.

About the Author

Arisika Razak, MPH, is professor emerita and the former Chair of the MA and PhD Women's Spirituality Program at the California Institute of Integral Studies, San Francisco California, where she also served as Director of Diversity. She is a former President of the American Academy of Religion, Western Region (AAR-WR), and she co-chaired the Womanist-Pan African Section of AAR-WR for five years. For over twenty years, Arisika provided midwifery care primarily to indigent women and women of color in the San Francisco Bay area, sparking her interest in multicultural feminisms, embodied healing methodologies and diverse spiritual traditions. She has led embodied healing and empowerment workshops for over thirty-five years and performed nationally and internationally as a spiritual dancer. Arisika is deeply committed to diversity, inclusion, cultural humility and anti-racist praxis; she has led numerous diversity trainings and served as a facilitator for groups in conflict. A presenter at the historic "The Gathering II," a historic celebration of seventy-five Buddhist teachers of Black African descent, and the (virtual) Black and Buddhist Summit, Arisika is a regular contributor to books and journals, writing on the subject of womanism, African-Diasporic spiritual traditions, Buddhism and Blackness, and embodied healing traditions. She currently serves as a core teacher at the East Bay Meditation Center where her teachings incorporate diverse spiritual traditions, movement, and contemporary diversity theory. Her film credits include: *Alice Walker: Beauty in Truth* by Pratibha Parmar; *Fire Eyes*, by Soraya Mire, the first full length feature film by an African woman on the issue of female genital cutting; and *Who Lives, Who Dies?* a PBS production on the provision of health care provided to underserved and marginalized communities in the USA.

2   Shekhinah: Transgendered or Transvestite? A comparison of the *Zohar* and *Sha'are Orah*

Emily Leah Silverman

Introduction

In this chapter I compare and contrast the views of Shekhinah from two thirteenth-century kabbalistic texts, the *Zohar* (*Book of Splendor*) and *Sha'are Orah* (*Gates of Lights*). Shekhinah, also known as Malchut (kingdom), is the tenth sefirah or emanation of God's attributes and is considered to be a feminine sphere and the feminine face of God.[1] Jewish feminists have renewed their interest in and relationship to her but not in a scholarly manner. A number of female Rabbis have invoked her and written about her from a spiritual perspective.[2] I am interested in the primary sources on Shekhinah and how the kabbalistic Rabbis viewed her. Here, I examine if it is possible to redeem her from the texts and investigate if kabbalistic sources are valid for Jewish feminist theologies. Many scholars and feminists do not think that Shekhinah is retrievable from Kabbalah because of the masculine nature of the Godhead.[3] The focus of my discussion is how each text portrays Shekhinah's mutable gender qualities. In this preliminary investigation of a complex subject, I examine the verbs and some of the symbols that each text uses to describe Shekhinah's channeling and changing nature.

A comparison of the verbs and symbols used in these texts leads to some fascinating questions about Shekhinah's gendered feminine and masculine qualities. First, what do the *Zohar* and *Sha're Orah* mean by feminine and masculine? This paper works from an assumption that masculine and feminine are socially constructed within a historical cultural context. By examining Shekhinah's movements in the two texts through the verbs and symbols, we can learn something about Shekhinah's masculine and feminine traits and the nature of her fluctuations.

How exactly do Shekhinah's gender fluctuations occur? Is she simply dressing up like a transvestite (wearing the clothes of the opposite gender), or is she undergoing a transformation and literally becoming a masculine quality or a different type of feminine quality? Does she have a dual nature consisting of both masculine and feminine traits?

Shekhinah clearly has a unique character that distinguishes her from all the other sefirot. She is always in flux between three worlds, the upper world of the higher sefirot, the lower world of creation, and the *sitra ahara* (the other side), which is the demonic underworld. She channels and reflects the energies of the upper sefirot to the lower world, so she is the divine mediator of these emanations to the lower world. She also moves upward and unites with the upper sefirot through Yesod and Tif'eret; this union depends on the positive deeds and thoughts of men in the lower world. She is only attached to the other side when a kabbalist has negative thoughts or actions. Thus, Shekhinah's ability to channel and her constant mutability are what make this sefirah so unique in comparison to the others.

In the mediation process, does Shekhinah embody the gender along with the qualities of the sefirah that she is channeling? Does she lose all of her femininity, part of her femininity, or take on a different aspect of feminine character? Or, is she just dressing up, meaning that some part of her feminine qualities remains intact as she embodies masculine qualities or different feminine qualities?

Sometimes Shekhinah channels sefirot that are considered feminine such as those of Binah, *GeVuRaH*, and Hod, while at other times she channels sefirot with masculine qualities such as Hokmah, Hesed, Tif'eret, Netzah, and Yesod. These sefirot are symbolized in many ways, including by body part, color, divine God name, and many other symbols of nature and life found in the Torah. In the first case, the sefirot symbolically represent primordial man. The three top ones—Keter, Hokmah, and Binah—are the head. Hesed is the right arm, *GeVuRaH* the left arm, Tif'eret the trunk, Netzah the right leg, Hod the left leg, and Yesod the phallus. This picture or map is essential if we are to grasp the gender assignments of the sefirot. The left side is feminine, the right side masculine, and the middle torso masculine.

The writings of the kabbalists take the words and verses of the Torah and decode their esoteric meaning through an understanding of how God's divine light flows and emanates to the lower world through the system of the sefirot. A person's thoughts and deeds influence the sefirot that Shekhinah emanates downward, whether masculine or feminine, and they also affect whether or not Shekhinah will move upwards and unite with Tif'eret. Both the *Zohar* and

Sha'are Orah were written with the intention of letting men know that their mitzvoth and prayers have a direct impact on the divine realm of the sefirot.

Zohar

The *Zohar* first appeared around 1286. *Sha'are Orah* was probably written before 1293, incorporating parts of the *Zohar*; however, the styles of the books are different, and so are their intentions.[4] The *Zohar* is written in medieval Aramaic and is intended to be a mystical commentary, or kabbalistic midrash, on the Torah, starting with Genesis and including chapters from Deuteronomy. Its goal is to reveal a mystical understanding of the Torah itself as God's emanation of divine light through the sefirot. That is to say, since Genesis described God's creative essence, the *Zohar* attempts to create the bridge between the text and the sefirot tree.[5] The *Zohar* also had a homiletic purpose, to show that by following the mitzvoth (religious laws) a person had an impact on the higher realms of the sefirotic system and thus on the divine.

Daniel Matt suggests that the surge of religious mysticism exemplified in the *Zohar* was a backlash against the secularizing influence of the rationalism characteristic of the "Golden Age" of religious tolerance and pluralism in Spain under Alfonso X (the Wise).[6] The probable author of the *Zohar*, Moses de Leon, attempted to overcome this secular trend by suggesting the cosmic importance of observance, describing the performance of mitzvoth as having a direct effect on the divine union of Shekhinah with Tif'eret, thus restoring her to her sacred state in the higher world. Matt says,

> Though it rarely discusses mystical experience, the *Zohar* is eager to highlight the mystical significance of the *mizwot*. Living according to the Torah is the surest way to encounter God. "When a human being observes the commands of Torah, *Shekhinah* walks with him constantly and never departs from him." (*Zohar* 1: 230a) The author speaks with the passion of a mystical moralist.[7]

Another scholar, Isaiah Tishby, points out that in the *Zohar*, "...man's religious task is to sustain this unification [Shekhinah's union with Tif'eret through divine intercourse] through devotion in prayer and the fulfillment of the commandments."[8] In other words, a man's actions and prayers have a direct effect on the unification of Shekhinah with Tif'eret and the upper spheres. A man's negative thoughts can separate and isolate the Shekhinah from the whole sefirot system. If a man thinks of cleaving to Shekhinah just for himself and separating her from the upper realms, it destroys her unity with Tif'eret and the rest of these realms. Adam's sin was separating the tree of knowledge [Shekhinah] from the tree of life [Tif'eret]. Adam's thoughts destroyed the divine unity. And just as Adam's thoughts destroyed this unity, so can a kabbalist's thoughts do the same. Tishby explains, "the thought of separation causes the forces in the Godhead actually to separate; the links that connect the Shekhinah to *Tif'eret* and to the other *sefirot* are severed, and the channels of influence are stopped up."[9] A kabbalist's actions and thoughts are so powerful that they totally affect the flow of the divine light of emanation and unification with the Godhead.

Sh'are Orah

In contrast to the *Zohar*, *Sh'are Orah* is written in medieval Hebrew from one kabbalist to another as a treatise on a method to open the mystical gates in order to experience the emanations of the divine light. Gikatilla, the author of the text, begins,

> You, my brother and soul mate, have asked me to show you the pathway to the Names of the Ever-Blessed God so you may derive what you will from them and reach the place that you desire. Even though your enthusiasm is far greater than your question, I still feel compelled to divulge to you the way the light is disseminated and how God wants us to reach it.[10]

These keys to the Names of God are the names of the sefirot and the qualities of each of their emanations. Gikatilla tells his student that when he learns how each is disseminated, "then God will answer when you call. You will be one of those who are truly close to Him and you will love Him with all your heart. Yes, you will delight in *YHVH*, and He will grant you all that you ask."[11]

The Tetragrammaton is considered the holiest of the holy names of God in the Torah, and contemplating the various names will allow the student to understand that all of the Torah is intrinsically tied to the Tetragrammaton. Gikatilla states, "Know that all the Holy Names in the Torah are intrinsically tied to the Tetragrammaton, which is *YHVH*."[12]

Dealing with the traditional injunction against using the holy names, Gikatilla argues:

> It is within the parameters of our historical covenant, however, that those who want their needs fulfilled by employing the Holy Names should try with all their strength to comprehend each Name of God as they are recorded in the Torah, names such as EHYE, YH, *YHVH*, A*D*o*N*a*Y*, EL, ELOH EL*o*HIM SH*a*D*a*Y, TZVAOT. One should be aware that all the names mentioned in the

Torah are the keys for anything a person needs in the world. When one contemplates these Names one will understand that all of the Torah and the Commandments are dependent upon them. Then when he knows the purpose of every Name he will realize the greatness of "He who spoke and thus the world came into being." He will be fearful before Him and he will yearn to cleave to Him through His blessed Names. Then he will be close to God and his petitions will be accepted, as it is written: "I will keep him safe, for he knows My Name. When he calls on Me I will answer him."[13]

This verse does not promise safety by merely mentioning His Name, but by *knowing* His Name. That is, by deep understanding, the petitioner is intrinsically linked to the divine and can thus draw on divine protection and power.

Gikatilla then cites examples of how the method works. Jacob called on El *SHaDaY* in Genesis 43:4: "And may El *SHaDaY* dispose man to mercy toward you."[14] Daniel invoked a different name, *ADoNaY*, who "show[s the] favour for the desolate."[15] Hannah prayed and petitioned God with a different name: "O ye, Y'Y TZVAOT, if you will look upon the suffering of your maidservant."[16] *Shaa're Orah* demonstrates which Holy Name is applied to which emanation, for each emanation has different qualities and therefore different utility for seeking divine union and divine aid.

Thus, both the *Zohar* and *Sha'are Orah* explain the inner meaning of Torah by identifying Torah with the inner system of emanations and disseminations of the divine light. Gikatilla focuses not only on interpreting Torah, but on finding a way to give ultimate meaning to Torah in order to "know" God.

Filling, Dressing, Robing, Changing, Connecting, Cleaving, and Bonding

To understand Shekhinah's gender performance,[17] I examine the way each kabbalist describes how Shekhinah mutates, is partially absorbed, or crosses over in terms of gender. To begin with, both texts use feminine metaphors to describe her shape, metaphors that are also used to signify the female genitals and organs in the medieval period. For instance, in medieval medical literature, an upside-down jar signified a woman's vagina and uterus. Joan Cadden, a scholar of medieval medicine, notes:

> ...the emphasis upon the womb as the central female organ was in harmony with the view of the women as essentially passive vessels. The word *vas* in the sense of "jar" or "vessel" occurs in medieval texts as a synonym for woman, and the image of the womb as an upside-down jar (dissociated from any person) is repeated in frequently copied illustrations of fetal position.[18]

It appears that to describe Shekhinah, the kabbalists inverted the medieval uterus in the shape of a jar and turned it right side up to face the higher realms and receive the semen of Tif'eret and Yesod. Both texts use the symbol of the well, a type of receptable. When the well, or uterus, is filled, then it overflows with semen down to the lower realms. Her cup runneth over.

According to one text in the *Zohar* interpreting the verse, "Drink water from your **cistern**, running water from your own well," (Prov 5:15, emphasis mine) when Shekhinah receives the influx from the upper masculine divine potencies, she is transformed from an empty **cistern (*bor*)** that has nothing of its own into a **well (*be'er*)** that is full and overflows to every side. Thus, in the *Zohar*, Shekhinah as uterus fills up with semen from the phallus, which overflows down to the lower world.

In *Sha'are Orah*, Gikatilla also uses the well symbol. Sometimes *ADoNaY* (the God name of Shekhinah) is referred to by its cognomen Be'er (well). Gikatilla writes, "the rationale for this [cognomen] is that *ADoNaY* can be seen as the 'well of living waters' where all the energy and the emanations from above gather, as it is written: '[You are] a garden spring, a well (Be'er) of fresh water, a rill of Lebanon.' (Songs of Songs 4:15) ".[19]

If the children of Israel are righteous and recite their hundred blessings a day as they should, this well will be filled with the living waters from the highest emanations. Men will be prosperous and full of all that is good as they draw what they require from the living waters. Sometimes the cognomen appears as Be'er Sheva (the well of seven) because seven rivers flow from it through the emanation known as Yesod Olam (Foundation of the Universe). These seven rivers draw from the seven highest emanations.

Gikatilla thus makes clear that Shekhinah is a divine receptacle, a well, just like a womb. The well fills with water just as the womb fills with the semen of the male. The well fills when the children of Israel recite their blessings. The seven rivers from Hokmah to Tif'eret flow into Yesod, symbolically the penis, which then channels the rivers down to Shekhinah, just as the semen of a penis fills a uterus when it ejaculates, from a medieval perspective.

These symbols of the well, the cistern, and the pool (the latter not discussed here) by which Shekhinah is described all imply some type of womb or vagina shape and image. But when there is total union of Tif'eret and Shekhinah, does this union cause Shekhinah to lose her receptacle shape? Does the jar metamorphose into a penis?

When we take a look at the two texts, we see that Shekhinah emanates the same sefirot but in different ways. In both there is a crossing back and forth between the two genders. We see Shekhinah's mutability when she channels the energies of higher sefirot downwards from *GeVuRaH* or Din

(Judgment, feminine) and her opposite Hesed (Love or Mercy, masculine), as well as when she moves upwards and unites with Tif'eret (Beauty, masculine) through Yesod (Foundation, masculine). When Shekhinah emanates the sefirot down, the texts note her new gendered qualities; when she moves upward to unite with Tif'eret, they also note her gender shifts. But what is actually happening in the in-between of Shekhinah's mutations? Is there a demarcation that would imply a bi-gendered being, or is there a total merging in which feminine is absorbed or transgendered into masculine? An examination of the verbs used by the two authors can tell us something about this fuzzy line between merging into one and maintaining a duality of energies. The texts use verbs such as filling, overflowing, dressing, robing, adorning, calling, changing, connecting, uniting, joining, bonding, and cleaving to connote Shekhinah's gender transitions when channeling the energies of the higher sefirot or when moving upwards to unite with Tif'eret.

I contend that Shekhinah is merely cross-dressing or donning a costume when a text uses the verbs "dresses" or "adorns." In contrast, when a text uses the verb "changes," Shekhinah is either merging with or being totally absorbed into the masculine; she literally becomes masculine. When a text uses the verb "to fill," Shekhinah has a bi-gendered character. She keeps her vessel-like shape but is filled with masculine energies or with another aspect of female energies. Finally, with verbs such as uniting, joining, cleaving, bonding, and connecting, there is a possibility that part of her has merged and another part of her has not. In geometric terms, this Shekhinah looks like a Venn diagram of the transitive property where there are two opposite sides and the middle is merged. I call this situation tri-gendered because one side of Shekhinah is feminine, the opposite side is masculine, and the middle is some sort of unification of masculine and feminine. The *Zohar* uses the symbol of the multi-colored flame of the candle, which I contend describes this type of tri-gendered situation.

Both texts describe how the emanations of energies flow through Shekhinah as she moves downward and upward. In *Sha'are Orah*, Gikatilla explains that *ADoNaY* [Shekhinah] receives energies from the higher sefirot. She acts upon the world with the energy of the sefirah that she receives, and she is called by that sefirah's God-name. Gikatilla writes,

> Know that this attribute, [Shekhinah] because it receives energy from higher powers, [once received] has various qualities: to give life, or bring death, to bring up or to bring down, to smite or to cure. All, however, is dependent upon the kind of energy that can be drawn to this attribute. It acts among all Creation according to the energy it receives…Since this attribute is **filled** with

the everflow from those attributes which reside above it, sometimes it is **called** by the name of one of these attributes from which it is **filled** at that particular time [emphasis mine].[20]

Gikatilla tells us that Shekhinah has tremendous powers, and, depending upon which sefirah she is filled with, she does all the above-mentioned things. To give life is the sefirah of *GeVuRaH*. To bring death is the sefirah of Din, the harsh side of *GeVuRaH*. To bring up is Shekhinah's ability to unite with upper sefirot when a kabbalist does mitzvoth that travel up to her. To bring down is to summon the energies of usually *GeVuRaH* or Hesed. To smite is again Din, and to cure is Hesed, which balances Din. This array of behaviors demonstrates Shekhinah's unique quality of mutability.

According to Gikatilla, when *ADoNaY* is filled with *GeVuRaH*, she is called by her God-name *ELoHIM*. *GeVuRaH* is a sefirah from the left side of the body or tree and is considered feminine. The question is, when she is called by the name *ELoHIM*, has she literally become *ELoHIM*, or is she just a channel for the attributes of *ELoHIM*? Is Shekhinah, in Star Trek terms, a shape shifter? Does she assume the shape of the sefirah that she channels? Or is her original form still intact like a vessel or tunnel that fills up with energies that then overflow downward to the lower world? Gikatilla goes on to explain how the channeling works.

> When the attribute of *GeVuRaH* decrees its judgment on the lower worlds for destruction, decimation and extinction, then the attribute *ADoNaY*, which is the storehouse for all things which descend from above, fills itself with the judgement [Din] that *ELoHIM* has decreed and dispenses the justice that *ELoHIM* has decreed on the lower world. During this time, *ADoNaY* is called *ELoHIM*; it is called by the Name which invokes the attribute *GeVuRaH*, which decreed its judgments on its subjects. It is as if the messenger is **called** by the name of him who sent the message. Thus, sometimes attributes may be known as *YHVH*, sometimes as *ADoNaY*, sometimes as *ELoHIM* and sometimes *SHaDaY*–everything happens in accord with the influencing attribute, its power and its qualities: if the quality be mercy or its opposite. Since the attribute **fills** itself from the source before it, it is called *SHaDaY* [*SHeh Day*, which means "it suffices"], which tells that there is enough, there is completeness, there is fullness. When this attribute is called *SHaDaY* all destructive forces are dispersed [emphasis mine].[21]

We thus learn that Shekhinah is a storehouse for all the emanations that descend from the sefirot above her from Yesod to Hokmah. The image is again of a vessel of some sort that can be filled up; for a storehouse, like a jar, holds something. The jar, as we have seen, was a medieval cultural symbol of the uterus.

When Shekhinah fills up with the attribute that she receives, then she is called by the God-name of that attribute, such as *ELoHIM* [*GeVuRaH*] or *YHVH* [Tif'eret] or *SHaDaY* [Yesod/Malchut]. *YHVH* is the power that channels the higher sefirot of *GeVuRaH* and Hesed down to Shekhinah.

In the map of the sefirotic body, as we have seen, *GeVuRaH* is the left arm and Hesed the right. They go down through Tif'eret, the torso, into the phallus, Yesod, and pour into Shekhinah. This is why the text states, "it is filled itself from the source."[22] The flow is coming out of Yesed, the penis, and fills the Shekhinah, now called *SHaDaY*. Day means "enough" in Hebrew, so she is filled to the brim. Because the higher sefirot flow through Tif'eret in order to reach Shekhinah, do feminine sefirah such as *GeVuRaH* lose their female qualities in the process of flowing toward Shekhinah? Because the masculine force is behind the emanation of sefirot downwards, are Shekhinah's gendered characteristics affected? What do these names tell us about her gender? Is she masculine when she is *YHVH*, and different aspects of feminine when she is *ADoNaY* and *ELoHIM*?

The image of filling up implies that there is a structure intact; Shekhinah's own structure is filled with a quality that can be masculine. Is Shekhinah therefore bi-gendered at the moment she is channeling? The vessel would be her femininity, the masculine sefirah of *YHVH* her masculinity, and *ELoHIM* an active (as opposed to receptive) feminine quality. When Shekhinah is filled up with *ELoHIM*, she is channeling a feminine sefirah. Yet her qualities are harsh, and she hands out judgments. *ELoHIM* is an active sefirah, not a passive one. She thus possesses a different type of feminine quality.

We get a clearer image of the nature of Shekhinah's channeling in *Sha'are Orah* when Gikatilla uses the verbs "robed" and "dresses" to describe her clothing of fire. He writes,

> We must reiterate that this attribute is **robed** in three kinds of fire as there are three different Names: *SHaDaY ELoHIM* and *ADoNaY*. All of these are fueled by the power of *YHVH*, which is responsible for all activity. When **it is called *SHaDaY* it dresses** as a consuming **black** fire which all destructive demons flee and legions of impure creatures do no have the strength to withstand [its consuming flame]. All are dispersed and are reduced to a pile of ashes. When **it is called *ELoHIM* it dresses** in **red** fire, the vision of a consuming, burning and destructive fire which comes to dispense justice sternly both above and below. It seals the judgment of both the wicked and the righteous. From here is where all those who dispense judgment are given licence to pass judgment

on all Creation. This attribute is able to bring death or life, to smite or heal, to make low or raise up by the power of the Name *YHVH* that dwells in its midst.

When it is called *ADoNaY* it **wears** a **green** flame from which all creatures are fearful and terrified. It then stands on the kingdom's throne, and all the heavenly legions above and below are anxious and full of supplication. It employs the strategems of the Kingdom as the master and ruler which rides and rules over all of the chariot [emphasis mine].[23]

When Shekhinah is dressed or robed, is her structure underneath the robes still female? Furthermore, when she takes on the color of different attributes, she does not change into that color, she puts it on as if it were a garment. When she is wearing the colored garment of the new attribute, then she is called by its name.

When someone is a transvestite, do we determine his or her gender by the appearance of the outer garment, or do we ascertain it by what is underneath the garment? "He is a transvestite," means that he dresses up as a she, just as "she is a transvestite," means that she dresses up as a he. What does this cross-dressing tell us about femininity and masculinity? Is wearing masculine clothing an indication that she is masculine? When she dresses in clothing of a different feminine style (as when she wears the color of a feminine sefirah, such as the red of Din), does she embody a different type of feminine quality?

Gikatilla writes, "It is as if the messenger is **called** by the name of him who sent the message,"[24] (emphasis mine). But the question remains, is she merely dressed up as *ELoHIM*, or is she literally *ELoHIM*? If Shekhinah is acting as *ELoHIM*, the fifth sefirah, then are we addressing our petitions directly to her, Shekhinah, or rather to *GeVuRaH ELoHIM*? The answer is implied by Gikatilla's language. When Shekhinah is **called** by the name *ELoHIM*, which is the attribute of *GeVuRaH*, the fifth sefirah, she **dresses** in red fire. She **dresses** in black fire when she takes the name *SHaDaY*, which is the attribute of the sefirah Malchut. When she is **called** *ADoNaY*, she **dresses** in green as Shekhinah. Therefore, is she a transvestite in masculine clothing or a fashion queen dressing in different feminine styles? If Shekhinah is merely dressing, then is her receptive shape still intact underneath the clothing? In that case, her vessel-like feminine form is merely being concealed.

The *Zohar*, in contrast to *Sha'are Orah*, takes a different approach. In it, Shekhinah changes gender and literally shape shifts. Being transgendered or a shape shifter is different from being a transvestite or wearing a different style of clothes. Nowhere is the total transformation of Shekhinah from feminine to masculine in the *Zohar* more apparent than in the metaphor of her as a rose changing into a lily.

> A Rose and A Lily (*Zohar* 1 221a)
> Come and see. At first she is green like a rose, whose leaves are green; afterward "a lily" (*shoshanah*) she is red with white colors. *Shoshanah* with six leaves, *shoshanah*, because she **changes (*ishtaniat*)** from color to color, and varies (*shaniat*) her colors. "A lily"—first a rose; when she wishes to **unite** with the king, she is called "rose"; after she has become **united** with him, with the King, with those kisses, she is called "lily," since it is written "His lips are as lilies" (Song of Songs 5:13). "A lily of the valleys," for she **changes** her colors, sometime for good, sometime for evil, sometime for Mercy, sometimes for Judgment [emphasis mine].[25]

The Zohar first tells us that Shekhinah is green like the leaves of a rose. There are six leaves on the flower representing the six lower sefirot: Hesed, *GeVuRaH*, Tif'eret, Netzah, Hod, and Yesod. She is called Shoshanah because the root word of Shoshanah means to change in Hebrew and Aramaic.[26] Before the rose (Shekhinah) has intercourse with the king (Tif'eret), she is green. Afterwards she changes into a lily, and she is red and white, meaning she is the balance of *GeVuRaH* (Judgment) and Hesed (Mercy). What is significant here is that unlike in *Sha'are Orah*, Shekinah has intercourse and literally metamorphoses or shape shifts from a rose to a lily. She has crossed over and taken on a new form. She is not dressed up as lily but has transformed into a lily. There is no question about her change of form.

Likewise, the *Zohar* uses the symbols of color and fire differently from *Sha'are Orah* to describe Shekhinah's metamorphosis. The *Zohar* describes the sefirot as the colored light of a candle. In *Zohar* 1.50b–51b, a passage entitled "The Unification of the Sefirot through the Mystery of the Light of the Lamp," we read,

> Whoever wishes to understand the wisdom of the holy unification, let him look at the flame that rises from a glowing coal, or from a burning lamp, for the flame rises only when it takes hold of some coarse matter. Come and see. In the rising flame there are two lights: one is a radiant white light, and one is a light that contains black or blue. The white light is above, and ascends in a direct line, and beneath it is the blue or black light, which is a throne for the white, and the white light rests upon it, and they are **connected** *together, forming one whole, and the black light, or* [that which has] *blue color, is the throne of glory for the white.* And this is the mystic significance of the blue. And this blue-black throne is **joined** to something else, below it, so that it can burn, and it stimulates it to grasp the white light. This blue-black [light] sometimes **changes** to red, but the white light above it never changes, for it is always white. However, the blue **changes** to these colors: sometimes blue or black, and sometimes red.

> This [light] is **connected** *on two sides*. It is connected above to the white light, and it is connected below to what is beneath it, to what has been prepared for it, so that it might illuminate and grasp it. This [light] devours continuously, and consumes whatever is placed beneath it; for the blue light consumes and devours whatever is attached to it below, what ever it rests upon, since it is its habit to consume and devour: for the destruction of the all, the death of all depends upon it and therefore it devours whatever is attached to it below… [But] the white light, which rests upon it, does not devour or consume at all, and its light does not change. Concerning this, Moses said "For the Lord your God is a devouring fire," really devouring, devouring and consuming whatever rests beneath it. That is why he said "the Lord your God," and not "our God," because Moses was [linked] to the white light above, which does not consume, and does not devour [emphasis mine].[27]

According to the *Zohar*, each part of the candle represents one of the sefirot, and the whole candle portrays the relationship between all of them. The higher part of the flame is the upper sefirah of Tif'eret, which is immutable. He is white. The lower part of the flame is Shekhinah, and she changes various colors from blue to black to red. The unchanging white light, the higher part of the flame, rests on the lower light. The lower light is either a blue or black throne for the white to sit upon. The throne shape implies some type of receptacle.

The words used here are "changes" and "connected." The verb "changes" implies a total transmutation of one color into another color, unlike *Sha'are Orah*, which describes Shekinah as "dressed" In the different colors of a flame. Yet changing and dressing are two different concepts. Changing implies shape shifting and transgendering, while dressing suggests transvestism. In transvestism, unlike transgendering, there is some type of form that is covered up by the garments; there is a shape underneath.

In the *Zohar*, not only does Shekhinah change, but she is connected on two sides. Above she is connected to the upper sefirah of Tif'eret (the white light), and below she is linked to the world of creation through the good deeds and thoughts of men and the smoke of the sacrifice. The concept of connection is an interesting one. It shows Shekhinah as a bridge between two worlds. When Shekhinah is connected on one side to Tif'eret and on the other to the lower world, what is going on in the in-between, the inter-space of the two worlds? Has she totally merged with the white light or is there a space in which Shekhinah is still intact? It appears that when there is a harmonious union between the two worlds, the lower flame of Shekhinah is blue because she is fulfilling two functions. She is bringing up the good deeds of man below, and this action causes her to bond to the white flame above and become blue. This transformation is explained more clearly in the next passage, which discusses the meaning of the rising smoke of the sacrifice. The smoke feeds the blue flame of Shekhinah so that she can rise up and cleave to the white flame of Tif'eret. The smoke is the esoteric substance that is lifted up by man's deeds to feed the flame. The *Zohar* explains,

> There too is the mystical significance of sacrifice, for the rising smoke stimulates the blue light to burn, and when it burns it **joins** with the white light and the flame burns as a single unity. And since it is the manner of the blue light to consume and devour what is attached to it beneath, so, when the will exists and the flame burns in single union, then it is written: "Then the fire of the Lord fell, and consumed the burnt-offering…" (I Kings 18:38)—then it is known that the lamp burns in a single union and in a single **bond**: the blue light **clings** to the white light, and they are one, [Then] it consumes the portions and offerings beneath it, for it consumes [the offerings] beneath it only when it burns, and is **joined** to the white light; and then there is peace in all the worlds, and all is bound together in a single unity. And when the blue light has finished consuming [the offerings] beneath it, the priests, the Levites, and Israel **cleave** to it beneath: some in joyful song, some with at willing heart, and others in prayer, and the flame burns above them, and the lights **cleave** to one another, and illumine the worlds, and the upper and lower realms are blessed…[emphasis mine].[28]

Here the *Zohar* illustrates the unification or joining of Shekhinah with Tif'eret, which happens when Shekhinah cleaves, clings, and bonds to Tif'eret. Tishby explains, "And since it is the manner of the blue light to consume and devour what is attached to it beneath, so, when the will exists and the flame burns in a single union.[29] This means that this is when intercourse takes place: "The "devouring" of the sacrifice is not a destruction that derives from the side of Judgment, but the binding of the upper and lower worlds at the moment of intercourse.[30]

When the children of Israel bring a sacrifice, the smoke rises upwards, which then stimulates Shekhinah to move upward and have intercourse with Tif'eret. At this point, she is described as being blue because the light from all of the upper sefirot is flowing into her. When Shekhinah and Tif'eret are having intercourse, the verbs used are "cleave," "cling," and "bond." They imply a sense of attachment to Tif'eret, which is also illustrated by the cleaving of the blue to the upper white light. According to the *Zohar*, Shekhinah is only blue when the system is united and in balance. Yet the light underneath the white has not been absorbed into the white light, and the whole burning flame of the candle is not one color but two. This example of the colors of the burning flame resembles the geometric Venn diagram of tri-gender that I mentioned earlier. The top of the candle remains white, while the bottom is blue. Is it thus masculine on top (Tif'eret), feminine on the bottom (Shekhinah), and something else in the middle at the point where white and blue connect? What then does the burning flame symbolize in terms of gender? Clearly, it is outside of the binary system of gender duality.

Conclusion

To conclude, what have we learned from the *Zohar* and *Sha'are Orah* about Shekhinah's feminine and masculine qualities and the nature her gender fluctuations? First, in both texts, we see that Shekhinah sometimes takes the shape of a receptacle such as a well. The well is similar in shape to a vase, which was a medieval symbol for a uterus. Shekhinah, in the form of a receptacle, is the recipient for the light of the higher sefirot. One of her major characteristics is thus her ability to receive and be receptive.

Shekhinah receives the light of the upper sefirot, which have either masculine or feminine qualities, in a number of ways. In the *Zohar*, Shekhinah totally transforms into the sefirah she is channeling, whether it be feminine or masculine. We see Shekhinah's shape-shifting ability most clearly in the symbol of the rose turning into the lily. Shekhinah is a green rose before she has intercourse. Once she has intercourse with Tif'eret, a masculine sefirah, she changes into a lily, or transforms from queen to king. Once she is king, then she can rule the lower world.

Likewise, in the Zoharic symbol of the burning flame of a candle, the lower blue flame changes to red or black. In other words, even when Shekhinah is channeling a sefirah with feminine attributes, she transforms into that sefirah without any trace of having been something else.

When the Zoharic Shekhinah unites with Tif'eret, on the other hand, the blue light and the white light are connected together, and the blue light cleaves or bonds to the white light. What do these verbs imply? The white light is always above and never changes, while the blue light below can change at any moment. But what about the inter space between the connection? The white light does not take over and go all the way down the wick. It only burns on top. This image implies that there is a part of the Shekhinah that has not been totally merged into the white. Maybe, therefore, she is tri-gendered. We are constrained in our analysis by the binary notion of gender, which limits our ability to fully understand what is going on with the burning flame.

In contrast to the *Zohar*, we learn from *Sha'are Orah* that Shekhinah does not change into but merely dresses as the color of fire of whichever sefirah she channels. Dressing is clearly a different type of action from changing. There is no metamorphosis or connection but rather some sort of dressing up—a fashion show of various styles of sefirot. When Shekhinah wears red flame, she is Din, and then she is called Elhoim. The sefirah of *ELoHIM*, although feminine, is not a passive but an active emanation that hands out judgment on the world. When Shekhinah dresses in black, she is called *SHaDaY* and is *GeVuRaH*. When she dresses in a green flame, she becomes a ruler.

Analysis of both texts demonstrates that kabbalistic definitions of gender are anything but clear-cut. Is it possible to define Shekhinah within a binary gender system at all? Traditionally, binary concepts of gender have been very limiting. If we take a new perspective and expand our concepts of masculine and feminine, we can perhaps see the qualities of Shekhinah in a new way. The queer community, for example, has a different way of talking about feminine and masculine. Lesbians divide feminine attributes into categories of Butch and Femme, and within these two categories, there are sub-categories that permit multiple expressions of gender identities. There are not just two but multiple genders, which mix conventional definitions of masculine and feminine.

Hence, I contend that in order to retrieve kabbalistic texts for Jewish feminist theologies, we will have to look at gender in a new way and outside of the typical binary duality of masculine and feminine.[31] I am suggesting that it might be possible to use queer identity as a tool to unpack the fuzziness of gender play in these texts, especially since the Kabbalah defines Shekhinah as a feminine Sefirah with amazing abilities. If we adopt the language of queerness as a tool of analysis, these texts might well be redeemable. Shekhinah is the gender which is not one—or even two.[32]

Notes

1 The first mention in the Torah of the root word from which *Shekhinah* derives, **Shachan,** the verb form of **Schanati** (to dwell) and the noun form **Mishkan** (tabernacle or dwelling place) is in the twenty-fifth chapter of Exodus: "And let them make Me a sanctuary ***v'ShaCHaNti*** (that I may dwell) among them. Like everything that I show you the form of the ***HaMishkan*** (Tabernacle) and the form of all its vessels, and so shall you do," (Exodus 25:8–9). Shekhinah is called Kingdom because she rules over the lower world of creation. The author of *Sha'are Orah*, Gikatilla, tells us her God name is Adonay because Adonay means lord or ruler. She is ruler of the lower kingdom.

The term sefirah was first coined in the *Sefer Yetsirah* (*The Book of Creation or Formation*) which, according to Scholem, was written sometime between the third and sixth centuries. It derives from the word **Sapor**, which means to count. *Sefer Yetsirah* postulated that the world was created by the primordial ten numbers and twenty-two letters of the Hebrew alphabet. In the *Zohar*, these ten sefirot become attributes, powers, or emanations of God's light. They are named as follows:

1. Keter Elyon (Supreme Crown)
2. Hokhmah (Wisdom)
3. Binah (Understanding)
4. Hesed (Love or Mercy)
5. Gevurah or Din (Judgment)
6. Tif'eret (Beauty)
7. Netzah (Lasting Endurance of God)
8. Hod (Majesty or Glory)
9. Yesod (Foundation)
10. Shekhinah or Malchut (Kingdom)

2. See Rabbi Lynn Gottlieb, *She Who Dwells Within: A Feminist Vision of a Renewed Judaism* (San Francisco: HarperSanFrancisco, 1995), and Rabbi Leah Novick, "Encountering the Schechinah, The Jewish Goddess," in *The Goddess Re-Awakening*, ed. Shirley Nicholson (Wheaton, IL: Theosophical Publishing House, 1989) 204–214.

3. In my discussion with Danny Matt, he stated that most scholars and rabbis do not think that Shekhinah is retrievable from Kabbalistic sources because of the sexist nature of the texts.

4. Gershom G. Scholem, *Major Trends in Jewish Mysticism* (New York: Schocken Books, 1961), 231.

5. The sefirot are portrayed not only as a body but as a mystical tree, with the right side (Hochmah, Hesed, Nezah) representing masculine emanations, the left side (Binah, Gevurah, Hod) representing feminine emanations. The middle of the tree, which is the trunk (Tiferet, Yesod), consists of masculine emanations and the base of the trunk (Shekhinah) is a feminine emanation.

6. Daniel Matt, "The Mystic and the Mizwot," in *Jewish Spirituality from the Bible through the Middle Ages*, ed. Arthur Green (New York: Crossroads, 1988), 386, and Daniel Matt, *Zohar* (Mahwah, NJ: Paulist Press, 1983), 5–7.

7. Matt, 386.

8. Isaiah Tishby, *The Wisdom of the Zohar* (Oxford: Oxford University Press, 1989), 374.

9. Ibid., 375.

10. Rabbi Joseph Gikatilla, *The Gates of Light—Sha'are Orah* (Walnut Creek, CA: AltaMira Press,1994), 3.

11. Ibid., 3.

12 Ibid., 6.
13 Ibid., 5.
14 Ibid., 5.
15 Ibid., 6.
16 Ibid., 6.
17 In recent queer theory discourse, the whole notion of gender has been challenged and deconstructed. Judith Butler argues that gender fluctuates and is a type of performance. See Judith Butler, *Gender Troubles: Feminism and the Subversion of Identity* (New York: Routledge, 1990).
18 Joan Cadden, *Meanings of Sex Difference in the Middle Ages: Medicine, Science and Culture* (Cambridge: Cambridge University Press 1993), 178.
19 Gikatilla, 19.
20 Ibid., 50.
21 Ibid., 50-51.
22 Ibid., 50-51
23 Ibid., 51-52.
24 Ibid., 51.
25 Tishby, 392.
26 Ibid., 392.
27 Ibid., 319-320.
28 Ibid., 321.
29 Ibid., 321.
30 Ibid., 321, ff139.
31 We can take this step based on Hans-Georg Gadamar's hermeneutical principles. When a reader engages with a text, a dialectic emerges between the two. The reader brings her own experience to the text. Twenty-first century Jewish feminists can thus bring their own experience to a reading of these texts. The interaction with the sefirot can have a whole different meaning for them than for the thirteenth-century kabbalists. See Hans-Georg Gadamer, *Truth and Method* (New York: Crossroads, 1982).
32 Before looking at these different ways of viewing gender, however, we need to grapple with our predecessors and deeply examine their analysis. The next step in this analysis is a close examination of Elliot Wolfson's suggestive chapter on gender in the Kabbalah, "Crossing gender boundaries in kabbalistic rituals and myth" in Mortimer Ostow's *Ultimate Intimacy: The Psychodynamics of Jewish Mysticism*, (London: Karnac Books, 1995) 255-347. Wolfson is the leading feminist reader of Kabbalah, and feminists wishing to retrieve Shekhinah need to understand why he argues that that there will always be a privileging of the masculine over the feminine in the different types of gender transformation in the Kabbalah. We also need to understand why Wolfson attacks his predecessors' (Scholem and Tishby) notions of the feminine.

References

Butler, Judith. *Gender Troubles: Feminism and the Subversion of Identity*. New York: Routledge, 1990.

Cadden, Joan. *Meanings of Sex Difference in the Middle Ages: Medicine, Science and Culture*. Cambridge: Cambridge University Press, 1993.

Gadamer, Hans-Georg. *Truth and Method*. New York: Crossroads, 1982.

Gikatilla, Joseph. *The Gates of Light—Sha'are Orah*. Walnut Creek, CA: AltaMira Press,1994.

Gottlieb, Lynn. *She Who Dwells Within: A Feminist Vision of a Renewed Judaism*. San Francisco: HarperSanFrancisco, 1995.

Matt, Daniel. "The Mystic and the Mizwot." In *Jewish Spirituality from the Bible through the Middle Ages,* edited by Arthur Green. New York: Crossroads, 1988.

———. *Zohar*. Mahwah, NJ: Paulist Press, 1983.

Novick, Leah. "Encountering the Schechinah, The Jewish Goddess." In *The Goddess Re-Awakening,* edited by Shirley Nicholson, 204–214. Wheaton, IL: Theosophical Publishing House, 1989.

Scholem, Gershom G. *Major Trends in Jewish Mysticism*. New York: Schocken Books, 1961.

Tishby, Isaiah. *The Wisdom of the Zohar*. Oxford: Oxford University Press, 1989.

Wolfson, Elliot R. *Circle in the Square*. Albany, NY: State University of New York Press, 1995.

———. "Crossing gender boundaries in kabbalistic rituals and myth." In Mortimer Ostow's *Ultimate Intimacy: The Psychodynamics of Jewish Mysticism*. London: Karnac Books, 1995.

About the Author

Kohenet, Dr. Emily Leah Silverman is a Visiting Scholar at the Graduate Theological Union, Berkeley, CA. She received Smicha (ordination) from the Hebrew Priestess Institute and is a recent Past President of the American Academy of Religion Western Region. Silverman has developed the field study of Feminist Theology of Spiritual Resistance. Her current research is on the Feminist theology of Spiritual Resilience and Resistance of Jewish Women during the Nazi Holocaust. She most recently was an invited lecturer at the University of Wales and was formerly a lecturer at San Jose State University and taught at the Graduate Theological Union. Dr. Silverman also investigates the reclaiming and retrieval of Hebrew Priestess lineage, their 12 spiritual pathways and practice. Dr. Silverman was the organizer of Rosemary Radford

Ruether Frestschrift and co-edited with Dirk Von der Horst and Whitney Bauman *Voices of Feminist Liberation: Writing in Celebrations of Rosemary Ruether.* Silverman has also published *Edith Stein and Regina Jonas: Religious Visionaries of the Death Camps.* Silverman is a sought after invited speaker. She holds a Master of Divinity from Harvard Divinity School and a Ph.D. from the Graduate Theological Union.

3 Aspects of Old and New Approaches to Feminism in Islam: A Focus on the Middle East

Souad T. Ali

Introduction

Since the beginning of the twentieth century, issues of modernity and authenticity have been at the center of debate in the Middle East. The place and role of women in new emerging societies of the Middle East have been a significant part of this debate. Concepts of Westernization, modernity (*hadathah* or *mu'asarah*), secularism (*'ilmaniah*), and authenticity (*asalah*) are elements of the shared concern among the different groups of participants in this ongoing debate. On the one hand, given the misogyny of the period immediately preceding the rise of Islam in Arabia where female infanticide (*wa'd al-banat*) was the norm of the day,[1] the history of early Islam speaks of a tradition that improved the status of women significantly and elevated their position in an unprecedented manner. On the other hand, Muslim women in subsequent centuries have been struggling in most of their own societies against many aspects of oppression that Islam had denounced since the seventh century, through Qur'anic scriptures that stipulated, in the clearest manner, powerful laws in favor of women.[2]

Women's movements in the Middle East, particularly in Egypt, have been increasingly active since the 1890s. Within a broader concept of pan-Arab feminism, the Egyptian Feminist Union (EFU, established by Huda Sha'rawi in 1923) has reached out to women in other Arab countries since the late 1930s, a key move that eventually led to the establishment of the Arab Feminist Union (AFU) that held its first meeting in Cairo in 1944.[3] However, as will be revealed within the course of this paper, Arab women's ideological orientations and approaches to feminism have been manifold. Many groups of Arab and Egyptian women activists and scholars reflect on and articulate this distinction in views and orientations. The debate within and among the ranks of Muslim women, in general, has recently reflected the fact that certain forms of cultural or political aspects of women's issues—which Muslim women share with Western women—have been perceived by certain groups as "foreign" and "non-authentic." In her article, "Islamic Traditions and the Feminist Movement: Confrontation or Cooperation?" Lois Lamya' al-Faruqi claims that:

> Whether living in the Middle East or Africa, in Central Asia, in Pakistan, in Southeast Asia, or in Europe and the Americas, Muslim women tend to view the feminist movement with some apprehension. Although there are some features of the feminist cause with which we as Muslims would wish to join hands, other features generate our disappointment and even opposition. There is therefore no simple…answer to the question of the future of cooperation or competition which feminism may meet in an Islamic environment.[4]

Al-Faruqi's assertion has clearly failed to take into consideration the different orientations and approaches of Muslim feminists themselves as she speaks of a sum total of "Muslim women" that she has overgeneralized. Perhaps she could have elaborated on what she specifically meant or whether or not she talked to a specific group of women. The distinction between Western and Arab feminism should, rather, be seen within its historical context. Historians have offered several theories to explain the origins of feminism in Western societies. Historians note changes in family structure due to industrialization as an important factor in the rise of the first wave of U.S. feminism that led to women's acquisition of the right to vote in 1920.[5] Victorians in demographic patterns also have been considered causes of feminism.[6] Contradictions between the ideologies of women's roles and their actual position in society have further been suggested as causes for the rise of feminism.[7] Conversely, the emergence of Egyptian feminism, as Soha 'Abdel Kader explains, was not the result of industrialization, demographic pattern transitions, or the contradiction between ideologies and practice, but, rather, was due to political factors, namely, the British occupation of Egypt in 1882.[8]

This paper discusses early feminist voices that emerged in Egypt, advocating a brand of feminism that has been deeply embedded in citizenship and Islamic heritage without finding difficulty coming to terms or conflict with modernity. Women's movements in Egypt and other parts of the Middle East have long been striving to articulate and shape their own version of feminism that shares many of the universal aspects of other feminist movements but has, nonetheless, been fashioned by its own cultural heritage. The paper will further address the developments, similarities and differences between the early writings on women, and some examples of the most recent writings by Muslim women scholars and activists from Egypt and other parts of the

Middle East, highlighting the deep-rooted conflict and disagreement that accompanied these movements since their inception.

Early Approaches

In contrast to the widely held view of Middle Eastern women as "submissive non-thinkers to whom feminism is a foreign concept," history reveals that a feminist ideology began to take shape in Egypt as early as the 1890s when pioneering Arab women engaged in discreet forms of feminist activism.[9] In her chapter "Independent Women: More Than a Century of Feminism in Egypt," Margot Badran corrects the misconception that Arab feminism drew on the most recent Western feminist tradition. She argues that there is more than a century-long unbroken tradition of feminism in the Middle East, maintaining that:

> In Egypt, feminism has been indigenous, and that there has been broader cross-class cooperation among feminists than commonly acknowledged. From the colonial era to the present day, women across the spectrum from right to left have continued to ground their feminism in Islam and nationalism, as they have persisted in challenging a patriarchy transcending, in different ways, political and class formations.[10]

Feminism and women's movements in Egypt thus emerged as part of the social differentiation that took place as an outcome of the 19th century nationalist and intellectual *Nahda* (Renaissance) discourse. Egyptian feminism grew out of an expanded body of knowledge and the observations that Arab women made of their own lives during times of great transformation. The Islamic Reform Movement and the *Nahda* discourse led by Muhammed Abduh[11] (1849–1905), Qasim Amin (1863–1908) and other men made women aware, as Margot Badran and miriam cooke explain in their book: *Opening the Gates: A Century of Arab Feminist Writing* "that certain so-called Islamic practices, such as veiling, segregation, and seclusion imposed upon urban women, were not ordained by Islam as they had been led to believe."[12]

Before delving into the discussion on early women's activism in Egypt, it is important and equally useful to shed light on Qasim Amin, who has been largely perceived as the father of Arab feminism. An Egyptian lawyer, young judge, and writer on social and women's issues, Amin made a marked impact on both Egyptian and Middle Eastern social life, especially in the field of women's liberation. His contribution is mainly manifested in his most celebrated books that include, *Tahrir al-Mar'ah* (*The Emancipation or Liberation* of Women) published in 1899, and *al-Mar'ah al-Jadidah* (*The New Woman*) that appeared a couple of years later in 1901. Although, as noted above, some Arab feminists currently claim Amin as the father of Arab feminism and women's rights, others—as will be discussed in the course of this paper—criticize him for being the son of Lord Cromer, the colonial British governor of Egypt (1882–1907).

In *Tahrir al-Mar'ah*, Amin argues that the liberation of women is an essential prerequisite for the liberation of Egyptian society from both harmful traditions to women as well as foreign domination. His main thesis is that the status of women is the single most important aspect of Egyptian society in need of reform, for the emancipation and thus salvation of the country is contingent upon the liberation of women. Amin believes that this liberation can most effectively be made through education. He dedicates the whole first chapter of his book, *Tahrir al-Mar'ah*, to *Tarbiat al-Mar'ah* (Educating Women, pp. 17–52). He argues:

> Education is the only means through which a human being's status rises from humiliation and corruption to the marvels of dignity and honor. Every soul has the right to improve its innate faculties to any limits it aspires to. All divine and natural laws address women and men in the same manner.[13]

After a thorough discussion of the issue, Amin presents his suggestions for how the situation can be rectified. He uses an approach that employs two arguments: one based on Islam and another based on tradition, to arouse awareness within Muslims and non-Muslims in Egypt, and to call for the improvement of the status of Egyptian women, indeed all Arab women, suffering similar circumstances.[14] His main point is reflected in the suggestions he draws for the improvement of the status of women. These suggestions come under two sections; the first one concerns itself with traditions, culture, customs and norms of behavior. His conclusion here is quite simple: all harmful customs and traditions must be abolished, especially those customs that are falsely and erroneously perceived as religious while they only corrupt religion.[15] The second suggestion focuses on the *Shari'a* and calls on those scholars and jurists who know its laws and *ahkam* (rules) to consider the needs of the Muslim *umma* (nation) to improve the status of women through the following: Firstly, in implementing *Shari'a*, they should not stop at, or be influenced by, the interpretation of only one *Imam* (of the advocates of the four *Madhahib*—schools of jurisprudence)[16] of Islamic law whose *ijithad* (independent inquiry) might have been in conformity with his time, not necessarily with our time. Secondly, they need to research meticulously any new developments that took place without necessarily deviating from *usul* al-Shari'a. He maintains that it is through education and determination (*bil 'ilm wal 'azimah*) that such reforms can be carried out to liberate women.¹⁷ In his elaboration on how education can be used in this regard, Amin emphasizes that education provides the means to know the needs of society; it helps in distinguishing between the good and bad customs and tradition. Most importantly, education helps us know that the Qur'an does not specifically state some of the *Shari'a ahkam* or rules.¹⁸ He maintains:

> Don't you see that the Qur'an did not specify even the most important obligations such as *ahkam al-Salat* [prayer rule or rituals], or the amount of *Zakat* [almsgiving], nor the *Hajj* [pilgrimage] rituals; but it was the *Sunnah* that shaped all these rules in their totality, then the *mujtahidun* [interpreters]¹⁹ specified all these *ahkam* and decided on their breaches.²⁰

Accordingly, maintains Amin, it is important to preserve the Qur'an and only what cannot be changed of the *Sunnah*; and to abolish the *ahkam* or rules that were based on harmful customs and traditions (*al-'adat wal taqalid al-darrah*) because these are changeable based on time, place and circumstances.²¹ He further adds that people claim that these bad customs are Islamic, but this is not true. If these people had the right education, they would know that these are merely traditions that have nothing to do with Islam. Conversely, he elucidates, "if any religion on earth had the *sultan* or authority over influencing customs and traditions, the Muslim women today would have been ahead of all women of the world because the Islamic *Shari'a* preceded all religions in determining the equality of women to men emphasizing women's liberation, independence, and their entitlement to [enjoy] full human rights."²²

Nonetheless, Amin's book triggered severe criticism from the Khedival palace, as well as from religious and political figures in Egypt, such as Tal'at Harb, and from journalists and other writers. Mostly, Amin's views were perceived as calling for abandoning indigenous traditions and cultures and adopting foreign ones, especially with regard to the issue of unveiling. Amin devotes a whole chapter (pp. 53–92) of *Tahrir al-Mar'ah* to discussing the *Hijab al-Nisa* (Veiling of Women). However, a close reading of Amin's chapter on *Hijab* renders the severe criticism launched on him somewhat exaggerated. Contrary to what these criticisms allege (that Amin demanded the abolishing of *Hijab*), ironically, he argues:

> Some might assume that I am asking women to totally unveil. However, the truth is contrary to that. I still defend the *Hijab*, and consider it a cardinal of good behavior that must be preserved. However, I am asking that the veil be consistent with what the *Shari'a* stated…if the Islamic *Shari'a* specifically stated for the veil to be what it is now among some Muslims, then nobody

should dispute that and I would never have written a word to challenge that.... However, we don't find anything in the *Shari'a* that specifies the *Hijab* the way we see it; it is a custom that came to them through mixing with other nations, [a custom] that they adopted, exaggerated, and gave it religious credence like all other harmful customs that influenced people in the name of religion. But religion is innocent of it. Thus, we see nothing wrong with researching it; [not only that, but] it is in fact a duty to know about it and to clarify *ahkam al-Shari'a* on it and the need to change it. [23]

In response to the attack targeting him and his book *The Liberation of Women*, Amin wrote his second book entitled *al-Mar'ah al-Jadidah (The New Woman)*, in 1901. Unlike *Tahrir al-Mar'ah*, *al-Mar'ah al-Jadidah* was perceived by some scholars, such as Soha 'Abdel Kader, as "more rigorous and spirited."[24] 'Abdel Kader maintains, in her book *Egyptian Women in a Changing Society: 1899–1987*, that not only did he [Amin] indulge in a wider intellectual argument for the emancipation of women, but also "for the advantages of Westernization in general."[25] Clearly, Amin, in his second book, tries to defend his first book and implicitly responds to the criticisms launched against it. However, in *The New Woman*, although Amin defends Islam, he focuses less on the Islamic tradition such as the Qur'an and *Sunnah*, apparently to avoid further criticism. Instead, he explicitly advocates a Western analytical approach, arguing that the real cause of the decline of Muslim community is not due to Islam. As Albert Hourani explains, according to Amin, the decline taking place in Muslim societies that directly affects the position of women "is not due to the natural environment, for there have been ages of flourishing civilizations in these same countries; it is not due to Islam, the decline of which is itself a result and not a cause of the decline of social strength."[26] Hourani maintains, paraphrasing Amin:

> The real cause of the decay is the disappearance of the social virtues, of "moral strength," and the cause of *that* is ignorance—ignorance of the true sciences from which alone can be derived the laws of human happiness. This ignorance begins in the family. The relations of man and woman, of mother and child, are the basis of society; the virtues which exist in the family will exist in the nation. "The work of women in society is to form the morals of the nation."[27] But in Muslim countries neither men nor women are properly educated to create a real family life, and woman has not the freedom or status necessary if she is to play her role.[28]

As noted above, while some Egyptian women scholars such as Soha 'Abdel Kader wrote favorable remarks about Amin's second book, Leila Ahmed attacked his first book, *Tahrir al- Mar'ah* arguing that it "represents the rearticulation in native voice of the colonial thesis of the inferiority of the Islamic culture and the superiority of the European."[29]

However, regardless of the controversy over his work (discussed below in much detail), nobody can dispute the fact that Qasim Amin made the debate on women's issues in Egypt a subject of national and political concern. As the following discussion will show, Amin's ideas continue to provoke intense dialogue between Arab and Muslim feminists right up to the present day. In her book, *Women and Gender in Islam: Historical Roots of a Modern Debate*, Leila Ahmed argues, sarcastically, against the fact that Amin's book has been traditionally considered as "marking the beginning of feminism in Arabic literature."[30] Conversely, she maintains that Amin's book "merely called for the substitution of Islamic-style male dominance by Western-style male dominance. Hence, far from being the father of Arab feminism, Amin might more aptly be described as the son of Cromer and colonialism."[31] She elucidates that Amin's call for a primary education for girls and for reforming laws pertinent to polygamy and divorce can hardly be "described as innovatory," because both Muhammed Abduh (1849–1905) and Rifa'ah Rafi' al-Tahtawi (1801–1873) argued for women's education and called for reforming marriage, divorce, and polygamy laws in the 1870s, 1880s "even earlier without provoking violent controversy," as Amin's book did.[32] She maintains that the anger and passion that Amin's book ignited become intelligible—not within the "substantive reforms" Amin recommended for women in terms of polygamy and divorce—but rather only within the "symbolic reform—the abolition of the veil—that he passionately urged and, second, the reforms, indeed the fundamental changes in culture and society."[33] Changing customs regarding women and changing their costumes (abolishing the veil in particular) maintains Ahmed, were central to Amin's thesis.[34]

To set the background of her critique of Amin's book, Ahmed argues that British colonial rule did not improve the status of women in Egypt. Conversely, she maintains that whatever legal reforms introduced by the British "did not affect the position of women," and were largely designed to serve Europeans themselves.[35] She further discusses the Western narrative of the typical "otherness and inferiority of Islam," especially with regard to women, beginning with Dante's *Divine Comedy* along with subsequent European accounts as detailed in Edward Sa'id's book *Orientalism*.[36] Lord Cromer, the British governor of Egypt from 1882–1907 whose thesis on the new colonial discourse of Islam centered on women, stated that Islam was innately and inherently oppressive to women, and this segregation, the veil in particular, epitomized that oppression.[37] Such customs were portrayed as "the fundamental reasons for the general and comprehensive backwardness of Islamic societies."[38] Hence, based on such flawed misconceptions, only when these customs were removed, Muslim societies could then "begin to move forward in the path of civilization."[39] Critiquing Cromer's anti-feminist stance in his own native land, Ahmed argues, ironically,

> ...the Victorian colonial paternalistic establishment appropriated the language of feminism in the service of its assault on the religions and cultures of Other men, and in particular on Islam, in order to give an aura of moral justification to that assault at the very same time that it combated feminism within its own society.[40]

Furthermore, "Male imperialists, such as Cromer, known in their own home societies for their intransigent opposition to feminism led the attack abroad against the 'degradation' of women in Muslim societies and were foremost champions of unveiling."[41] Those like Cromer raised the banner of women's liberation in Muslim societies while assuming a misogynist stance in their own countries. Ahmed provides historical evidence regarding Cromer's opposition to feminism in the British Parliament. She also refers to Cromer's policies in Egypt that were detrimental to women, such as those policies that hindered girls' education and discouraged the training of women doctors. Christian missionaries exhibited the same belief that the indigenous culture was inferior to justify their attack on Islam. And, hence, whether it was patriarchal men or feminists, the ideas of Western feminism essentially functioned to morally justify the attack on native societies and to support this notion of the superiority of the European.

Leila Ahmed's synthesis in this regard is that, the "ideas to which Cromer and the missionaries gave expression formed the basis of Amin's book. The rationale in which Amin, a French-educated upper-middle-class lawyer, grounded his call for changing the position of women and for abolishing the veil was essentially the same as theirs."[42] She quotes many parts of his book, *Tahrir al-Mar'ah*, to substantiate her point. Thus, in lieu of these ideas she reiterates: "Amin's book...represents the rearticulation in native voice of the colonial thesis of the inferiority of the native and Muslim and the superiority of the European."[43]

To confirm her point further, Ahmed refers to examples of opponents of Amin's book, such as Tal'at Harb, whom she describes as more "national" in their call for liberating women.[44] Leila Ahmed's ultimate conclusion is that, "Amin's book, then, marks the entry of the colonial narrative of women and Islam—in which the veil and the treatment of women epitomized Islamic inferiority—into mainstream Arabic discourse. And the opposition it generated similarly marks the emergence of an Arabic narrative developed in resistance to the colonial narrative."[45]

On the other hand, many scholars and intellectuals, later viewed Amin's book as the discourse that paved the way to women in Egypt to express their struggle and activism in their own voices.[46] This, however, is further challenged given the fact that, at the personal level, women in Egypt started writing about their own experiences and liberations as early as the 1860s (even before the publication of Amin's first book in 1899). Ahmed's *Women and Gender in Islam* shows that Egyptian women wrote in these various women's journals published between 1860–1922, such as *Fatat al-Sarq* (*The Girl of the East*), *Fatat al-Nil* (*Woman of the Nile*), among others, as documented by these journals' records available in *Dar al-Kutub al-Misriyyah*. Badran and cooke claim that Arab women produced a discourse that can be identified as feminist before there was an explicit term for feminism. They maintain that, historically, a term connoting feminism first appeared in the Arab world in 1909, when Malak Hifni Nassef, the first Egyptian female writer to contribute articles to the mainstream press, published a collection of articles and speeches in a book entitled *Al-Nisaiyat*.[47] The content of Nassef's book was feministic, advocating the improvement of women's lives, new educational and work opportunities, and the reinstatement of freedoms understood to be granted by Islam. Since the Arabic word "nisai" conventionally signifies something related to, by, or about women, Badran and cooke believe that it was an Arab woman who introduced the term "feminism" to the world. The term was then adopted by the Egyptian Feminist Union EFU (1923) and was used by its members unambiguously as feminism.[48]

During the 1900s, Egyptian women's literary, intellectual, and political life started a period of enormous vitality during which varieties of feminist activism emerged as an integral part of the nationalist sentiment in Egypt. It was, hence, no accident that the heroic days of nationalism were also those when educated Muslim women, led by Huda Sha'rawi, abandoned the veil and first took part in public life. Even during the early stages of Egyptian feminism, conservative trends that followed a conservative Islamic line, represented, for instance, by The Society for the Advancement of Women (1908), developed with liberal trends that followed Amin's orientations.[49] Huda Sha'rawi (1879–1947), the most famous Egyptian activist, founded "The Intellectual Association of Egyptian Women" in 1914. Many other organizations followed suit, most important of which was the Egyptian Feminist Union (EFU) founded in Cairo by Huda Sha'rawi in 1923, as noted earlier. The organizational and political success of the EFU helped bring about significant gains for women. The main aim of the EFU was to raise women's intellectual and moral levels and to enable them to attain political, social, and legal equality. In response to feminist pressures, the parliament even decreed education compulsory for both boys and girls.[50]

The most fundamental outcome of the Egyptian feminist movement was the establishment of the Arab Feminist Union (AFU) and its movement towards a broader concept of Pan-Arab/African feminism. In the first Arab Feminist Conference, convened in Cairo in 1944, fifty resolutions addressing political, social, and economic goals and emphasizing gender equality were produced. Further, Badran and cooke noticed that a "resolution aiming at eliminating gender distinctions in language…foreshadowed more recent attempts in other languages, such as English, to eradicate sexism in language."[51]

From a religious standpoint, the conference emphasized its total rejection of the oppression of women and called for the exposition of colonialist laws that deprived Muslim women of the rights they obtained at the time of the Prophet Muhammed during the great days of Islam. In her opening and closing remarks, Huda Sha'rawi, the President of the Union said:

> Islam has given her [the Muslim woman] the right to vote for the ruler and has allowed her to give opinions on questions of jurisprudence and religion. The *Shari'a* [Islamic Law] gave her the right to education and to fight in the ranks of warriors and has made her equal to the man in all rights and responsibilities.… The woman demands with her loudest voice to be restored her political rights, rights granted to her by the *Shari'a* and dictated to her by the demands of the present. [Women] will not agree to be chained in slavery or pay for the consequences of men's mistakes.[52]

Huda Sha'rawi, later followed by Doria Shafiq (1914–76), promoted feminism in the rhetoric of "secularism" and democracy. However, having said that, it is critical to note, as Margot Badran has earlier reminded us, that from the rise of Arab feminism to the present, its advocates across the spectrum from left to right have consistently employed Islam and nationalism as legitimizing discourses.[53] It becomes clear that, although the Sha'rawi version of feminism was "secular," broadly speaking, it was embedded in Islam (her demands for social reform did not advocate for reforms lacking Islamic sanctions). This can be seen more clearly in the way she dealt with such issues as polygamy and divorce. When protesting against polygamy, for instance, she recognized the exceptions for polygamy that are granted by the Qur'an. Further, Sha'rawi's demand for equal education for girls was also based on the teachings of Islam.

Unlike Sha'rawi, Malak Hifni Nassef (1886–1918) was an advocate for a conservative Islamic feminism. Her version of feminism differed from Huda

Sha'rawi's, mainly in her strong opposition to unveiling. As the daughter of Hifni Bey Nassef, a distinguished member of Muhammed Abduh's circle, Nassef was trained under more liberal standards. Despite Qasim Amin's noted influence over her, she declared in one of her poems that she did not belong to his way of thinking. She was more conservative than Amin and repeatedly emphasized her allegiance to Islam and condemned imitation of the West.[54] Nassef thus choose to express a version of feminism that did not affiliate itself with Westernization and rejected unveiling. Apparently, as Ahmed has observed, she was aware of the misogyny in contemporary male texts and the politics of male dominance being re-enacted through the debate over the veil. She believed that unveiling was a mere expression of male corruption, as she made clear in one speech:

> How can you men of letters…command us to unveil when any of us is subject to foul language if she walks in the street, this one throwing adulterous glances at her and that one bespattering her with his despicableness. [Given] a collection of men such as we have at present, whose abuse and shamelessness a woman should not be exposed to, and a collection of women such as we have today, whose understanding is that of babes, for women to unveil and mix with men would be an innovation that would lead to evil.[55]

However, despite their different approaches to feminism, both Sha'rawi and Nassef pushed for fundamental reforms to improve the status of women. In Egypt, the first political action that women became involved in occurred during the 1919 revolution, when women marched through the streets of Cairo in support of the revolution against the British. Huda Sha'rawi and the wives and relatives of prominent Egyptian politicians were among the leaders of that march. It was at that time that Huda Sha'rawi cast off her veil and thus inspired other women to do so. In 1910, Malak Hifni Nassef presented to the Legislative Assembly ten points that she considered should form the basis for women's reforms. These points included the teaching of true religion and domestic science, the establishment of theoretical and practical health laws, and the training of children. She also asked for a sufficient number of girls to be trained in medicine and education to meet the needs of women in Egypt.[56] Sha'rawi, as discussed earlier, made several demands to elevate the status of Egyptian and Arab/African women, first through the EFU and later through the AFU.

A few years later, a more radical Islamist feminist voice made its way into the political arena of the Middle East. Led by Zeinab al-Ghazali, an Egyptian Muslim fundamentalist (1917–2005), this group campaigned for women's rights in strict Islamic terms. Al-Ghazali's conviction of the superiority of the

Islamic culture, a conviction vigorously nurtured in her childhood and later solidified by her involvement in the Islamist movement in Egypt, seems to be a psychological replication of her worth as a Muslim and a determination to find feminism within Islamic, as opposed to Western, values. Given the bitterness over the Palestinian issue at the time (the 1940s) and the anti-Western feeling, this group considered the developing situation to be a Western imperialist and Zionist crusade against Arab, African, and Islamic nations. Hence, the militancy in their total rejection of the West because of what they perceived as its antagonism toward Islam. Nevertheless, their main rejection was specifically directed towards Western women. The Muslim Brotherhood, of which the fundamentalist feminist movement is an affiliate, rejected Western women as a model for Muslim women, arguing that the West had exploited women and female sexuality to increase profit in the service of capitalism.[57]

Overall, from its broadest to its most specific trends, Arab feminism reflects the conflicting ideologies that shaped the earlier *Nahda* movement. In this sense, the debate over women's liberation and their rights has led to a threefold divergence in outlook and ideology.

First, Islamic Feminism: This movement is derived from the teachings of early Islam and draws its arguments from the claims of the Islamic Reform Movement about the rights of women in Islam. The basic argument of this school, which is derived from the *Nahda* discourse about women's rights in Islam, is twofold:

1. Based on the fact that Islam has liberated women, Muslim women—within a true interpretation of Islam—have considerably more rights than women in other cultures, eastern or western. Representatives of this school emphasize the gains women attained during the early days of Islam; hence their feminist interpretation of the Qur'anic Scriptures and the living conditions of women during the rise of Islam.
2. This school blames the social problems, gender inequalities, and the unfavorable conditions of Muslim women today, in general, on what they perceive as the corruption that came to Islam from outside, on the one hand, and to the misinterpretation of the Qur'an by some male jurists, on the other.

Secondly, Secular Feminism: The program of the secular feminist school was also embedded in the *Nahda* discourse. It included under its aegis Muslim, Christian, and Marxist women alike. This trend took more radical steps after the Second World War, when leftist and feminist factions became increasingly interested in addressing problems, particularly those that reflect prejudicial treatment with regards to job salaries, education, and family life. New voices and leadership emerged out of the ranks of the Egyptian left movement. Feminist leaders, such as Inge Aflatun and Latifa al-Zayat, worked vigorously to locate the gender issue in egalitarian terms. Under the late Egyptian leader, Nasser, this feminist voice was subdued. It was suppressed even further under the regime of the late president Sadat. It is only within the last few years that the secular feminist movement has been fully revived. Nevertheless, it has predominantly been rejected by different segments of the society for its open advocacy of secularism.

Thirdly, and ironically, "Fundamentalist" or Islamist Feminism: This trend represents a movement that endorses a full distancing from Western discourse. The Society of Muslim Sisters sprang up in the 1940s as a strong branch of the Muslim Brotherhood. Although they stressed that Islamic education was essential to women chiefly in helping them fulfill their roles as wives and mothers, this was not their sole objective. This trend also promoted the return to Islamic dress. Although over the middle decades the veil virtually disappeared from the Arab urban scene, it reappeared as the visible emblem of Islamists in the latter part of the twentieth century. One factor that particularly contributed to the spread of the veil was Sadat's active endorsement, in the 1970s, of the Muslim to serve as a base of opposition to his opponents—the leftists. The Islamic fundamentalist feminists justified their claim by maintaining the idea that the veil symbolizes dignity and validity of all native Islamic customs as well as female autonomy. Recent studies show that veiling has also been connected with the emotional comfort of bringing the values of Islam to the Westernized urban cities of the area. Islamic dress, in its various styles, seems to be growing more popular in the Islamic world, and studies indicate that its use is particularly widespread among university students. However, Islamic fundamentalists have been criticized for articulating a different version of the religion—one that is intolerant of all understandings of Islam except its own.

Recent Approaches

Recent writings on Muslim women's issues in the Middle East reveal that their methodology, although consistent in its advocacy of feminism, differs significantly from the approach adopted by earlier women. This difference becomes understandable given the fact that the writings of nineteenth century women were influenced by the circumstances that governed their lives in an age of major transformations in the Middle East, as reflected in the experience of

Egyptian women discussed above. Recent studies on Muslim women's issues, as reflected, for example, in such books as Fatima Mernissi's *The Veil and Male Elite: A Feminist Interpretation of Women's Rights in Islam* have been more concerned with discussing the legal status of women.[58] Mernissi, for instance, digs so deeply into the original literature of Islam trying to find out whether or not the oppression of women in Muslim societies is sanctioned by Islam. As part of the Muslim feminist movement, Mernissi, a Moroccan sociologist, scholar, university professor, and activist was dynamically involved in articulating a discourse on women on a broader sociopolitical level. Raising the economic awareness and improving the legal, social, and political status of women seems to be the primary aim of such discourses. However, as I have argued elsewhere, feminism within the sphere of Muslim women has other forms and shapes. In addition to what I have just described of the most recent Muslim feminist movement, represented here by Mernissi, there are other women's groups (some of whom have also been projecting themselves as "feminists") but these are what I refer to here as "fundamentalist" or Islamist feminists. This group is represented by the Egyptian Islamist activists Zeinab al-Ghazali and Safinaz Qazim. In dealing with recent studies on women's issues, I will use Mernissi and Ghazali/Qazim as contrasting models to represent these two forms of feminism.

The Veil and the Male Elite: A Feminist Interpretation of Women's Rights in Islam, published in 1991, is Mernissi's attempt to research the position of women in Islam from its primary sources composed and collected by early Muslim historians and scholars including *al-Tabari* (838–923), *Ibn-Hisham* (d. 834), *Ibn-Hajar* (1372–1449) and *Ibn Sa'ad* (d. 844). Mernissi's approach in dealing with feminist issues differs from the approaches of earlier feminists, such as Sha'rawi and Malak Nassef, in that, while the latter's feminism did not clearly deal with the problem of interpreting early Islamic literature, especially the *Hadith*, Mernissi has been quite explicit in challenging what she labels as "a tradition of misogyny" in *Hadith* fabrication and forgery. One of the main themes of the book revolves around Mernissi's question of whether "Islam is opposed to women's rights," and her conclusion is that it is not. She goes a step further to argue that: "if women's rights are a problem for some modern Muslim men, it is neither because of the Koran, nor the Prophet, nor the Islamic tradition, but simply because those rights conflict with the interests of the male elite."[59] Mernissi, thus, deals heavily with the issue of women's political rights, especially regarding their right to leadership. She discusses this through a controversial *Hadith* claimed to have been said by the Prophet Muhammed. The *Hadith* states that: "Those who entrust their affairs to a woman will never know prosperity,"[60] an argument that Mernissi refused to take for granted. After thoroughly researching the source, origin, circumstances, and transmitters of the *Hadith*, Mernissi reveals interesting facts that might constitute grounds for eliminating the transmitter of the *Hadith* as she simultaneously casts doubt on the authenticity of this specific *Hadith* even though it was included in *Sahih al-Bukhari* (d. 870), perceived to be one of the most "authentic" of *Hadith* collections. Finding justification in *Malik, Ibn Hajar and Tabari*, she concludes by attacking and severely criticizing what she describes as misogynous tendencies within *Hadith* forgery.

In the *Veil and the Male Elite*, Mernissi shows an awareness of her worth as a Muslim woman and feminist, an awareness that was clearly lacking in her earlier book *Beyond the Veil* (1973). Almost twenty years after the publication of this book, Mernissi wrote *The Veil and the Male Elite*, declaring her departure from her old approach to discussing women's liberation in Muslim societies. To set the tone of the theme of her book, and in what is apparently a response to some of the prevalent misconceptions in this context, Mernissi maintains:

> Any man who believes that a Muslim woman who fights for the dignity and right to civilization excludes herself necessarily from the *umma* and is a brainwashed victim of Western propaganda is a man who misunderstands his own religious heritage, his own cultural identity. The vast and inspiring records of Muslim history so brilliantly completed for us, by scholars such as Ibn Hisham, Ibn Hajar, Ibn Sa'ad, and Tabari, speak to the contrary. We Muslim women can walk into the modern world with pride, knowing that the quest for dignity, democracy, and human rights, for full participation in the political and social affairs of our country, stems from no imported Western values, but is a true part of the Muslim tradition.[61]

Critiquing what she perceives as many Muslim men's misinterpretation of Islam with regard to women, Mernissi argues that neither the Qur'an nor the Prophet, as the main and primary sources of Islamic law, desired anything other than equality between the sexes. However, as noted earlier, she maintains, explaining the current prevalent oppression of women in Muslim societies, that "…if women's rights are a problem for some modern Muslim men, it is neither because of the Koran nor the Prophet, nor the Islamic tradition, but simply because those rights conflict with the interests of the male elite."[62] I have deliberately emphasized this point for its importance; yet what appears to have triggered Mernissi's concern regarding such a misinterpretation is the previously mentioned *Hadith* narrative allegedly attributed to the Prophet Muhammed: "Those who entrust their affairs to a woman will never know prosperity."[63] Given the fact that the *Hadith* included in the *Sahih* of al-Bukhari, Mernissi elucidates, "it is *a priori* considered true..."[64] However, Mernissi was not convinced and decided to do her own research in early Islamic literature of *Hadith* tradition to verify the authenticity of a *Hadith* that has disturbed her given the fact that the Qur'an never mentioned anything to this effect. As part of her research Mernissi consulted the respected seventeen volume biographic study of the *Fath al-Bari* by Ibn Hajar al-'Asqalani, highlighting the fact that it includes a line-by-line commentary for each *Hadith* on al-Bukhari regarding historical clarifications, the political events that served as background, a description of the battles, the identity of the conflicting parties, the identity of the transmitters and their opinions, and the debates regarding their reliability.[65] According to Abu Bakra, the original transmitter of that *Hadith*, the Prophet said this *Hadith* "when he learned that the Persians had named a woman to rule them."[66] Given the fact that al-Bukhari does not elaborate on this *Hadith* apart from reporting the words of Abu Bakra, the content of the *Hadith* itself, Mernissi embarks on another mission. Thus, to find more on Abu Bakra, she decides, "we must turn to the huge work of Ibn Hajar al-'Asqalani."[67] As documented by Ibn Hajar, Abu Bakra claimed to have recalled this *Hadith* after the Battle of the Camel, twenty-five years after the Prophet's death. This was when 'Aisha, the Prophet's wife, was calling for Muslims to join her in the Battle against 'Ali Ibn Abi Talib:

> When he was contacted by 'A'isha, Abu bakra made known his response to her: he was against fitna. He is supposed to have said to her (according to the way he told it *after the battle*): 'It is true that you are our umm [mother, alluding to her title of *Umm al-Mu'minin* "Mother of Believers," which the Prophet bestowed on his wives during his last years]; it is true that as such that you have rights over us. But I heard the Prophet say: "Those who entrust their affairs to a woman will never know prosperity."[68, 69]

Not only did Abu Bakra remember the *Hadith* a quarter of a century after the Prophet's death, but Mernissi was able to find more discrediting information recorded by one of his biographers, that he (Abu Bakra) was convicted by the second Caliph, 'Umar Ibn al-Khattab, based on the fact that he lied in accusing an innocent man of *zina* (adultery).[70] Finding justification in Malik Ibn Anas (d. 795), Mernissi concludes: "If we have to apply this rule to Abu Bakra, he would have to be immediately eliminated."[71, 72]

Mernissi's criticism of this alleged *Hadith* falls within the realm of a debate that has been active amongst Muslim scholars throughout the centuries regarding the problem of *Isnad*, or the science of *Hadith* transmission in Islamic law. Her point is supported by the fact that *Hadith* has undergone a series of criticisms by early Muslim scholars themselves. As well as the fact that, within

Hadith, the area that has been subjected to close scrutiny is *Isnad*, which deals with the chain of transmitters of each individual *Hadith* and through which a number of unauthentic *Hadith* have been eliminated. The challenge Mernissi is posing is: even some of the *Hadith* that are considered authentic and included in one of the most trusted among the canonical tradition—*Sahih* of al-Bukhari—might be problematic, especially when it is clearly not corroborated by Qur'anic Scriptures. Hence, Mernissi's call for "redoubled vigilance when, taking the sacred as an argument, someone hurls at the believer as basic truth a political axiom so terrible and with such grave historical consequences."[73]

Conservative Voices

On the other side of the spectrum, there are other voices equally claiming to advocate women's rights within Islamic terms. However, while the brand of feminism advocated by Mernissi is constantly calling for correcting what she perceives as the injustices inflicted on women's lives through the misinterpretation of Islam, the other voices identify such injustices as *Jahiliyya*, ignorance, and in many instances succumb to them under the pretext that these are "pre-Islamic legacies." In addition to Zeinab al-Ghazali, this group includes such Islamist women as Safinaz Qazim. Given the fact that I have already discussed Zeinab al-Ghazali as part of earlier voices, I will confine this last part to discussing Safinaz Qazim as an Islamist voice of a younger generation, claiming to advocate women's rights, while she openly denounces feminism. For Qazim, feminism is a movement—not for women's liberation—but a movement that chains women and alienates them from their humanity. Given this, she maintains that feminism is "unnecessary." With regard to such issues as equality, Qazim argues that, "Allah gave certain different blessings to men and women, but these are partial differences that do not mean inequalities."[74] While Zeinab al-Ghazali's linkage with Hasan al-Banna (1906–1949), the founder of the Muslim Brotherhood in Egypt, has lent her some of the latter's allure and legitimacy, Qazim can claim no such historic and deep link to the Muslim Brotherhood in its entirety. However, like al-Ghazali, Qazim's main criticism has been against all aspects of Muslim society that she perceives as being "ape imitations of the West," thus she rejects what she perceives as the West's attempt to impose, discredit, and eliminate cultural authenticity and religion within the Muslim world.[75] Qazim's point of departure from Zeinab al-Ghazali's discourse is that she openly admits that women are and continue to be oppressed. However, she attributes this oppression to their ignorance of religion and rights. She maintains:

> There has been oppression against women, but that is a result of ignorance (Jahiliyya) and barbarism (hamajiyya). These are pre-Islamic legacies. It is very important to make a distinction between our heritage (*irth*) and what actually takes place. It is not the oppression of man to woman, but the oppression of someone who does not fear God to a fellow human being.[76]

However, Qazim believes that there are issues that are far more serious than women's oppression, such as fighting Western ideologies against Islam. Most significant is Qazim's opposition to feminism; she admits to being "one of its most ardent enemies."[77] She justifies this antagonism by claiming that feminism is "the embodiment of much misinterpretation and harm to women [because] feminism ultimately leads to a fight between two camps: men and women."[78] Hence, her conclusion, alluded to earlier, is that feminism is unnecessary—since it is not for women's liberation as much as for chaining them to certain erroneous ideas that alienate them from their humanity.

Before concluding, the contradiction inherent in the Islamist discourse on women is valuable to review. A close look at the rhetoric of Zeinab al-Ghazali and Safinaz Qazim reveals that, despite their antagonistic views to feminism, both seem (at the individual and personal level) to lead quite a feminist way of life, while publicly advocating contrary discourses for other women. This is by no means strange to the Islamist ideology they adhere to. For instance, the contradiction between al-Ghazali's public discourse on women and her private life is striking. She wrote in one article, "a woman asking her husband for divorce is a crime that deserves punishment, for is there anything more terrible than a woman threatening the nest of her marriage and her motherhood?"[79] Conversely, not only did she ask her first husband for divorce, but she admits that she insisted on having the *'ismah* (right to divorce) in her hand upon her second marriage contract, stipulating that her husband should never interfere in her Islamist activism. As Azza Karam has noted: "in view of this, it becomes increasingly obvious that al-Ghazali seems to apply double standards: one for herself and the other for other Muslim women. Her own, essentially public role, and her private life contradict what she preaches."[80]

Conclusion

In conclusion, it is evident that Middle Eastern and Egyptian women's movements have followed a particular path. Beginning in the 1890s, Middle Eastern societies experienced deep social changes in areas of civil, cultural, and political life in search for an indigenous reinvented identity that could be utilized to confront new challenges. Women's movements in Egypt, as well as other parts of the Middle East, represent an evolution in correlation to this profound growth and change. The leaders of these movements, men and women, through the ages, constructed their vision of the world, grounded in Islam and Arab culture. Eventually and inevitably, more than one type of articulation, approach, and political practice emerged. Recently, these movements have branched into three broad trends: Islamic, Islamist, and secular. Each of these movements continued to develop and branched into several others that deserve to be studied more at length in a separate project.

Although the focus of this study is on Muslim feminist approaches in Egypt and the Middle East, it is worth noting that expanded literature has recently been coming out from American Muslim women's experiences that take inspiration from these Egyptian and Middle Eastern earlier movements. Examples of such literature are reflected in the writings of amina wadud, Kecia Ali, Juliane Hammer, Asma Barlas, Nimat Barazangi, among others. To avoid changing the scope of this paper which is so importantly focused on the specific Middle East region and history, including the colonial history, a different future study focused on the literature on American Muslim women's experiences will certainly do justice to such important writings by Muslim American and other scholars.

As this paper has demonstrated, the debate on each one of the three approaches of feminism discussed—Islamic feminism, Islamist feminism, and secular feminism—has been handled at the highest levels of social and intellectual life in Egypt as well as other parts of the Middle East (as in the case of the Moroccan Mernissi). While most, if not all, of these movements might be similar in embodying a strategy that emphasizes particular and general aspects of Middle Eastern heritage, other varieties of these movements may be attributed to the distance of each one of them from political Islam as a governing ideology.[81]

Notes

1. The Qur'an has clearly criticized and banned female infanticide in many *Ayahs* (verses) such as the following: "when the female infant, buried alive, is questioned for what crimes she was killed," chapter 81. In this *Surat (al- Takwir)*, female infanticide is singled out as the most brutal, unjust, culpable sin. As the Qur'an details, in pre- Islamic society the crime was committed in the guise of social plausibility in secret collusion and no questions were asked. But in the Day of Judgment full questions will be asked and the victim herself will be able to testify and to give evidence, for she had committed no crime.

2. Numerous Qur'anic *Ayahs* spell out women's rights to education, marriage, divorce, inheritance, economic independence, etc.: examples can be found in chapters 4, 2, 5, among others. In addition, such themes of equality between men and women are reflected in such *Ayahs* as 35 of chapter 33 of *Surat al-Ahzab*, and *Ayah* 124 of *Surat al-Nisa* among other examples.

3. In her book *Women and Gender in Islam: Historical Roots of a Modern Debate* (Yale 1992), Leila Ahmed elaborates on the emergence and development of both the EFU and the AFU, respectively.

4. Lois Lamya' al-Faruqi, "Islamic Traditions and the Feminist Movement: Confrontation or Cooperation?" http://www.salaam.co.uk/wp-content/uploads/2019/09/islamic-traditions-feminist-movement.pdf

5. In her book *The Politics of Women's Liberation* (1975) Jo Freeman explores this first wave of American feminism.

6. See for example R. J. Evans, *The Feminists: Women's Emancipation Movements in Europe, America and Australia* (1977).

7. Juliet Mitchell discusses this theory in her book *Women's Estate* (1971).

8. Soha 'Abdel Kader, *Egyptian Women in a Changing Society: 1899–1987* (Boulder, CO: Lynn Rienner Publishers, 1987), 50.

9. Booklist. Review excerpt on book cover. Badran, Margot, and miriam cooke, editors. *Opening the Gates: A Century of Arab Feminist Writing.* Bloomington: Indiana University Press, 1990.

10. Margot Badran, "Independent Women: More Than a Century of Feminism in Egypt" in *Arab Women: Old Boundaries, New Frontiers*, ed. Judith E. Tucker (Bloomington, IN: Indiana University Press, 1993), 129.

11. Abduh was the most forceful 19th century advocate of Islamic liberalism. Among the reforms he suggested, his critique of polygamy has been remarkable. He argued, "in nothing does Islam maintain its fitness to be considered a modern world religion than in the high position of honor it accords to women. According to the Qur'anic teachings, men and women are equal before God in all essential aspects. Polygamy, although permitted in the Qur'an, was a response to existing social conditions and was given with the greatest possible reluctance.... The practical impossibility of [justice and impartiality in treating more than one wife] indicated that the Divine Law, in its intent, contemplated monogamy as the original and ideal state of marriage. The evils of polygamy and of the easy and frequent divorce

were an outcome of ignoring the original intent of the Qur'an, in this and other aspects. It therefore was necessary that all unfavorable conditions affecting the lives of women be corrected in the spirit of the religion of Islam." (Qtd. in 'Abdel Kader (1987), pp. 53–54).

12 Margot Badran and miriam cooke, "Introduction," in *Opening the Gates: An Anthology of Arab Feminist Writing*, 2nd ed. (Bloomington, IN: Indiana University Press, 1990), xxxv.

13 Qasim Amin, *Tahrir al-Mar'ah* (Cairo: Tarqqai Publisher, 1991), 22. See also his entire argument on the education of women pp. 17–52. All translations are mine unless otherwise stated.

14 Ibid., 153.

15 Ibid., 9.

16 These are: the Hanafi, the Maliki, the Shafi'i, and the Hanbali.

17 Amin, *Tahrir al-Mar'ah*, 153.

18 Amin's ideas and suggestions on education are further detailed on pp. 133–161 of *Tahrir al-Mar'ah*.

19 The noun *ijithad* denotes "independent inquiry"; similarly, the plural active participle *mujtahidun* and *mufasirun* synonymously denote interpreters of the Qur'an or the *Sunnah*.

20 Ibid., 157.

21 Ibid., 11.

22 Ibid., 11.

23 Ibid., 53–56.

24 Soha 'Abdel Kader, *Egyptian Women in a Changing Society: 1899–1987* (Boulder, CO: Lynn Rienner Publishers, 1987), 60.

25 Ibid., 60.

26 Albert Hourani, *Arabic Thought in the Liberal Age, 1798–1939* (Cambridge: Cambridge University Press, 1983), 164.

27 Amin, *al-Mar'ah al-Jadidah*, 124, translated by and quoted in Hourani, *Arabic Thought*, 162.

28 Hourani, *Arabic Thought*, 162.

29 Leila Ahmed, *Women and Gender in Islam: Historical Roots of a Modern Debate* (New Haven, CT: Yale University Press), 162.

30 Ibid., 145.

31 Ibid., 162–163.

32 Ibid., 144.

33 Ibid., 145.

34 Ibid., 144–145.

35 Ibid., 146.

36 Ibid., 149.

37 In one of his passages on Islam and women, Cromer audaciously argued that: "The attitudes of Muslim women to their religion are milder than those of men. This is not surprising as the roots of the differences in attitude between Christian and Muslim women lies in the intrinsic differences between Christianity and Islam. Islam gives men a status far above that of women. It is therefore natural that Muslim women are not too enthusiastic about their religion" (Qtd. in 'Abdel Kader's *Egyptian Women*, 57).
38 Ahmed, *Women and Gender*, 152.
39 Ibid., 152.
40 Ibid., 152.
41 Ibid., 237.
42 Ibid., 155.
43 Ibid., 155–158, 160.
44 Ibid., 162.
45 Ibid., 163.
46 See 'Abdel Kader, *Egyptian Women*, 64.
47 Malek Hifni Nassef, *Al-Nisaiyat* (Cairo: Matbaat al-Jaridah, 1910).
48 Badran and cooke, *Opening the Gates*.
49 Ahmed, *Women and Gender*, 177.
50 Ibid., 177–178.
51 Badran and cooke, *Opening the Gates*, 337.
52 Ibid., 338.
53 Badran, "Independent Women," 129.
54 'Abdel Kader, *Egyptian Women*, 64, 66.
55 Ahmed, *Women and Gender*, 180.
56 'Abdel Kader, *Egyptian Women*, 67.
57 Ahmed, *Women and Gender*, 194–195.
58 Fatima Mernissi, *The Veil and the Male Elite: A Feminist Interpretation of Women's Rights in Islam*, trans. Mary Jo Lakeland (New York: Perseus Books, 1991).
59 Ibid., ix.
60 Sahih Bukhari, vol. 4, p. 226.
61 Mernissi, *The Veil and the Male Elite*, vii–viii.
62 Ibid., ix.
63 Ibid., 49.
64 Ibid., 49.
65 Ibid., 50.
66 Ibid., 49.
67 Ibid., 50.

68 Ibid., 56.
69 'Asqalani, Fath al-Bari, vol. 13, p. 46, quoted in Mernissi, *Veil and the Male Elite*, 56–57.
70 Mernissi, *Veil and the Male Elite*, 60–61.
71 Ibid., 60.
72 In his approach of documentation of *Hadith*, Malik Ibn Anas, who was born in the year 93 of Hijra, 8th century CE, is quoted as saying: "There are some people I reject as narrators of Hadith…just simply because I saw them lying in their relations with other people, in their daily relationships that had nothing to do with religion" (qtd. in Mernissi, *Veil and the Male Elite*, 60).
73 Mernissi, *Veil and the Male Elite*, 61.
74 Azza M. Karam, *Women, Islamisms, and the State: Contemporary Feminisms in Egypt* (New York: St. Martin's Press, 1998), 219.
75 Ibid., 216.
76 Ibid., 218.
77 Ibid., 218.
78 Ibid., 219.
79 Ibid., 213.
80 Ibid., 213.
81 Unfortunately, the remarkable activism of the Egyptian Feminist Union that gave birth to the Arab Feminist Union has been curbed in recent years by state-controlled policies. What had been born out of independent feminist activism in the mid 1940s had come by the 1950s and 1960s to be harnessed by states to serve their purposes. However, there was still regional structure in place. As patriarchal forces have regrouped—whether as "state patriarchy," "social patriarchy," or "family patriarchy"—so have feminist forces regrouped in Egypt, as elsewhere in the Arab world. Both at home and within this wider struggle the Egyptian Feminist Union's legacy has been enduring, as Margot Badran explains in her book, *Feminists, Islam, and Nation: Gender and the Making of Modern Egypt* (Princeton, NJ: Princeton University Press, 1995), 224–250.

References

'Abdel Khader, Soha. *Egyptian Women in a Changing Society: 1899–1987*. Boulder and London: Lynne Rienner Publishers, 1987.

Ahmed, Leila. *Women and Gender in Islam: Historical Roots of a Modern Debate*. New Haven: Yale University Press, 1992.

Amin, Qasim. *Tahrir al-Mar'ah* (The Emancipation of Women). Cairo: *Tarqqai* Publisher, 1991.

———. *Al-Mar'ah al-Jadidah* (The New Woman). Cairo: *Sinai* Publisher, 1987.

Badran, Margot. "Independent Women: More than A Century of Feminism in Egypt." In *Arab Women: Old Boundaries, New Frontiers*, edited by Judith E. Tucker. Bloomington: Indiana University Press, 1993.

———. *Feminists, Islam, and Nation: Gender and the Making of Modern Egypt*. Princeton, New Jersey: Princeton University Press, 1995.

Badran, Margot, and miriam cooke, editors. *Opening the Gates: A Century of Arab Feminist Writing*. Bloomington: Indiana University Press, 1990.

Evans, Richard J. *The Feminists: Women's Emancipation Movements in Europe, America and Australia: 1840–1920*. London: Croom Helm, 1977.

Faruqi, Lois Lamya' al-. "Islamic Traditions and the Feminist Movement: Confrontation or Cooperation?" http://www.salaam.co.uk/wp-content/uploads/2019/09/islamic-traditions-feminist-movement.pdf

Freeman, Jo. *The Politics of Women's Liberation*. New York: David McKay, 1975.

Ghazali, Zeinab al-. *Ayyam Min Hayti*, 12th edition. Cairo: Dar al-Shuruq, 1978.

Hourani, Albert. *Arabic Thought in the Liberal Age: 1798–1939*. Cambridge: Cambridge University Press, 1983.

Karam, Azza M. *Women, Islamisms and the State: Contemporary Feminisms in Egypt*. New York: St. Martin's Press, 1998.

Mernissi, Fatima. *The Veil and the Male Elite: A Feminist Interpretation of Women's Rights in Islam*. Translated by Mary Jo Lakeland. New York: Perseus Books, 1991.

Mitchell, Juliet. *Women's Estate*. Harmondsworth, Middlesex: Penguin Books, 1971.

Nassef, Malek Hifni. *Al-Nisaiyat*. Cairo: Matbaat al-Jaridah, 1910.

About the Author

Professor Souad T. Ali is head of Classics and Middle Eastern Studies, founding chair of the Arizona State University Council for Arabic and Islamic Studies; coordinator of Arabic Studies; associate professor of Arabic literature and Middle Eastern/Islamic studies in the School of International Letters and Cultures (SILC). She is simultaneously an affiliate graduate faculty member in English, women and gender studies, religious studies, and justice and social inquiry; as well as an affiliate faculty member in the Center for the Study of Religion and Conflict, African and African-American studies, Center for the Study of Race and Democracy, Institute for Humanities Research, and Arizona Center for Medieval and Renaissance Studies. A scholar with international recognition, Professor Ali is a recipient of several awards including, the ASU Faculty Women's Association Outstanding Graduate Mentor Award (2017); the ASU Outstanding Advisor of the Year (2019), among others. A Fulbright Scholar, Professor Ali is the author of *A Religion, Not A State:*

Ali 'Abd al-Raziq's Islamic Justification of Political Secularism (University of Utah Press 2009), *The Road to Two Sudans*, an edited volume of which she is the lead editor, has been published internationally by Cambridge Scholars Publishing (2014). Ali's third book is *Perspectives of Five Kuwaiti Women in Leadership Roles: Feminism, Islam and Politics* (CSP, 2019). Professor Ali's impressive scholarship also includes over 30 scholarly articles in several languages, and more than 100 scholarly conference presentations. With degrees from prestigious institutions such as the University of Utah and Brigham Young University, as well as the University of Khartoum and the Polytechnic of North London, Professor Ali brings a wealth of knowledge and expertise to her work. She has held several key leadership roles, including serving as the past president of the American Academy of Religion/Western Region (AAR/WR), president of the Sudan(s) Studies Association of North America, and executive committee member of the International Association of Intercultural Studies (IAIS) in Cairo, Egypt and Bremen, Germany.

4 Of Strange Strangers: Interconnected Others in Religion and Ecology

Kimberly Carfore

Throughout the 20th century, many schools of thought contributed to the representation and emancipation of subjugated voices by relying on concepts of the ethically compelling force of encounters with otherness, also known as "alterity." This is evident in feminism, beginning with Simone De Beauvoir, extending to phenomenologists including Emmanuel Levinas, to postcolonial theorists and works of deconstruction including Jacques Derrida. In this work I argue that such contributions to an ethics of alterity can be beneficial to the field of religion and ecology.

In order for it to be applicable to the field, an ethics of alterity must meet two criteria. First, it must not be conceived in exclusively secular or atheistic terms and must account for the significant role that otherness plays in religious phenomena, especially in definitions of the sacred as "wholly other." The second criterion is that alterity must not be conceived in exclusively anthropocentric terms, but must also include the alterity of nonhuman members of the Earth community. The deconstruction of Jacques Derrida meets these criteria, although Derrida is not explicit in his inclusion of nonhuman members into his concept of alterity. However, Timothy Morton's ecological philosophy (what he calls his "ecological thought") draws out Derrida's philosophy to include nonhuman others.

In what follows, I trace the concept of alterity beginning with feminism, extending into ecofeminism, and moving to phenomenology, postcolonial theory, and deconstruction. I then demonstrate how the work of Derrida—specifically his concept of the *arrivant*, or "newcomer,"—and Morton's extension of the *arrivant* as the "strange stranger," embedded in the planetary "mesh," meet the criteria for an ethics of alterity that includes both humans and nonhumans, as well as secular and non-secular elements.

The integrity of the Other is maintained through concepts of alterity and practices of alterity. Attending to alterity is a way to respect the singularity of all others, including non-human others. Feminist theorists have accomplished much by way of bringing more attention to alterity, specifically in relationship to the Otherness of gender and sexuality. Many feminist scholars articulate ways in which the patriarchal structures of Western civilization objectify the alterity of women, subjugating and subordinating women to the subjective agency of men. In other words, are there spaces where women can merely be themselves? Or is their identity and identity formation always subject to the patriarchal gaze? Consider internalized patriarchy which occurs independent of the presence of men in the room. I'm not merely speaking of individual women subjecting themselves to individual male gazes, but rather, in addition to this, existing in the collective systems and structures of patriarchy co-opts feminine energies and agency.

One cannot simply step outside of patriarchy because patriarchy is the ideology that informs the systems and structures we exist under, around, and within. Pointing out the patriarchal ideology that informs Western civilization would be like trying to communicate to a fish that water deeply shapes its being. (In this example, water is patriarchy.) For women who seek liberation from patriarchy, swimming in the waters of patriarchy can feel like swimming in a polluted home. Where are the spaces where women can simply be themselves? And how do we know that this selfhood hasn't been already co-opted by patriarchal norms, roles, and expectations? Where, and how, do we attend to this alterity?

To attend to the alterity of women, womanhood, and femininity, welcoming it on its own terms is to subvert the domination of women that has marked the history of patriarchy. In *The Second Sex*, Simone de Beauvoir recognizes this subversive power in her classic work of feminist philosophy when suggesting that "the very fact that woman is *Other* challenges all the justification that men have ever given" for assimilating women into their own identity.[1]

Ecofeminist theorists extend feminist concerns with the domination of the alterity of women to address the domination of all others—human and nonhuman. In other words, ecofeminism offers an intersectional lens that analyzes not just the domination of women, but rather, it draws attention to the underlying logic that instills oppressive hierarchies and asymmetries.[2] This underlying logic—the "logic of domination"—has been used to justify the historic domination of women, nature, racial and ethnic minorities, the poor, and indigenous communities. The logic of domination, as outlined by Karen Warren, demonstrates how sexism, speciesism, racism, classism, and ethnocentrism all follow the same philosophical logic to justify colonial behavior. Accepting the logic of domination as natural order (e.g. women are naturally weaker than men, therefore men need to dominate them) is the attitude up for analysis.

While it is true that many men tend to have more upper body strength and higher levels of testosterone than many women, the logical conclusion drawn from this premise does not imply that therefore men are intrinsically more capable of leading a country, business, or household. There is no implicit connection between testosterone and power, other than physical strength (since testosterone is the hormone responsible for increased muscle mass). The cultural standards are what instill and naturalize this attitude. As the Doctrine of Discovery legalized the genocide of Native Americans, the underlying attitude justifying this domination was the intrinsic superiority of the Christian religious tradition over what Christian missionaries considered pagans. In addition, just because nature doesn't have a voice and can't represent herself in a court of law doesn't mean her resources are available for extraction and exploitation.

Respecting the alterity of human and Earth Others does not call for differences to be erased and Otherness to be incorporated so that everybody is the same. In other words, to respect the alterity of humans and nonhumans alike at a time when patriarchal rule is under fierce critique doesn't mean that all men and women erase their differences (biological, anatomical, cultural) and become one and the same. While this is the path some are navigating, it would be silly to expect all humans to embark on this. To expect this type of conversion would be perpetuating the same problematic universalistic attitude that underlies the logic of domination. On that same note, as we have learned from the first and second waves of feminism, another problematic attitude that continues to perpetuate the sticky logic of domination is to assume that to fix patriarchy we simply reverse the hierarchy, where women are assumed to be better than men, or women assume positions of power and domination over men. That would be what the ecofeminist philosopher Val Plumwood calls an "uncritical reversal," and it is this behavior that reinforces the very structure we are working to do away with.[3] While perhaps it might benefit organizations to include women in positions of power, this doesn't promise that the desired or necessary change will be made in order to address all the problems of patriarchy.

As Warren outlines the logic of domination, Val Plumwood offers her own interpretation through an analytical lens—the logic of colonization. For Plumwood, the answer in resolving the dualisms of patriarchy is to cultivate continuity *with* difference, where we recognize both the interconnectedness of things as well as their alterity. In other words, we can affirm that men and women do have differences while affirming that gender is influenced and constructed by societal and cultural expectations, roles, and norms. These are a bit more flexible than biological and anatomical differences, although as we have seen in recent cultural shifts there is flexibility in those as well. In the remainder of this essay, I will apply these reflections on sex and gender to the emerging field of religion and ecology.

In response to the emerging environmental crisis, changing climate, and spiritual dimension of our planetary changes, the field of religion and ecology was founded by Yale professors Mary Evelyn Tucker and John Grim. The field was informed by the spiritual insights of geologian and Catholic priest Thomas Berry, mathematical cosmologist Brian Thomas Swimme, and Jesuit paleontologist Pierre Teilhard de Chardin. One of the goals of the field is to use the insights of our world's religions and wisdom traditions to learn to inhabit this planet together with love and respect for our nonhuman neighbors and family members. It is a big task we have ahead of us. Thomas Berry considers this the great work of our time—to learn to live together on this planet though mutually beneficial relationships.

As patriarchy is built on extractive relationships and economies—women's unpaid labor, slavery, petrocultures, to name a few—learning to live together on this planet doesn't only mean changing our attitudes but, also, changing our material relationships. In other essays I have focused on changing material relationships, but for the remainder of this essay, I will focus on the necessary change in attitude. As we inhabit the logic of colonization through the air we breathe, the media we watch, and the simple act of existing in technoindustrial, patriarchal cultures, it is almost impossible to step outside of this world to regain a vision for the future. This is what the work of environmental philosopher Timothy Morton can offer, as philosophy can build imaginary worlds, and imagination can inform the material world (policies, architecture, law, etc.).

To affirm a continuity with difference, Morton's philosophy can give us the imaginary tools—whether that be insightful for gender relations, affirming one's "divinanimality" (a term offered by Derrida to affirm both our divinity and animality), or our paradoxical local and global presence on this planet. In Morton's terms, to affirm both continuity *with* difference means recognizing every being as part of the interconnected "mesh" (or continuity) and as a strange stranger (difference).[4] This also resonates with the work of the feminist theorist Donna Haraway, particularly her category of "companion species," which figures the co-evolutionary interconnectedness between species while also affirming the "significant otherness" of species.[5] As some ecological queer theorists like to do away with categorical species boundaries, I believe these lines of difference are important to maintain.

We can problematize the social construction of boundaries and categories while also affirming that differences and boundaries exist. While species lines can be arbitrary and fluid, we have to be careful not to project too much of our human-made categories and ideas of nature onto the natural world. Species differences do exist in nature. The labels humans give to the natural world many times do not reflect the characteristics of the actual beings—consider how many birds are named after European men who "discovered" them. However, completely doing away with species difference is ideologically driven. A more accurate way forward would be to return to the indigenous names of plant, animal, and landscapes. Indigenous language is tied to the land and soundscapes of a place.

To avoid the logic of colonization, attuning to continuity with difference in the natural world, while bracketing one's own ideological projections onto nature, so as to welcome in the Real takes practice. It takes encountering the natural world, asking questions, and developing a dialogical relationship to nature while being open to a response that might not fit one's preconceived desires, or ideology. Haraway develops this practice of contact with "companion species" through her dog.[6] Articulated in her book *When Species Meet*, Haraway asks, "Whom and what do I touch when I touch my dog?"[7] This contact calls into question the "who" or "what" of the dog, leaving the alterity of the dog untouched and intact. Recall that alterity leaves space for divinity, and an encounter with this divinity leaves open the question.

The concept of companion species enforces the importance of relationship and engagement with the Other in co-evolutionary entanglements. According to Morton, relationship is the "mesh," and suggests both a "hardness and delicacy...a complex situation or series of events in which a person is entangled."[8] There is no definite foreground and no definite background, as this would be ascribing to a dualism implicit in the logic of colonization. Affirming fluidity between the "strange stranger" and the "mesh" is affirming a continuity with difference. The "strange stranger" therefore is the embedded Other entangled in the "mesh"—these life forms we find ourselves connected to. For the ego, this interconnected entanglement can be an attack on its very existence. But those versed in Freud or Buddhist philosophical wisdom traditions know that the ego isn't the only game in town. And a threat to the ego, or ego-death, signifies a trace of divinity.

For Morton, the relationship between the alterity of the strange stranger and the interconnected entanglements of the mesh are "at the limit of our imagining."[9] This is not to say the "strange stranger" is placed at the end of a long list of imagined "earth others"—human, anteater, wombat, tube worms…strange stranger. It is entangled within and without life forms. For the ego, or the part of the self that compartmentalizes, analyzes, and understands, adding a new concept, creature, or ecological species would be adding it to the end of a list. Just as we have learned in previous versions of feminism—we can't just add women to the systems and structures of patriarchy and stir. This won't fix patriarchy. Rather, to truly imagine femininity at the core of every patriarchal structure would be to deconstruct the very essence of its being.

To truly affirm the depth at which the multi-faceted ecological crisis is a spiritual emergence, one might imagine the strange stranger at the very center of every co-evolutionary entanglement. Humans aren't as neatly placed above nature as the logic of domination has taught us to previously consider. The bacterium in our stomachs helps break down our food which then transforms into our flesh. Our history of domestication is entangled with the domestication of dogs, not to mention the fact that we share fifty percent of our genetic information with a banana.[10] The boundaries between strange strangers are muddled. This complexifies ethics.

What does Morton say about an ethics involving the strange stranger? In his book *The Ecological Thought* Morton states, it "comes as close as possible to the strange stranger, generating care and concern for beings, no matter how uncertain we are of their identity, no matter how afraid we are of their existence."[11] This fear and uncertainty is characteristic of the strange stranger, for it is uncanny. Haraway agrees that our relational entanglements are weird and messy—that companion species are "messmates" derived from the Latin *cum panis*, meaning "with bread."[12] They are symbiogenetic relationships that should indeed cause indigestion. In fact, Haraway states that "[e]ating one another and developing indigestion are…one kind of transformative merger practice."[13] Eating with and being eaten are two practices that move away from human exceptionalism and toward "becoming with" companion species, or significant others—others that include strange strangers.

Cohabiting a world with strange strangers, in a sense, puts humans back in the food chain, as the strange stranger includes climate change, microbial viruses, global capitalism, and plutonium (what Morton refers to as *hyperobjects*). Although being threatened by climate change is uncanny indeed, Morton affirms, "the fact that the strange stranger may bite is the least of our worries…. It is more like [how] feminist Luce Irigaray puts it, when she imagines the nonhuman as a teacher and the nonhuman–human relationship as a model for future ways of human being."[14] If the nonhuman–human relationship is a model for future ways of being, how do we enact this change?

Let's start at the meeting point. The meeting of strange strangers is a paradoxical relationship, creating an opening or gap. This openness is the place of politics and ethics. The meeting of two "others" is the entrance point toward an ethics of alterity. Phenomenologist Emmanuel Levinas agrees as he considers face-to-face the place of ethics. The sheer thisness and immediacy of the face-to-face encounter calls for response. We see in the face of the other an "infinite that blinks."[15] However, a Levinasian ethics of alterity is anthropocentric. In an interview he admits, "I don't know if a snake has a face. I can't answer that question."[16] Ecophenomenologist Edward Casey extends Levinasian ethics to include the environment. He is explicit in stating, "If the face is to play a role in environmental ethics it must be dehumanized.... [I]t is in landscape that the face of the place-world shows itself."[17] For Casey, the imperative for ethical action lies not in the face, but rather in the intensity of the encounter, moving from simply noticing to being compelled. Therefore, according to Casey, an object such as climate change indeed has a face based upon the intensity of the ethical imperative it speaks.

It is the face-to-face encounter that interrupts solipsistic consciousness. Derrida opens this encounter with the Other to its religious dimensions. In his essay "Violence and Metaphysics," Derrida states, "It is the encounter, the only way out, the only adventuring outside oneself toward the unforeseeably-other.... Face to face with the other within a glance and a speech which both maintain distance and interrupt all totalities.... Levinas calls it religion.... It opens ethics...it is respect for the other."[18] This ultimate respect for the other is not only ethics, it is religion. The absolute alterity of the other must remain ineffaceable in the name of justice, the impossible, and a future "to come."

Affirming a justice to come would be opening to the unique imperatives issued from the otherness of every other. For Derrida, "Every other is altogether other." The French translation is palindromic: "tout autre est tout autre," which means both "every other is altogether other," and "altogether other is every other."[19] To maintain the ineffable mark of otherness in every other would be to affirm the "absolute singularity of every other."[20] Welcoming the arrival of the singularity of every other through an ecological lens is completely overwhelming. It would be a mix of a Jain worldview and a Buddhist hell realm. I have seen friends and colleagues crippled by opening to the call of justice issued from every single other. The simple act of choosing an ethical soap, or cleaning one's house (as keeping myself safe means killing bacteria, micro-organisms, and insects) can leave one paralyzed. The impossible task of opening to an event of justice is not meant to paralyze, but rather, it is particularly the structure of the possible that leaves open the space for the possible.

For Derrida, this event of justice is always to come, infinitely exceeding the limits of presence. In other words, welcoming the other, the wholly other, foreigner or stranger, is a welcoming of an impossible event, a justice that exceeds the coordinates of what we currently understand to be possible. According to Derrida, this call for justice, this arrival of the wholly Other which interrupts, in its absolute and unpredictable singularity, is the *arrivant*.[21] In the hope and promise to one day bring about justice, the *arrivant* continues to arrive, as an unpredictable force that haunts us with its compelling alterity. Morton is explicit in that his phrase "strange stranger" is his translation of Derrida's *arrivant*: "the ultimate arrival to whom one must extend ultimate hospitality."[22] He suggests that we should welcome all beings as "strange strangers."

The *arrivant* is a guest or newcomer. It is the messianic future and the coming of justice without a determinate Messiah and without a determinate messianism, whether Jewish, Christian, or otherwise. To welcome the *arrivant* is to practice what could be called a postsecular "religion without religion," opening up to the Otherness or "alterity" that overflows properly marked boundaries—believers from nonbelievers, saints from sinners, the saved from the damned, the sacred from profane, etc. Welcoming the stranger marks the arrival of an event of justice, an event that implodes these otherwise neatly categorized boundaries: sacred/profane, religious/secular, familiar/foreign, self/Other.

One of these neatly categorized boundaries, religious/secular, is included in Morton's ecological thought. "Animism under erasure" is his version of Derrida's "religion without religion." Although every Other is wholly Other, we do not experience this in a Pollyanna type way, or as something that fits just right since the human cannot unknow what it already knows.[23] In a world filled with strange strangers—quarks, DNA, black holes, the unconscious, climate change, global capitalism, Styrofoam, and plutonium—the task of the human is to coexist. One of the first steps towards a mutually enhancing coexistence between human and earth Others is "admitting our coexistence with toxic substances we have created and exploited."[24]

In our dedication towards coexistence with a multitude of strange strangers, I end with the words of Morton—"[w]hat a fine mesh we've gotten ourselves into."[25]

Notes

1 Simone De Beauvoir, *The Second Sex*, trans. Constance Borde and Sheila Malovany-Chevallier (New York: Random House, 2009), 10.
2 Kimberly Carfore, and Sam Mickey, "Planetary Love: Ecofeminist Perspectives on Globalization," *The Journal of New Paradigm Research* 68, no. 2 (2012): 123.
3 Karen Warren, "The Power and Promise of Ecological Feminism: Revisited" in *Environmental Ethics: Readings in Theory and Application*, 5th edition, ed. Louis Pojman and Paul Pojman, (Belmont, CA: Thomson Wadsworth, 2008), 33–48.
4 Val Plumwood, *Feminism and the Mastery of Nature* (New York: Routledge, 1993), 31.
5 Timothy Morton, *The Ecological Thought* (Cambridge, MA: Harvard University Press, 2010), 15.
6 Donna J. Haraway, *When Species Meet* (Minneapolis: University of Minnesota Press, 2008), 90, 97, 165.
7 Ibid., 4.
8 Ibid., 3.
9 Morton, *Ecological Thought*, 28.
10 Ibid., 17.
11 Paul Waldau, *Animal Studies: An Introduction* (New York: Oxford University Press, 2013), 215. Waldau describes the chimpanzee/human DNA relationship. For facts on the banana/human genetic relationship see Sanjida O'Connell, "Are Human Beings Impossible to Ape?" Retrieved from http://www.telegraph.co.uk/science/evolution/5695045/Are-human-beings-impossible-to-ape.html.
12 Morton, *Ecological Thought*, 18–19.
13 Haraway, *When Species Meet*.
14 Ibid., 31.
15 Morton, *Ecological Thought*, 81.
16 Ibid., 42.
17 Alison Ainley, et. al., *The Provocation of Levinas: Rethinking the Other*, trans. A. Benjamin and T. Wright, eds. R. Bernasconi and D. Wood (London: Routledge, 1998) 172, quoted in Christian Diehm, "Natural Disasters," in *Eco-Phenomenology: Back to the Earth Itself*, eds. Charles S. Brown and Ted Toadvine (Albany: State University of New York Press, 2003), 172.
18 Edward Casey, "Taking a Glance at the Environment: Preliminary Thoughts on a Promising Topic," in *Eco-Phenomenology: Back to the Earth Itself*, eds. Charles S. Brown and Ted Toadvine (Albany: State University of New York Press, 2003), 202–203.
19 Jacques Derrida, "Violence and Metaphysics" in *Writing and Difference*, trans. Alan Bass (Chicago: The University of Chicago Press, 1978) 95–96.
20 Ibid, 195n37.

21 Jacques Derrida, *Specters of Marx: The State of the Debt, the Work of Mourning, and the New International*, trans. Peggy Kamuf (New York: Routledge, 1994), 28.
22 "I develop the concept of the strange stranger from Derrida's *arrivant*, the ultimate arrival to whom one must extend ultimate hospitality," (Timothy Morton, *Ecological Thought*, 140n39).
23 Timothy Morton, *Hyperobjects: Philosophy and Ecology after the End of the World* (Minneapolis, MN: University of Minnesota Press, 2013), 172.
24 Ibid., 109.
25 Morton, *Ecological Thought*, 61.

References

Carfore, Kimberly. "The Paradox of Homecoming: Home is where the Haunt is." In *Resisting the Place of Belonging: Uncanny Homecomings in Religion, Narrative, and the Arts*, edited by Daniel Boscaljon, 61–72. New York: Routledge, 2013.

Carfore, Kimberly, and Sam Mickey, "Planetary Love: Ecofeminist Perspectives on Globalization." *The Journal of New Paradigm Research* 68, no. 2 (2012): 122–131.

Casey, Edward. "Taking a Glance at the Environment: Preliminary Thoughts on a Promising Topic." In *Eco-Phenomenology: Back to the Earth Itself*, edited by Charles S. Brown and Ted Toadvine, 187–210. Albany: State University of New York Press, 2003.

De Beauvoir, Simone. *The Second Sex*. Translated by Constance Borde and Sheila Malovany-Chevallier. New York: Random House, 2009.

Diehm, Christian. "Natural Disasters." In *Eco-Phenomenology: Back to the Earth Itself*, edited by Charles S. Brown and Ted Toadvine, 171–185. Albany: State University of New York Press, 2003.

Derrida, Jacques. *Specters of Marx: The State of the Debt, the Work of Mourning, and the New International*. Translated by Peggy Kamuf. New York: Routledge, 1994.

———. *Writing and Difference*. Translated by Alan Bass. Chicago: The University of Chicago Press, 1978.

Haraway, Donna J. *When Species Meet*. Minneapolis: University of Minnesota Press, 2008.

Morton, Timothy. *Hyperobjects: Philosophy and Ecology after the End of the World*. Minneapolis, MN: University of Minnesota Press, 2013.

———. *The Ecological Thought*. Cambridge, MA: Harvard University Press, 2010.

O'Connell, Sanjida. "Are Human Beings Impossible to Ape?" *The Telegraph*. Retrieved December 8, 2013, from http://www.telegraph.co.uk/science/evolution/5695045/Are-human-beings-impossible-to-ape.html.

Plumwood, Val. *Feminism and the Mastery of Nature*. New York: Routledge, 1993.

Waldau, Paul. *Animal Studies: An Introduction*. New York: Oxford University Press, 2013.
Warren, Karen. "The Power and Promise of Ecological Feminism: Revisited." In *Environmental Ethics: Readings in Theory and Application*, 5th Edition, edited by Louis Pojman Paul Pojman, 33–48. Belmont, CA: Thomson Wadsworth, 2008.

About the Author

Kimberly Carfore teaches in both the Environmental Studies and Theology and Religious Studies Departments at the University of San Francisco. She received her PhD in Philosophy and Religion with a focus on Ecology. She is on the Advisory Board at the Forum of Religion and Ecology at Yale for eco-justice and ecofeminism. Dr. Carfore is co-chair of the Religion and Ecology Unit of the American Academy of Religion.

PART II

Centering Marginalized Voices

5 Sufism, the *Shatahat*, and a New Examination of Al-Ghazali's Writings

Souad T. Ali

Writing in his famous memoir, *al-Munqidh min al-Dhalal* (*The Deliverance from Error*), Abu Hamid al-Ghazali[1] (d. 1111) immortalized his admonition of Sufis that claimed to achieve union with God. "In general, what they manage to achieve is nearness to God," he writes, "some, however, would conceive of this as [incarnation] (*hulul*), some as "union" (*ittihad*), and some as "connection" (*wusul*) – all that is erroneous."[2] Acknowledging this, it is certainly reasonable to assume, as some scholars have already done, that al-Ghazali must have rejected the so-called "intoxicated" mysticism of Bayazid al-Bistami (d. 874) or Abu Mansur ibn al-Hallaj (d. 922). For instance, al-Hallaj is reported to have publicly declared "I am the Truth" while enraptured in a mystic state. Such ecstatic or intoxicated utterances are known as *Shatahat*. However, as we will see, al-Ghazali did not in fact reject the *Shatahat* at all, but rather defended such Sufi utterances against traditionalist critics within the framework of Sunni Islam.

There was a great deal of controversy among scholars in the twentieth century over al-Ghazali's attitudes toward mysticism. At the core of this controversy was the perceived failure among scholars to consider the full range of al-Ghazali's treatises on Sufism, and from there disputes further arose over the authenticity of those treatises.[3] This study offers a new examination of al-Ghazali's many writings on Sufism based on the original Arabic texts, and affirms their authenticity. In particular, it analyzes sections of al-Ghazali's mystical treatise, *Mishqat al-Anwar* (*The Niche of Light*), and addresses the two areas of Sufism where al-Ghazali's influence has been most significant. The first relates to his re-articulation of the early Sufi notion of union with God. The second is his explanation of the state of intoxication that Sufis experience temporarily after which they regain their consciousness and realize that "what they experienced was not the reality of unification, but that it was similar to unification."[4] Contrary to erroneous assumption that al-Ghazali rejected the *Shatahat*, or intoxicated utterances of such Sufis, crystallizing the distinction between "sober" and "intoxicated" mysticism, he defended them by arguing that what they said was not what was perceived, and that the speech of God's lovers is not to be revealed but "should be concealed and not spread out."[5]

It is generally believed that the famous Persian Sufi, Bayazid (or Abu Yazid) al-Bistami, was the first to speak openly about ecstatic annihilation of the individual self in the Oneness of God, known as *fana*. Among his most controversial public declarations was: "Praise be to me! How great is my majesty!" To the outsider, especially austere Sunni jurists, unfamiliar with the experience of *fana*, such statements could be interpreted as blasphemous claims of divinity. Such was the case with fellow Persian mystic, al-Hallaj, who was just a young man at the time of al-Bistami's death in 874, but studied under the great Sufi master, al-Junayd, in Baghdad. In the early 10th century, sociopolitical tensions were high around the Abbasid capital of Baghdad and popular preachers and mystics like al-Hallaj became a target of the authorities. His infamous public proclamation "I am the Truth" provided them with ample justification for his imprisonment and, later on, his gruesome execution. Al-Hallaj, his accusers insisted, had declared that he was God. In the wake of this incident, the line separating Sufism and Shari'a-oriented Sunni Islam seemed almost irreproachable. That is until the brilliant Persian scholar, al-Ghazali, emerged on the scene in the late 10th century to reconcile the two.

In his book, *Islam,* Fazlur Rahman (d. 1988) argued that, "al-Ghazali has puzzled many a modern writer. Some have wondered whether he was essentially a mystic or a theologian, although he is described as both."[6] Other scholars, such as W. Montgomery Watt, concur with Rahman's view, indicating the complex intricacies involved in writing about al-Ghazali. In his book, *Muslim Intellectual: A Study of Al-Ghazali*, Watt explained: "the difficulty of writing about al-Ghazali is well-illustrated by the various comments and criticisms that have been made of the works by Julius Obermann, A. J. Wensinck, Margaret Smith and Farid Jabre."[7] Some of the reasons for this difficulty may stem from the huge volume of al-Ghazali's writings, the complexity of the subjects he dealt with, and the influence his writings have had on scholars in the East and West, as well as Muslim intellectual and religious life. In his book, *al-Ghazali wa 'Alaqat al-Yaqin bil 'Aql* (*al-Ghazali and the Relationship of Certainty to the Intellect*), Muhammad Ibrahim al-Faiyyoumi further reflects on the ingenuity of al-Ghazali's unique persona: "Imam al-Ghazali… is one of the pioneers in [the field] of truth and knowledge."[8]

Of all al-Ghazali's many writings, *al-Munqidh min al-Dhalal*[9] is among the most important for this analysis because it constitutes a major part of al-Ghazali's work on Sufism, including his reconciliation of Sufism with Shari'a-oriented Sunni Islam. In the words of T. J. Winter:

Al-Munqidh min al-Dhalal, is one of the most remarkable personal documents to have come down to us from Islamic civilization. The Imam describes his education and his intellectual crisis which left him so paralyzed by doubt that he was forced to resign the most distinguished academic appointment of his day. His faith returned after years of wandering and seeking during which he achieved direct knowledge of God in the form of the illuminative experience of the Sufis.[10]

A thorough reading of *al-Munqidh min al-Dalal* reveals that, when al-Ghazali experienced his famous crisis of spiritual doubt, he eventually reached the point where he found *yaqin* ("certainty") and *iman* ("faith"). He recounts that his *yaqin* did not come to him through any instruction or rational proofs "but through light that God Most High has thrown in the heart" (*bal bi-Nur qadhafahu Allah Ta'ala fi al-Sadr*).[11] This, however, was not the end of al-Ghazali's doubts. Soon another doubt preoccupied him. Al-Ghazali's new doubt was related to how he could apply his *iman* (faith) with regard to the three cardinals of faith given the diversity of claims made by theologians, philosophers, and mystics. He believed that answering this question would ultimately determine what approach he would follow. Given his extensive studies and knowledge, he realized that all truth-seekers claim to know the way to salvation, and thus he began to contemplate which one of them was correct. As he pondered these questions, he decided that the best way to deal with this challenge was to narrow down the approaches of the truth-seekers. Al-Ghazali classifies the truth-seekers into four groups: (1) The *Mutakalimun*, or scholastic theologians, who argue that they are men of independent judgment and reason; (2) The *Batiniyya*, who claim to be the unique possessors of *al-Ta'lim* (gnosis) and the privileged recipients of knowledge acquired from *al-Imam al-Ma'sum*, the infallible Shi'ite Imam; (3) The philosophers, who maintain that they are the men of logic and apodictic demonstration; (4) The Sufis, who claim to be the familiars of the Divine Presence and the men of mystical vision and illumination.[12]

According to al-Ghazali, the "Truth cannot transcend these four categories, for these are men who are following the paths of the quest for the truth. Hence, if the truth eludes them, then there remains no hope of ever attaining it."[13] In his book, *Freedom, Modernity, and Islam: Toward a Creative Synthesis*, Richard Khuri argues that al-Ghazali makes it clear that, "given the nature of the audience, any appropriate method is acceptable for bringing its members closer to the truth."[14] He further explains that al-Ghazali warned against the dangers of theological or mystical truth falling into the wrong hands. What is more important here is that, because al-Ghazali "wants to ensure that no one would be led astray through immersion in an inappropriate discipline, he recommends that theology, for instance, be restricted to initiates. Sufism and esotericism [*batin*] are naturally restricted and not much emphasis is needed on that."¹⁵ Eventually, Khuri maintains: "although all the different temperaments were catered to, so that those more attuned to theology could feel as much at home as those more attuned to mysticism, the various disciplines, paths, and methods were sequestered."¹⁶

In his study of the four groups, al-Ghazali dismissed the *Mutakalimun* for their failure to provide an effective means to dispel the darkness of those aspiring to find the truth. For the *Mutakalimun*'s argument merely focused on exposing or revealing the contradictions of their opponents and confuting them by means of their accepted premises. Such an argument, al-Ghazali maintains, had little value for someone who only admits self-evident truth. But al-Ghazali also gave the theologians credit for their attempts to provide an answer for those seeking the truth, maintaining that his purpose is not to express disapproval of anyone who sought a cure in *Kalam* (theology). As he states, "healing remedies differ as the sickness differs, and many a remedy helps one sick man and harms another."¹⁷ Yet, the scholastic theology of the *Mutakalimun* "could not satisfy me nor heal the malady I have been suffering from."¹⁸

The second group al-Ghazali addresses in his book is the philosophers, which al-Ghazali describes as committing "evil and mischief."¹⁹ As such, the works of the philosophers are said to be harmful and to contain "deceit and danger" for the believers.²⁰ Al-Ghazali goes a step further to warn that the uninitiated must be kept away from pursuing philosophy, just as an unskilled swimmer must be kept away from the slippery river bank.²¹

A close reading of the *Munqidh* and *Tahafut* in Arabic clarifies that, from the very beginning, al-Ghazali classified the philosophers into three categories: (1) the *al-Dahriyyun*, or Materialists, who denied the existence of God and held that the world existed by itself; (2) the *al-Tabiyyun*, or Naturalists, who believed in God's existence but denied his relevance and judgment; (3) the *al-Ilahiyyun*, or Theists, such as Plato and Aristotle and their partisans among the Muslims, such as al-Farabi and Ibn Sina. Within the last category, al-Ghazali argues that "the sum of what we regard as the authentic philosophy of Aristotle, as transmitted by al-Farabi and Ibn Sina, can be reduced to three parts;" a part which must be regarded as unbelief; a part which must be branded as innovation; and a part which must not be repudiated at all.²² At first glance, these classifications and divisions of the philosophers and their beliefs might seem confusing, especially with regard to al-Ghazali's conclusion in *Tahafut al-Falasifa: The Incoherence of the Philosophers* (detailed below). However, this confusion might be clarified by weighing the two accounts from the *Munqidh* and *Tahafut*.

In *Tahafut al-Falasifa*, al-Ghazali launches his severest attack on the philosophers' assertions that the universe is eternal and uncreated, their restriction of God's knowledge to universals rather than particulars, and their denial of bodily resurrection in the afterlife. Nonetheless, he simultaneously acknowledges their contribution to the fields of logic and the sciences and steps back as he says, "we prefer not to plunge into [the question] of pronouncing those who uphold heretical innovations as infidel."[23] This is a significant point of departure given al-Ghazali's description of each of the philosophers' three assertions as "unbelief," and sometimes as even "disbelief," in *al-Munqidh*. Yet, his conclusion in *Tahafut* is not to pronounce them as infidels. Further, his choice of describing them as *ahl al-bida'* not as (*kuffar*) is important enough and quite consistent with his other description of the philosophers as theists, *Ilahiyyun* in *al-Munqidh*. This implies that al-Ghazali, unlike most theologians, draws a distinction between disbelief and "infidelity" for, in each of the three charges he maintains that the philosophers are in disbelief, yet this apparently does not necessarily make them "infidels" or "*kuffar*." In other words, from within the context of al-Ghazali's discussion on the philosophers in the *Munqidh*, much that has been unclear can be explained. That, as mentioned above, "unbelief" in al-Ghazali's perspective does not necessarily amount to "infidelity," hence his three categories of the philosophers, on the one hand, and his further divisions of the Neo-Platonic theories of al-Farabi and Ibn Sina into three parts, on the other. In summary, the wording of the original Arabic text of both *al-Munqidh* and the *Tahafut* implies that al-Ghazali finds some of the philosophers in disbelief in some areas, yet that does not justify labeling them as "unbelievers" inherently as has been widely interpreted. This reading in fact is consistent with the insights obtained from the analysis of al-Ghazali on the Sufis' temporary state of intoxication (detailed below), because it has similarly been largely misinterpreted by some of al-Ghazali's critics and scholarly interpreters.[24]

The Batinites'[25] doctrine did not satisfy al-Ghazali's quest for truth either. Their doctrine was quickly dismissed as an attempt "to deceive the common folk by showing the need for the authoritative Imam."[26] He ridicules the Batinites' inability to establish a sound proof for the designation of the Imam, arguing that Islam already has a teacher, the Prophet Muhammad. Thus, he maintains, "when we had had experience of them, we also washed our hands of them."[27]

It was not until he studied Sufism towards the end of his life, that al-Ghazali concluded that Sufism[28] was the best path to a positive knowledge of God compared to the first three approaches. He made his declaration public when he wrote:

> I knew with certainty that Sufis were masters of states, not purveyors of words, and that I had learned all I could by way of theory. There remained, then, only what was attainable, not by learning and study, but by fruitional experience and actually engaging in the way.... What became clear to me of necessity from practicing their way was the true nature and special character of prophecy.[29]

In pursuit of the meaning expressed by al-Ghazali above, one needs to understand the basic ideas behind this statement. Despite the fact that Sufis have varied stages, seven of these are identical in almost all Sufi schools of thought. According to Abu Bakr al-Kalabadhi (d. 995), the Sufi stages are more than seven, including repentance, abstinence, patience, poverty, humility, fear, piety, sincerity, gratitude, trust, satisfaction, certainty, recollection, intimacy, nearness, union, and love.[30] Here al-Kalabadhi has clearly combined both the *maqamat* ("stages") and *ahwal* ("states") in his definition. However, in his book *Kitab al-Luma'* (*The Book of Flashes*), Abu Nasr al-Sarraj (d. 988) lists the primary seven *maqamat* as: *Tawba* (repentance); *Wara'* (watchfulness); *Zuhd* (renunciation); *Faqr* (poverty); *Sabr* (patience); *Tawakkul* (trust); and *Rida* (acceptance).[31]

Though highly intellectual and even philosophical, al-Ghazali's journey towards attaining "the Truth" is in many ways analogous to the traditional initiation of the Sufi into the *ahwal* and *maqamat* ("states" and "stages"). Although he did not go through an initiation into Sufism in the traditional sense through a particular Sheikh, as does a Sufi disciple, the numerous points of comparison are indeed valid. Al-Ghazali's speculative interest was transformed significantly after he embraced the Sufi path. After he acquired a sure and certain faith in God, the Prophetic mediation of revelation, and the Last Day, al-Ghazali announced that "these three fundamentals of our faith had become deeply rooted in my soul."[32] This is his first stage in the Sufi path of *Tawba*, or repentance, after a very long journey of doubt. Al-Kalabadhi quotes al-Junayd (d. 910) who, when asked "what is repentance?" replied: "It is the forgetting one's sin." Al-Kalabadhi maintains "the saying of al-Junayd means that the sweetness of such an act so entirely departs from the heart that there remains in the conscience not a trace of it."[33] When al-Ghazali was experiencing the *maqam* of repentance, he obtained "illumination" and thereafter understood that the first requirement of repentance "is the total purification of the heart from everything other than God Most High."[34] Following this, his only hope for salvation in the afterlife, al-Ghazali realized, was through "piety and self-restraint" which marks the second stage, *Zuhd*, or renunciation. Sarraj argues that there are three ranks of *Zuhd*. For the first rank, he quotes al-Junayd, who said renunciation is "that the hands are free of possession and that the hearts are free of craving."³⁵ When Ruwaym ibn Ahmed (d. 915) was asked about renunciation, the second rank according to Sarraj, he said: "It is the giving up of all goods or benefits for the self from whatever exists in the world."³⁶ For the third rank, Sarraj quotes Shibli who, when asked about renunciation, said: "Renunciation is neglect, because the world is nothing and renunciation of nothing is neglect."³⁷ Al-Ghazali had clearly gone through all three ranks when he declared:

> The beginning of all…was to sever my heart's attachment to the world.… Then I reflected in my intention in public teaching, and I saw that it was not directed purely to God, but rather was instigated and motivated by the quest for fame and widespread prestige.³⁸

He eventually renounced the world and entered into seclusion, the ultimate reflection of *Zuhd*. His third stage in the Sufi path is *Faqr*, or poverty. Sarraj lists three ranks of poverty, all of which include the *fuqara*, referring to the poor, those who do not own anything, or who do not seek anything from anyone whether outwardly or inwardly."³⁹ Al-Ghazali, the prestigious professor and jurist, announced that he was departing from Baghdad to enter seclusion in Syria after "I had distributed what wealth I had.… My excuse for that was the money of Iraq was earmarked for the welfare of the people, because it was pious bequest in favor of Muslims."⁴⁰

Al-Ghazali's journey on the path of *Ahwal*, or the Sufi states, is best explained in his book, *Fear and Hope*, which is one of the books included in his major work, *Ihya 'Ulum al-Din* (*Revival of the Religious Sciences*). He writes:

> Hope and fear are two wings by means of which those who are brought near fly to every commendable station, and two mounts on which every steep ascent of the paths of the next world is traversed. And nothing but the reins of hope will lead to the vicinity of the Merciful and the joy of the Gardens. …Nothing shall avert from the fire of Gehenna and the painful punishment the man who is encompassed with the blandishments of lusts and the marvels of pleasures except the scourges of threatening and the assaults of violence. Consequently, there is nothing for it but an expression of the essence and merits of the two of them, as well as the way of arriving at a junction between the two of them, in spite of their polarity and mutual antipathy.⁴¹

Yet, because of the expectations of what seems desirable, "hope is the relief of the heart."⁴² Heart is compared to the earth, and faith is compared to the seed in the heart. Hence, for the Sufi al-Ghazali, hope is planted in the heart because the masters of hearts teach that the present world is the field of the next world. Thus, through obedience the earth, meaning the heart, is cleansed.

Fear, on the other hand, is portrayed as "an expression of the suffering of the heart and its conflagration by means of the anticipation of what is abhorred as a future contingency."[43] Indeed, this has also been made clear "in the exposition of the essence of hope." The image and metaphor of the future combines both fear and hope. Eventually, within this connection, "whoever is intimate with God, whose heart is ruled by truth and who lives in the present through his seeing the majesty of truth perpetually, no longer turns to the future and is possessed of neither fear nor hope."[44] Interestingly, al-Ghazali brilliantly used a Sufi *Maqam*, that is *Sabr* ("patience"), to cure the state of fear, or *halat al-khawf*. Because "patience is only possible after the attaining of fear and hope," it becomes the most suitable therapy for fear since the first of "the stations of religion is assurance, which is an expression for strength of faith in God and the Last Day and the Garden and the Fire; and this assurance necessarily excites fear of the Fire and hope of the Garden, and hope and fear fortify patience."[45] In juxtaposition, it is interesting to refer here to the Qur'anic passage that has apparently inspired al-Ghazali with regard to his creative employment of the station of *Sabr* ("patience") as a cure for the state of *Khawf* ("fear"). We read in the Qur'anic *Surat al-Baqarah* (Qur'an chapter 2, the Cattle) that the believers are advised "to be firm and patient in pain (and suffering) and adversity and throughout all periods of panic. Sure [these] are the people of Truth, the God-fearing."[46]

Despite the fact that much has been said about al-Ghazali's position regarding certain aspects of Sufism, a closer look at al-Ghazali's original Arabic writings, as opposed to some of his translated works, reveals that some of these views have been somewhat distorted or simply misinterpreted (perhaps inadvertently). This brings us to al-Ghazali's conceptualization and identification of the state of *Sukr*, or intoxication. He provides a useful analysis of the temporary nature of this "intoxication" that is immediately followed by a "sober" state, not only in the milder case of the dervishes "dancing," but even in such extreme examples as in al-Hallaj and al-Bistami's *Shatahat* or intoxicated utterances, "I am the Truth" (*ana al-Haqq*), and "glory be to me" (*subhani*), respectively. In *Mishqat al-Anwar* (*The Niche of Light*), al-Ghazali provides a convincing analysis of these two states of sobriety and intoxication, maintaining:

> The 'Arifun (mystics), after having ascended to the heaven of reality, agree that they see nothing in existence save the One, the Real.... They become intoxicated with such an intoxication that the ruling authority of their rational faculty is overthrown. Hence, one of them says, "I am the Real!" another, "Glory be to me, how great is my station!" and still another, "There is nothing

in my robe but God!" The speech of lovers in the state of intoxication should be concealed and not spread about. When this intoxication subsides, the ruling authority of the rational faculty—which is God's balance in His earth—is given back to them. They come to know that what they experienced was not the reality of unification but that it was similar to unification.[47]

Abul Qasim al-Junayd (d. 910) seems to agree with al-Ghazali that, as paraphrased by Annemarie Schimmel: "mystical experience and thought cannot be rationalized and that it is dangerous to speak openly about the deepest mysteries of faith in the presence of the uninitiated."[48] In this context, Junayd's rejection of al-Hallaj's utterances, and indeed Ghazali's denunciation of the notion of union with God, are apparently rooted in al-Hallaj's violation of what seems to be, for both Junayd and al-Ghazali, the rule of thumb in Sufism, namely that the temporary "state of intoxication should be concealed" because of its danger vis-à-vis the "uninitiated" in the path and knowledge (*ma'raifa*) of Sufism. The misinterpretation of such a state of *Sukr* has manifested itself in the claim that al-Hallaj and al-Bistami belonged to a separate genre of "intoxicated Sufism" as opposed to a "sober Sufism," as scholars such as William Chittick have alleged.[49] Al-Ghazali's original Arabic writings on Sufism suggest that this dichotomy is fundamentally flawed.

W. Montgomery Watt (d. 2006) cast doubt regarding the authenticity of al-Ghazali's authorship of the third part of *Mishqat al-Anwar*,[50] which is significant for our interest in his understanding of the *Shatahat*. However, another scholar, Abdel-Rahman Badawi (d. 2002), refuted Watt's allegations. In his book, *Nadharat fi Fikr al-Ghazali* (*Glimpses into al-Ghazali's Thought*), 'Amir al-Najjar writes, quoting Badawi's *Mu'alaffat al-Ghazali* (*al-Ghazali's Publications*):

> In a paper that he presented at the Orientalists conference in Paris in 1948 (later published in the *J.R.A.S.*, 1949, pp. 5–22), W. Montgomery Watt claimed that the third part of *Mishqat al-Anwar* with regard to the saying of the Prophet, peace be upon him, that "God has seventy veils of light and darkness, if he revealed them would burn the face of whoever...." We say he assumed that this third part is *manhul* [spurious] and is injected in the original text of the *Mishqat al-Anwar*.... I responded to him after he had presented his paper at the Orientalists conference and told him that "there is a hand-written (*Nuskhah Makhtutah*) of the *Mishqat al-Anwar* book in group number 1712 at the Shahud Ali Pasha Library in Istanbul; and that the date of this group was 509 [Hijjri] in the handwriting (*wa malak*) of Abdel Majid ibn al-Fadl al-Fazari al-Tabari, and there is a photocopy of it in *Dar al-Kutub al-Misriyya* (Egyptian House of Books and National Archives) under the number 3662

Tasawwuf (Sufism), which means this was [done] four years after al-Ghazali's death and included the third part [of the *Mishqat*]." And this is *Hujja Qati'ah* (a decisive proof) that invalidates his [Watt's] allegation, for there is no room for doubt regarding the authenticity of this *Makhtutah* (hand-written copy), not to mention the fact that al-Ghazali himself referred to this [third] part in the introduction of the *Mishqat*.[51]

It is also important to mention that Abu al-'Ala al-'Afifi also wrote a refutation of Watt's argument regarding this very point in his introduction to the *Mishqat*. 'Amir al-Najjar also elaborated on Badawi's rebuttal. Furthermore, there appears to be yet another argument that renders the third part of the *Mishqat* authentic, yet this important point apparently has not been discussed by these scholars. This relates to the observation that al-Ghazali's discussion of the Sufi state of intoxication in this section of the *Mishqat* is quite consistent with the analysis offered in his book *al-Maqsad al-Asna fi Sharh Ma'ani Asma Allah al-Husna* (*The Noblest of Aims in the Explanation of God's Finest Names*). In this text, al-Ghazali further discussed the intoxicated utterances, or *Shatahat*, of al-Bistami and al-Hallaj within the context of poetic metaphors. He writes:

> The identification of two things is impossible.... Whenever one speaks of identification and declares "this is identified with this," it can only be by way of the extension and allowance proper to the usage of the Sufis and the poets. For in order to make what is said more pleasing to minds they follow the way of metaphorical usage, as the poet says: "I am the one I love, and the one I love is I." That is the poet's interpretation for he does not mean thereby that he is really the beloved, but it is as though he were, because his interest is as absorbed by the beloved as it is by himself: so he expresses that state by "identification" through [poetic] license. In the same way one ought to interpret the utterances of Bayazid al-Bistami [and al-Hallaj].[52]

This is almost identical to al-Ghazali's analysis in the third part of *Mishqat al-Anwar* regarding the *Shatahat* of al-Hallaj and al-Bistami. In the *Mishqat*, al-Ghazali uses the example of poetic verses, in addition to the example of "wine" that he uses in both texts. We read in the *Mishqat* that the intoxicated Sufis:

> ...Come to know that what they experienced was not the reality of identification, but that it was similar to identification. It was like the words of the lover during a state of extreme passionate love: "I am He whom I love, and He whom I love is I."[53]

Finally, this discussion would not be complete without a brief word about al-Ghazali's *Ihya 'Ulum al-Din*, which contains so much of al-Ghazali's teachings to the extent that Imam al-Nawawi compared it to the Qur'an in importance, saying "the *Ihya* were about to be a qur'an" (Mahmoud 1965: 19). The *Ihya* also includes *Kitab al-Munjiyyat* ("The Book of Salvations or Redemptions") in which al-Ghazali discusses the Sufi *maqamat* and *ahwal*. Part of the *Ihya*'s significance is the fact that al-Ghazali used a style of rhetoric in his writings that was acceptable to most Muslims, especially those who perceived Sufism unfavorably. Al-Ghazali himself seemed to be quite proud of the *Ihya*, noting that many books had been written before the *Ihya*, but that his book is distinguished from them by five characteristics: (1) that it made clear what they had made complex; (2) that it organized what they had scattered; (3) that it summarized what they had prolonged; (4) that it eliminated what they had repeated; (5) and finally that he researched and wrote about difficult and ambiguous issues that were not easy to understand, such issues that had never before been discussed in books.[54] Scholars have admired the *Ihya* and praised it extensively for the major influence it has had on them. The *Ihya* is divided into four sections, each containing ten books: (1) *'Ibadat (Fiqh)*; (2) *'Adat*: Habits, or ways of acting; (3) *Muhlikat*: Things that lead to perdition or destruction; (4) *Munjiyyat*: Salvations or things that lead to salvation. The fourth section of the *Ihya*, called *al-Munjiyyat*, is the section that includes the main Sufi themes, namely *tawba, sabr, shukr, khawf, rajaa, faqr, zuhd, tawhid, tawakkul, mahabba-shawq-uns* and *ridha; niyya, sidq, ikhlas; muraqaba-muhasaba-tafkeer* and *dhikr al-mawt* and what comes after it. It is interesting to note that in the *Ihya* al-Ghazali also related his belief that the corruption of peoples and nations is first and foremost the responsibility of the 'ulama and *rijal al-din* (legal scholars and men of religion) to remedy, because the 'ulama are the salt of the nation, thus if the salt goes rotten what else would be good [*idha fasad al-malh fama al-ladhi yasluh?*][55, 56] For al-Ghazali, Sufism was a key part of that remedy (when handled appropriately), not the source of such corruption as many traditionalist 'ulama have alleged by erroneously invoking the "heretical" claims of al-Hallaj and al-Bistami.

This notion becomes especially significant when we recognize the enormous impact which al-Ghazali has had on the Muslim community. Watt himself referred to this point in his book, *Muslim Intellectual: A Study of al-Ghazali*, when he noted that, although al-Ghazali never produced any tidy theory, nor did he reform "the intellectual class, he seems to have had a wide influence."[57] He further states:

> By largely removing the tension between Sufism and the "Islamic sciences," he brought the community much nearer to accepting a modified ideation suited

to the situation in which it found itself.... It was a new conception of the function of the religion in the life of a society.[58]

Above all, Watt maintains, al-Ghazali has "made the individualistic aspect of religion intellectually respectable [even though] in his practice he effects a genuine integration of individualism and communalism," a reflection of an important aspect of Islam that teaches its adherents their responsibility towards oneself, group, and the community at large.[59]

Although, as Fazlur Rahman noted above, al-Ghazali may have "puzzled many a modern writer;" and although he had his share of criticism, one fact remains certain: al-Ghazali's impact on Islamic thought as the best-known theologian, jurist and Sufi—not only of his time, but of subsequent centuries— is a fact on which all biographers concur. Of all his enormous intellectual contributions, it is al-Ghazali's contributions to Sufism which are perhaps his most enduring, and, as we have seen, perhaps most misunderstood. His success at reconciling Shari'a-oriented Sunnism with Sufism and defending the mystics against their traditionalist detractors has shaped the course of Islamic history. Without him, the two strains of Islamic thought may have diverged into separate religions entirely, which is a far more radical outcome than the dichotomy of "sober" versus "intoxicated" Sufism articulated by some. Yet, scholars must approach this legacy with caution and diligence. The complexity of his thought on such subjects as the *Shatahat* can easily lead to misreadings and misinterpretations. This is the problem that I have addressed here, by returning to al-Ghazali's own writings and words, in order to truly understand the thought of one of Islam's greatest scholars and mystics.

Notes

1   Abu Hamid Muhammad Ibn Muhammad al-Tusi al-Ghazali (1058–1111) is perhaps the best known jurist, theologian, religious intellectual, and Sufi of Sunni Islam, hence his unique nickname *Hujjat al-Islam*, (the Proof of Islam). He was born in Khurasan at the city of Tus in Northeastern Iran, where he also died. He was a prolific writer and a great thinker whose works and ideas have influenced generations of Muslims and non-Muslims through the ages. Al-Ghazali is the author of an impressive body of literature including *Ihya 'Ulum al-Din* (*Revival of Religious Sciences*) and the timeless spiritual classic, *al-Munqidh min al-Dhalal* (*Deliverance from Error*). Abu-Hamid Ghazali's other books include, *Tahafut al-Falasifa* (*The Incoherence of Philosophers*); *Maqasid al-Falasifa* (*The Aims of Philosophers*); *Mishqat al-Anwar* (*The Niche of Light*) and *al-Maqsad al-Asna fi Sharh Ma'ani Asma Allah al-Husna* (*The Noblest of Aims in the Explanation of God's Finest Names*), among others. The Reference section in this chapter includes a wide range of publications by and on al-Ghazali.

2 W. Montgomery Watt, *The Faith and Practice of al-Ghazali*, (Oxford: Oneworld, 1994), 64.

3 See B. Carra de Vaux, *Gazali*, Paris, 1902; P. Crone, "Did al-Ghazālī Write a Mirror for Princes?" *Jerusalem Studies of Arabic and Islam* 10, 1987, pp. 167–91; M. Asín Palacios, *La espiritualidad de Algazal y su sentido cristiano*, 4 vols., Madrid and Granada, 1931–41; D. B. Macdonald, "Life of al-Ghazzālī with Special Reference to His Religious Experiences and Opinions," *JAOS* 20, 1899, pp. 71–132; J. Obermann, *Der philosophische und religiöse Subjektivismus Ghazālīs*, Vienna and Leipzig, 1921. M. Smith, "Al-Risālat al-Laduniyya. By Abū Hāmid Muhammad Al-Ghazzālī (450/1059 –505/1111)" *JRAS* 1938, pp. 177–200, 353–74; A. J. Wensinck, *La pensée de Ghazzālī*, Paris, 1940.

4 Abu Hamid Al-Ghazali, *Mishqat al-Anwar: The Niche of Light*, trans. David Buchman (Provo, UT: Brigham Young University Press, 1998), 18.

5 Ibid., 18

6 Fazlur Rahman, Islam, 2nd ed. (Chicago: University of Chicago Press, 1966), 95

7 W. Montgomery Watt, *Muslim Intellectual* (Edinburgh: Edinburgh University Press, 1963), vii.

8 Muhammed Ibrahim Faiyyoumi, *Al-Imam al-Ghazali wa 'Alaqat al-Yaqin bil 'Aql* (Cairo: Anglo-Egyptian House Publishing, 1976), 10. The original text was in Arabic. English translation is mine.

9 Although the term *dhalal* might be one of the Arabic nouns that is resistant to translation into English, there seems to be a problem with the awkward but apparently widely accepted translation of "the Deliverer or Deliverance from Error," even though it hardly reflects the Arabic *Munqidh min al-Dhalal*, the original Arabic title. The Word "savior" or "redeemer" is perhaps a more accurate translation of *Munqidh*; and *Dhalal* simply denotes "going astray," as in the Qur'anic "*wala al-Dhalin*" that has mostly been translated as "those who have gone astray," not those who have "erred." Accordingly, "The Savior (or Redeemer) from Going Astray," seems to be closer to the Arabic meaning *al-Munqidh min al-Dhalal* than "the Deliverer/Deliverance from Error," given the fact that, in Arabic, the word "error" mostly denotes *khata'*, not *dhalal* and there is definitely a major difference between the two words.

10 T. J. Winter is Professor of Islamic Studies at the Faculty of Divinity, Cambridge University. He made his comment as part of his evaluation of McCarthy's translation of *al-Munqidh min al-Dalal* (Fons Vitae Publishing, 2000), found on the Fons Vitae website for the book https://fonsvitae.com/product/hardback-al-ghazali-deliverance-error-al-munqidh-min-al-dalal-works-copy/

11 بل بنور قذفه الله تعالى في القلب

12 Abu Hamid Al-Ghazali, *al-Munqidh min al-Dhalal*, 5th ed. (Cairo: Modern Books Publishing House, 1965), 67

13 Ibid., 67

14 Richard K. Khuri, *Freedom, Modernity, and Islam: Towards a Creative Synthesis* (Syracuse, NY: Syracuse University Press, 1998), 98

15 Ibid., 98

16. Ibid., 98
17. Al-Ghazali, *al-Munqidh*, 69
18. Ibid., 69
19. Ibid., 81
20. Ibid., 80
21. Ibid., 80–81
22. Ibid., 71–72
23. Al-Ghazali, *Tahafut al-Falasifa: The Incoherence of the Philosophers*, trans. Michael E. Marmura (Provo, Utah: Brigham Young University Press).
24. See W. H. T. Gairdner ("The Christian Church as a Home for Christ's Converts from Islam," *The Muslim World* 14 (1924): 235–246)
25. Al-Ghazali's full account on the Batinites is explained in his book *Fada'ih al-Batiniyya wa Fada'il al-Mustazhiriyya*, found in *Deliverance from Error*, 2nd ed., trans. and annotated Richard Joseph McCarthy (Louisville, KY: Fons Vitae, 2000).
26. Al-Ghazali, *al-Munqidh*, 83–85, 89
27. Ibid., 83–85, 89
28. Although Sufism has largely been conceived in the West as the spirituality or mysticism of Islam, it is important to mention that Sufism can best be explained as the inner experiential aspect of Islam. In other words, referring to Sufism as mysticism might be misleading given the fact that a mystic can belong to different religious traditions, that mysticism is mostly associated with spiritual experiences as they relate to the belief or doctrines of the mystics in different religious traditions. However, Sufism does not exist outside the boundaries of Islam. Alternatively, as William Stoddart put it: "One cannot be a Sufi without being a Muslim. There is no Sufism without Islam" (*Sufism: The Mystical Doctrines and Methods of Islam*, revised ed. (New York: Paragon House Publishers, 1985), 19).
29. Al-Ghazali, *al-Munquidh*, 90, 96.
30. Abu Bakr al-Khalabadhi, *Kitab al-Ta'arruf li-Madhab Ahl al-Tasawwuf* (*The Doctrine of the Sufis*) trans. A. J. Arberry (New York: Cambridge University Press, 1935), 82–112.
31. Abu Nasr al-Sarraj, *Kitab al-Luma'*, trans and ed. in Michael Anthony Sells' *Early Islamic Mysticism: Sufi, Qur'an, Mi'raj, Poetic and Theological Writings* (New York: Paulist Press, 1996), 196–211.
32. Al-Ghazali, *Al-Munquidh*, 1965: 91
33. Al-Kalabadhi, *Kitab al-Ta'arrof*, 91
34. Al-Ghazali, *Al-Munquidh*, 94
35. Al-Sarraj, *Kitab al-Luma'*, 203
36. Ibid., 203
37. Ibid., 203
38. Al-Ghazali, *Al-Munquidh*, 91.
39. Al-Sarraj, *Kitab al-Luma'*, 204

40 Al-Ghazali, *Al-Munquidh*, 93.
41 Al-Ghazali, *The Book of Fear and Hope*, in *The Revival of the Religious Sciences Ihya 'Ulum al-Din*, trans. Leon Zolondek, (Leiden: E.J. Brill, 1963), 1.
42 Al-Ghazali, *The Book of Fear and Hope*, 2.
43 Ibid., 25
44 Ibid., 25
45 Ibid., 51
46 Qur'an 2:177.
47 Al-Ghazali, *Mishqat al-Anwar*, 18.
48 Annemarie Schimmel, *Mystical Dimensions of Islam*, (Chapel Hill, NC: University of North Carolina Press, 1975), 59.
49 See William C. Chittick, *Sufism: A Short Introduction* (London: Oneworld Publications, 2000).
50 Watt, *Muslim Intellectual*.
51 Badawi quoted in 'Amir al-Najjar, *Nadharat fi Fikr al-Ghazali* (Cairo: al-Safa Publishing and Translation Company, 1989), 43–44. English translation is mine.
52 Al-Ghazali, *Al-Maqsada Al-Asna fi Sharh Ma'ani Asma Allah al-Husna*, trans. David B. Burrell and Nazih Daher (Cambridge: The Islamic Text Society, 1992), 357.
53 Al-Ghazali, *Mishqat al-Anwar*, 18.
54 Al-Najjar, *Nadharat*, 20
55 إذا فسد الملح فما الذي يصلح؟
56 Al-Najjar, *Nadharat*, 28
57 Watt, *Muslim Intellectual*, 179.
58 Ibid., 179.
59 Ibid., 180

References

Asín Palacios, Miguel. *La Espiritualidad de Algazal y Su Sentido Cristiano*. 4 vols. Madrid-Granada: Estanislao Maestre, 1931–1941.

Carra de Vaux, Bernard. *Gazali*. Paris: F. Alcan, 1902.

Chittick, William C. *Sufism: A Short Introduction*. London: Oneworld Publications, 2000.

Crone, Patricia. "Did Al-Ghazali Write A Mirror For Princes?" *Jerusalem Studies in Arabic and Islam*, no. 10 (1987): 167–191.

Faiyyoumi, Muhammed I. al-. *Al-Imam al-Ghazali wa 'Alaqat al-Yaqin bil 'Aql*. Cairo: Anglo-Egyptian House Publishing, 1976.

Ghazali, Abu Hamid al-. *Al-Maqsad al-Asna fi Sharh Ma'ani Asma Allah al-Husna. The Ninety-Nine Beautiful Names of God.* Translated by David B. Burrell and Nazih Daher. Cambridge: The Islamic Text Society, 1992.

———. *Al-Munqidh min al-Dhalal.* Fifth edition, with an introduction by Dr. Abdel Halim Mahmoud. Cairo: Modern Books Publishing House, 1965.

———. *Mishqat al-Anwar. The Niche of Light.* Translated by David Buchman. Provo, Utah: Brigham Young University Press 1998.

———. *Ihya 'Ulum al-Din. The Revival of the Religious Sciences: The Book of Fear and Hope.* Translated by Leon Zolondek. Leiden: E.J. Brill 1963.

———. *Tahafut al-Falasifa. The Incoherence of the Philosophers.* Translated by Michael E. Marmura. Provo, Utah: Brigham Young University Press, 1997.

Khalabadhi, Abubakr al-. *Kitab al-Ta'arruf li-Madhab Ahl al-Tasawwuf.* Translated by A. J. Arberry. New York: Cambridge University Press, 1935.

Khuri, Richard K. *Freedom, Modernity, and Islam: Toward a Creative Synthesis.* New York: Syracuse University Press, 1998.

Macdonald, Duncan B. "Life of al-Ghazzali with Especial References to His Religious Experiences and Opinions." *Journal of the American Oriental Society* 20 (1899): 71–132. Mahmoud, Abdel-Halim. *Al-Munqidh min al-Dhalal li Hujjat al-Islam al Ghazali.* 5th edition. Cairo: Modern Books Publishing House, 1965.

McCarthy, Richard J. *Freedom and Fulfillment: An Annotated Translation of al-Ghazali's al-Munqidh min al-Dhalal,* 2nd edition. Boston: Twayne Publishers, 2000.

Najjar, 'Amir al-. *Nadharat fi Fikr al-Ghazali.* Cairo: al-Safa Publishing and Translation Company, 1989.

Obermann, J. *Der philosophische und religiöse Subjektivismus Ghazalis.* Wien and Liepzig: Braumüller, 1921.

Rahman, Fazlur. *Islam.* 2nd edition. Chicago: University of Chicago Press, 1966.

Sarraj, Abu Nasr al-. *Kitab al-Luma'.* Translated and edited in Michael Sells' *Early Islamic Mysticism: Sufi, Qur'an, Mi'raj, Poetic and Theological Writings.* New York: Paulist Press, 1996.

Schimmel, Annemarie. *Mystical Dimensions of Islam.* Chapel Hill, NC: University of North Carolina Press, 1975.

Smith, Margaret. *Al-Ghazali the Mystic: A Study of the Life and Personality of Abu Hamid Muhammad al-Tusi al-Ghazali, together with an account of his Mystical Teaching and an estimate of his place in the History of Islamic Mysticism.* Lahore: Hijra International Publishers, 1983.

———. "Al-Risalat Al-Luduniyya. By Abu Hamid Muhammad Al Ghazali 450/1059-505/1111." *Journal of the Royal Asiatic Society* (1938): 177–200, 353–74.

Watt, W. Montgomery. *Muslim Intellectual: A Study of al-Ghazali.* Edinburgh: Edinburgh University Press, 1963.

———. *The Faith and Practice of al-Ghazali.* Oxford: Oneworld Publications, 1994.

Wensinck, A. J. *La pensée de Ghazzālī.* Paris: Adrien-Maisonneuve, 1940.

About the Author

Professor Souad T. Ali is head of Classics and Middle Eastern Studies, founding chair of the Arizona State University Council for Arabic and Islamic Studies; coordinator of Arabic Studies; associate professor of Arabic literature and Middle Eastern/Islamic studies in the School of International Letters and Cultures (SILC). She is simultaneously an affiliate graduate faculty member in English, women and gender studies, religious studies, and justice and social inquiry; as well as an affiliate faculty member in the Center for the Study of Religion and Conflict, African and African-American studies, Center for the Study of Race and Democracy, Institute for Humanities Research, and Arizona Center for Medieval and Renaissance Studies. A scholar with international recognition, Professor Ali is a recipient of several awards including, the ASU Faculty Women's Association Outstanding Graduate Mentor Award (2017); the ASU Outstanding Advisor of the Year (2019), among others. A Fulbright Scholar, Professor Ali is the author of *A Religion, Not A State: Ali 'Abd al-Raziq's Islamic Justification of Political Secularism* (University of Utah Press 2009), *The Road to Two Sudans*, an edited volume of which she is the lead editor, has been published internationally by Cambridge Scholars Publishing (2014). Ali's third book is *Perspectives of Five Kuwaiti Women in Leadership Roles: Feminism, Islam and Politics* (CSP, 2019). Professor Ali's impressive scholarship also includes over 30 scholarly articles in several languages, and more than 100 scholarly conference presentations. With degrees from prestigious institutions such as the University of Utah and Brigham Young University, as well as the University of Khartoum and the Polytechnic of North London, Professor Ali brings a wealth of knowledge and expertise to her work. She has held several key leadership roles, including serving as the past president of the American Academy of Religion/Western Region (AAR/WR), president of the Sudan(s) Studies Association of North America, and executive committee member of the International Association of Intercultural Studies (IAIS) in Cairo, Egypt and Bremen, Germany.

6 Surprise! Four Jewish Thinkers' Views of the "Other"

Emily Leah Silverman

The major ideas of the Jewish philosophers Rosenzweig, Buber, Levinas, and Arendt took shape during the darkest times of the twentieth century. The principal texts of Rosenzweig and Buber emerged in response to World War I, those of Levinas and Arendt to World War II. Rosenzweig started writing *The Star of Redemption* (published in 1921) from the trenches of Macedonia, sending his thoughts to his friends and family on postcards. It is therefore not surprising that his book begins with death, although it is equally significant that it ends with life. At this same time, Buber was writing his first draft of *I and Thou* (published in 1923). In 1952 Buber, speaking on *I and Thou*, said, "During the First World War it became clear to me that a process was going on which before I only surmised. This was the growing difficulty of genuine dialogue, and most especially of genuine dialogue…between man and man [that] threaten[ed] ever more pitilessly to become unbridgeable. I began to understand at that time, more than thirty years ago, that this is the central question for the fate of mankind."[1]

Levinas wrote *Time and the Other* in 1947 and *Totality and Infinity* in 1961. Like Rosenzweig in *The Star of Redemption*, he challenged the old notion of grand totalities, which he found useless when faced with war and unspeakable horrors. For Levinas, the demand of literally facing up to the Other and gazing into her eyes replaced grand universal notions.

Arendt, for her part, did more than put a face on the Other. She too laid to rest the notion of grand universal generalities such as the concepts of "nation" and "people." But in doing so she showed us the uniqueness of the Other. She pointed out that we come to know the unique Other through answering the question of "who" she is as opposed to "what" she is. And we come to know her as who she is through witnessing her speech and action in the world. In her speech and action, we encounter her unique being.

In this light we can appreciate poet Karl Wolfskehl's description of his encounter with a paralyzed, disease-stricken Franz Rosenzweig. The poet's encounter with Rosenzweig was nothing like what he had imagined. It was a type of "surprise," which is the primary concept to be examined here. I contend that these four thinkers, Rosenzweig, Buber, Levinas, and Arendt, all describe the moment of surprise when one is truly present with and encounters the Other.

The life narratives of all four philosophers had an impact on how they approached and recognized the Other and realized this moment. Each thinker describes the encounter from a different perspective, which can be demarcated by a notion of time and a structure of language. Yet each thinker is getting at the same paradoxical moment of experiencing and living in the present, the only moment in which we can truly engage with the Other. In this paper I describe in chronological sequence these four philosophers' views of the Other and how they all lead to a sense of wonder and surprise. Surprise leads us to see the Divinity of the Other, or, in the case of Arendt, her distinct uniqueness.

Introduction

The poet Karl Wolfskehl wrote this observation on his visit with Franz Rosenzweig:

> Whoever stepped over the threshold of Franz Rosenzweig's room entered a magic circle and fell under a spell, gentle yet potent—in fact, became himself a charmed being. The solidity and the familiar forms of every-day life melted away and the incredible became the norm. Behind the desk, in the armchair sat, not as one had imagined on climbing the stairs, a mortally sick, utterly invalid man, almost totally deprived of physical force, upon whom salutations were lost and solace shattered; behind the desk, in the chair, Franz Rosenzweig was throned. The moment our eyes met his, community was established. Everything corporeal, objects as well as voices and their reverberations, became subject to a new order, were incorporated without strain, conscious effort or need for readjustment, into that wholly genuine, primordially true kind of existence irradiated by beauty. It simply couldn't have been otherwise, for what reigned here was not pressure and duress, but utter freedom…
>
> It was not only that all petty human feelings, anxieties and embarrassments were wiped out. It was not only that all the paltry, complacent pity of well-being was purged away. What happened here was much more: in the presence of this man, *well* in the fullest sense, one's own welfare was assured, wholly and in accord with the spirit. Near Franz Rosenzweig one came to oneself, was relieved of one's burdens, heaviness, constriction. Whoever came to him,

he drew into a dialogue, his very *listening* was eloquent in itself, summoned, confirmed and guided, even if it were not for the unforgettably deep and warm look of the eyes…[2]

Karl Wolfskehl's encounter with Rosenzweig is an example of the experience of embracing the Other, a fundamental Jewish philosophical perspective also described by Martin Buber, Emmanuel Levinas, and Hannah Arendt. The encounter involves an element of "surprise," as Rosenzweig draws the "I" and "Thou" into dialogue through his own intense listening. The incredible becoming the norm is equally an aspect of Buber's perception of the Other, in which there is a total encounter and merging of transcendence and immanence. All objectification of the Other is erased, and the objective "It" of the Other becomes a subjective "Thou." The experience is one of "utter freedom," radiating from the Divinity. All the boundaries and projections upon the Other are broken. As Nahum Glatzer states (again in reference to Rosenzweig), "It is the freedom of man before God."[3] When Wolfskehl writes, "The moment our eyes met his, community was established," he reveals his experience of the Other and establishes the basis for the ethical responsibility not only to identify with, but also to care for the Other. In the same way, Emmanuel Levinas would go on to argue for the ethical responsibility toward the Other.

Levinas, in the preface to *Totality and Infinity*, writes, "We were impressed by the opposition to the idea of totality in Franz Rosenzweig's *Stern der Erlösung*, a work too often present in this book to be cited."[4] Rosenzweig bases his opposition to the concept of totality on his distrust of grand universal schemes, meta-narratives, and structures that everything fits into (which might earn him a nomination as the first post-modernist). Instead, he recommends *Sprachendenken*, or "speech-thinking." Speech-thinking is what two people do when they enter into dialogue with each other and are present in the dialogue encounter. The concept is a type of grammatical structure that allows the element of time to play an important role in the encounter.

Speech-thinking is necessary because thinking in grand universal schemes does not allow one to see the individual or the particular. According to Rosenzweig, we can never gain any direct knowledge from universal schemas. We only gain knowledge through our relationship to the Other. As Arendt also argues, the Other is a unique person whom we come to know and engage with through her actions and speech in the public space.

In speech-thinking there is an invocation to the Other that acknowledges the Other's presence. The invocation demands a response, which takes time. Rosenzweig insists that we need to wait for the Other's response and not project our own response onto the Other. Waiting creates a space where the

Other is able to respond. The invocation of the Other demands a total presence and a total openness. In waiting with no projection or expectation about the response of the Other, there is the gift of a surprise because one cannot know in advance how the Other will respond. The surprise that one encounters when hearing the speech of the Other is time-dependent.

For his part, Buber theorizes that the I and the ordinary "You" experience both the transcendence and the immanence of the Other from a Divine perspective through the simultaneous experience of the I and Thou. The I-and-Thou can only be achieved through a demand of absolute presence of the individual to the Other. For Buber, the experience of the Other occurs when we are in the absolute present moment, which is outside of the normal time–space continuum. It is a transcendent moment, which is also immanent. This idea is different from Rosenzweig's because, for the latter, the duration of time is what brings the individual into the present.

The third philosopher, Levinas, adds to the mix the concept of the face of the Other. He demands that we be able to look into the eyes and face of the Other. This ethical demand literally to face up to the Other produces an immediate sense of caring for the Other as we gaze into her eyes. His strategy is the reverse of Rosenzweig's, for Rosenzweig realized his own dependence on the Other through waiting for her response. Levinas, however, states that the Other becomes immediately dependent on us. This dependence of the Other when she faces us demands that we totally care for all of her basic needs. This caring only happens, according to Levinas, when a sense of the future is embedded in the present. Since the future is unknowable, this sense of the future is a surprise. As we dialectically engage and gaze into the Other's face, we do not know how the encounter will unfold. Finally, Hannah Arendt introduces the concept of the uniqueness of the Other. We learn who the Other is through the space of appearance created by her speech and action in the world. The Other's uniqueness, which is revealed through this space of appearance, is a surprise because we do not know what she will say and how she will act.

Thus, for all four thinkers, the encounter of the Other produces a sense of wonder and surprise, which can only happen in a paradoxical moment of being totally present with and for the Other. Each thinker describes this moment of engagement and encounter a little differently. Rosenzweig, using his concept of speech-thinking, describes it as a form of revelation, which is an invocation in the imperative tense. Buber sees the encounter of the I and Thou as creating a moment of transcendence–immanence. Levinas shows us the face of the Other, and Arendt develops the concept of the Other's uniqueness in the space of appearance. All of these linked concepts are investigated here, and their distinctions described in terms of time and grammatical structure.

Rosenzweig

For the last seven years of his short life (1922–29), Franz Rosenzweig was confined to his attic apartment due to the debilitating effect of Lou Gehrig's disease, which left his mind locked in a paralyzed body. Unable to write and barely able to speak, he and his wife Edith developed a system of communication using a specialized typewriter, which enabled her to interpret his personal shorthand, thus allowing him to produce his many books and essays.

In Rosenzweig's books *The Star of Redemption* and *The New Thinking* (first published in 1925 as an introduction to *The Star*), he explores his concept of the Other using the new methodology of *Sprachendenken,* which he developed in discussion and response to Eugen Rosenstock-Huessy, a contemporary ethicist and convert to Christianity. This notion of speech-thinking is Rosenzweig's major contribution to the philosophy of the Other.

Rosenzweig considered the speech-thinking methodology to be a turning point in the history of philosophy, and in fact "new thinking." One of the premises of the old philosophy was its concern for grand systems, which consisted "of a logic, an ethic, an aesthetic and a philosophy of religion."[5] The old basic question of philosophy had always been: what is the essence of something? How do we know a chair is a chair? Is it possible ever to know the essence of things? Emmanuel Kant questioned whether we can ever know the thing-in-itself and concluded that we never can, but that all knowledge arises out of experience. These questions have guided the history of epistemology. Two centuries later, Husserl and his students furthered the project by asking the question, can essentialism form a basis for ontology?

Rosenzweig makes a clean break with this thinking, moving from ontology to existentialism and relationship-based philosophy. He writes,

> Experience, no matter how deeply it may probe, will discover again and again in man only what is human, in the world only what is worldly, in God only what is divine. And only in God that which is divine, only in the world that which is worldly, only in man that which is human. *Finis philosophiae*? If it were [the end], so much the worse for philosophy! But I do not think that things will be as bad as that. On the contrary, it is at this point, where philosophy to be sure, would come to the end of [its way of] thinking, that experiential philosophy (*erfahrende Philosophie*) can begin.[6]

Rosenzweig demonstrates the techniques of this new type of understanding as speech-thinking and the awareness of our dependence on the Other through the grammatical structure of language. The first volume of *The Star of Redemption*, which he calls "The Elements," lays the foundation for this philosophy by showing that God, World, and Man [sic] are irreducible. Since they can never be reduced to one, they must be in relationship to each other. They connect to each other through God's creation of the world, God's revelation of herself to humans, and humans' redeeming themselves in the World. The creation of the world is an act that is described in the past tense, or in the narrative form. God reveals herself to Man, but how does God reveal herself? It is through the imperative tense and the invocation of a human proper name, which is found in the moment. The old philosophy is timeless in that being and beings are outside of time, or as Rosenzweig puts it, "essence wants to know nothing of time."[7] But the new philosophy is based on a grammar that is keyed to a transitive verb, a "time word" that moves forward or back from the moment of encounter but always remains embedded within it. Rosenzweig gives an example, which is relevant to his own embodiment:

> Everyone knows that for the attending physician, for instance, the treatment is present, the getting sick past, and the certification of death future, and that it would make no sense if out of fancy of timeless knowledge he wanted to eliminate learning and experience in the diagnosis, cleverness and stubbornness in his therapy, and fear and hope in his prognosis.[8]

In other words, God's act of creation is the getting sick, her revelation to Man is the treatment relation between doctor and patient, and the redemption of the human in the world is the prognosis of death. These different tenses of relationship are known as indicative, imperative, and cohortative. Following the pattern of this analogy, in an indicative relationship, the patient tells the doctor the story of his sickness. In an imperative relationship, the doctor's diagnosis takes the form of naming and addressing the patient, thus establishing a dialogue. In a cohortative relationship, both parties recognize the eventuality of death, but set it off as a future event. Speaking of the interrelationships among God, Man, and World, Rosenzweig says, "in their relationships only in creation, revelation, redemption, do they open up."[9] He goes on to say:

> Now this great world-poem is retold in three tenses. Actually told only in the first, the book of the past. In the present the story yields to the direct exchange of speech, for of those who are present, be they human beings or God, they cannot speak in the third person, they can only be heard and addressed. And

in the book of the future there reigns the language of the chorus, for even the individual grasps the future only where and when he can say We.[10]

Rosenzweig explains how grammar is a type of performance. Speech-thinking provides the structure to express the relationship. This relationship is shown in the following chart, after Robert Gibbs:[11]

Rosenzweig's Grammar

Theological Concept	Mood	Tense	Pronouns
Creation	Indicative	Past	He, She, It
Revelation	Imperative	Present	You, I
Redemption	Cohortative	Future	We

In revealing what is concealed by the process that takes place, first there is an invocation by God to Abraham, "Where art Thou?" This call marks the shift from the interior to the exterior; it is the call to the Other. Not only is there an invocation to the Other, but God calls out to Abraham by his proper name. Abraham responds, saying, "Here I am." God then commands the *Ve ahavta*, "Thou shalt love the Lord thy God with all thy might and with all thy soul." The command to love can only happen in a reciprocal revelatory relationship, which is present. Levinas comments:

> As the movement of God toward man and human singularity—that is, ipseity—revelation is immediately recognized as love: love opens up that singularity… [Rosenzweig's] revelation is love from the start…the love of God for human uniqueness is commandment to love. Only love can command love. Love orders to love in the privileged *now* of its loving, so that the commandment to love is repeated and renewed indefinitely in the repetition and renewal of the very love that commands love. And thus the *present* is the time of the Revelation.[12]

The present, which includes the categories of the imperative, the nominative case of the substantive, and the singular and the proper name, clearly illustrates revelation. These categories, however, function not as species or types, but entirely as definite individual considerations. The dialogue between God and man moves, as Else Rahel-Freund puts it, "from real word to real word."[13] Rahel-Freund goes on to say:

> This dialogue is one of the most beautiful and profound portrayals of man's encounter with the living God that is possible to express in words. It locates

speech in its most innate realm as "vital back and forth interconnection of address passing to and fro."[14] Further, it is the basis of speech thinking per se in as much as it demonstrates speech thinking's character as existential thinking by the inclusion of the "other."[15]

Time is the key element that defines Otherness for Rosenzweig. In his philosophy, thinking is a solitary activity not bound by time. One interacts only with oneself, and when one shares one's thoughts with another, it is not for the purpose of dialogue, but instead to confirm or raise objections that one has been thinking out alone. Thinking is not bound to time as a conversation is bound to time and the present moment. This temporal dimension, he states, is the difference between the new thinking and the old. Speech is in the present moment where dialogue takes place:

> The method of speech takes the place of the method of thinking, as developed in all earlier philosophies. Thinking is timeless and wants to be timeless. With one stroke it wants to make a thousand connections; the last, the goal, is for it the first. Speech is bound to time, nourished by time, [and] it neither can nor wants to abandon the ground of nourishment; it does not know beforehand where it will emerge; it lets itself be given its cues from others; it actually lives by another's life, whether that other is the one who listens to a story, or is the respondent in a dialogue, or the participant in a chorus; thinking, by contrast, is always solitary, even if it should be in common, among several "symphilosophers": even then, the other is only raising the objections I should actually have made myself.[16]

Therefore, traditional philosophy is not true dialogue but rather *a priori* deductive thinking that does not need a dialogue. There is no exchange, just objections or confirmations to arguments. We might make a modern analogy to the computer, which does not dialogue, but merely confirms or rejects instruction. Rosenzweig goes on to state the difference between thinking and speech-thinking:

> In actual conversation something really happens. I do not know beforehand what the other will say to me, because I do not even know beforehand what I will say; perhaps not even whether I will say anything at all; it could well be that the other begins, that being most often the case in the genuine conversation; a fact of which one will easily be convinced by taking a comparative look at the Gospels and the Socratic dialogues. Socrates most often just sets the conversation in motion, on the course of a philosophical discussion. The thinker plainly knows his thoughts in advance; that he "expresses" [*ausspricht*] them is only a concession to the defectiveness, as he calls it, of our means of

communication. This does not consist in the fact that we need speech, but rather in the fact that we need time.[17]

It is the element of time that leads to what I call surprise, or Rosenzweig's notion of not knowing and not being able to predict beforehand what the Other will say, or even whether she will say anything at all. It is the unexpected and therefore the surprise that leads to a type of openness that is not possible with thinking (as opposed to speech-thinking). This element of surprise helps us to stop projecting our expectations upon the Other. In contrast, thinking is more like a chess game that I could possibly play by myself. I could figure out my strategy beforehand and anticipate my counter-moves before I even move my chess pieces. In conversation, on the other hand, in Rosenzweig's sense, one cannot anticipate what the Other will say. What makes the surprise possible is that in conversation we need time, which makes us dependent on the Other. Rosenzweig writes, "To need time means: not to be able to presuppose anything, to have to wait for everything, to be dependent on the Other for what is ours. All this is entirely unthinkable to the thinking thinker, while it alone suits [entspricht] the speech-thinker."[18]

Rosenzweig is not saying that there is no inner dialogue that takes place in the thinking thinker's mind. Of course, that happens. But there is no need for the Other. One can process silently in one's own head. The Other, however, is very much required for a speech-thinker, and the way she depends upon and concretizes the Other is by speaking and waiting for the Other to speak, a process that requires the passage of time.

For the speech thinker, this new speaking thinking is also thinking, just as the old thinking-thinking did not come about without inner speech. The difference between the old and new, the logical and grammatical thinking, does not lie in sound versus silence, but in the need for an Other and for taking into account the passage of time.

Here "thinking" is taken to mean thinking for no one in particular and speaking to no one in particular (for which one can substitute "everyone in general"). But "speaking" means to speak to someone and to think for someone; and this someone is always a very definite Someone, or as Rosenzweig puts it, someone who "doesn't merely have ears like the general public, but also a mouth,"[19] and can therefore speak back, which is a time-dependent activity. The reason he states that no one individual can be substituted for the "everyone" that constitutes what he calls the "general public" is that a collective group cannot speak to a person in conversation the same way that a specific "someone" can converse in a one-to-one relationship and correspondence with the Other.

Going back to the opening quote describing poet Karl Wolfskehl's encounter with Rosenzweig, we can see the concept of speech-thinking as Rosenzweig's own personal embodiment, given that his paralysis forced him into the time-dependency of waiting for the Other to speak just as it forced the Other to listen carefully to and wait for his response. Rosenzweig's illness reified in his own body his philosophy of speech-thinking.

Buber

> Independently of those mentioned [Eugen Rosenstock *Angewandte Seelenkunde*, Hans Ehrenberg's *Fichte*, Victor Von Wiezsacker *Philosophie des Artzes*, and Rudolph von Wiesacker *Theoretical Biology*] and of each other, Martin Buber in *Ich und Du* [*I and Thou*] and Ferdinand Ebner in *Das Wort und die geistigen Realitäten* [*The Word and the Spiritual Realities*], a text produced at precisely the same time as my work, made their own advance on the focal point of the new thought, the one that is treated in the middle book of *The Star*.[20]

In his biography of Buber, Maurice Friedman suggests that *I and Thou* originated in three experiences that deeply affected Buber. Prior to World War I, Buber had a premonition of a great world catastrophe. As a result, in April 1914 he attended a three-day interfaith meeting that took place in Potsdam. Also present were Frederik van Eeden, Gustav Landauer, Eric Gutkind, Florens Christian Rang, Poul Bjerre, Henri Borel, and Theodor Gustav Norlind. Friedman says, "The conversations of the group, Buber testified, were marked by an unreserve whose substance and fruitfulness he had scarcely ever experienced so strongly. This reality of group presence and presentness had such an effect on all who took part that the fictitious fell away and every word was an actuality."[21] At this meeting Buber had a profound exchange with Florens Christian Rang, in which Buber told Rang that "the Jews knew [Jesus] from within, in the impulses and stirrings of his Jewish being, in a way that remains inaccessible to the peoples submissive to him."[22] Maurice Freedman writes of this landmark in Jewish-Christian dialogue:

> Rang stood up; Buber stood up; each looked into the heart of the Other's eyes. "It is gone," Rang said and before everyone Buber and Rang gave each other the kiss of brotherhood. "The discussion of the situation between Jews and Christians had been transformed into a bond between the Christian and the Jew," Buber later commented.[23]

In this meeting Buber had the experience of the complete encounter of the Other in a dialogue form. He and Rang were literally able to embrace each other in an I–Thou relationship.

The second event that had a major impact on Buber was a meeting with Reverend William Hechler, a friend and supporter of Theodor Herzl, which took place in May 1914. Hechler, who had predicated the pending World War, asked Buber if he believed in God. This question caused Buber to contemplate deeply. He realized:

> If to believe in God means to be able to talk *about* him in the third person, then I do *not* believe in God. But if to believe in him means to be able to talk *to* him, then I do believe in God.... The God who gives Daniel such foreknowledge of this hour of human history, this hour before the "world war," that its fixed place in the march of the ages can be predetermined, is not my God and not God. But the God to whom Daniel prays in his suffering is my God and the God of all.[24]

To talk about God in the He/She/It form is to discuss God as an object bounded in time–space by what Rosenzweig would consider to be the narrative form of speech-thinking, that is, the way an event is talked about. We describe God's qualities and story, but we do not experience God. God is not a Thou living in the moment, but instead God is an It, objectified when we talk about her. For Rosenzweig the past tense is a narrative language construct. The narrative tells us how something happened or was created. The narrative tells us about the something. For Buber the past tense is tied to objectifying. We turn our relationship into the I and It when we talk about the other as an It (human, animal, plant, work of art) as opposed to being present in a relationship to the Thou. The God with whom the I can dialogue is an immanent God, a God in the present moment. This experience of an immanent God is God's revelation to Man. To be able to pray to God is the future and the experience of Redemption in Rosenzweig's sense. Prayer expresses the hope that "We," the community, have a future.

The third event that Friedman suggests was pivotal to Buber's understanding of *I and Thou* was the impact of a meeting with a young man named Mehe who had come to Buber to address life-and-death questions. On the day of the visit, Buber, who was a student of Hassidic mysticism, had been engaged in meditative practices that put him into a state of mystical rapture. Therefore, during this meeting with an Other in the person of Mehe, Buber was not as engaged in the present as he could have been, as he was still feeling the effects of his otherworldly mystical journey. Buber gave Mehe the best attention he could at the time, but Buber felt that he had not been fully present to the young man with his mind and body. A few months later, one of Mehe's friends came to see Buber and told him that Mehe had died at the Front. He further told Buber that Mehe's visit to Buber had been prompted by the kind of despair that may be defined partially as "no longer opposing one's own death."[25] Buber's guilt over his failure to help the young man, which he attributed to his not being fully present with his whole being in his dialogue with Mehe, served as a conversion experience for Buber. Henceforth he redirected himself to being in the world as opposed to being apart from the world, which is where mystical rapture leads.

This commitment is what I consider to be Rosenzweig's concept of absolute empiricism demanding total presence at all moments of encounter and dialogue. As Buber states:

> Since then I have given up the "religious," which is nothing but the exception, extraction, exaltation, ecstasy; or it has given me up, I possess nothing but the everyday out of which I am never taken. The mystery is no longer disclosed; it has escaped or it has made its dwelling here where everything happens as it happens. I know no fulness but each mortal hour's fulness of claim and responsibility. Though far from being equal to it, yet I know that in the claim I am claimed and may respond in responsibility, and know who speaks and demands a response.[26]

Buber writes *I and Thou* out of his guilt for not being in the world, his experience of dialogue with the Other, and the question, "Do I believe in God?" Buber's lack of embodiment and presence during World War I, like Rosenzweig's contrasting embodiment of death at the same time, forced him to grapple with conversation. Both thinkers came to the same conclusion—that it is through the face of the Other that we see the face of God.

In the final part of *The Star*, Rosenzweig explained how the six-pointed star, a symbol specifically associated with Judaism, is the symbol of both the human face and God's countenance. The face is inscribed with the two triangles that make up the star. The first triangle descends from the center of the forehead to the plane of the nose, which processes scent, and the ears, which receive speech. Both of these senses and their facial triangle are receptive. The second triangle, inverted and superimposed on the first, is the active one, made up of the two eyes and mouth. The eyes play a double role as both gaze and vision. The mouth is capable of speech, invocation, silence, and the kiss. Stéphane Mosès suggests that in biblical symbolism, the kiss "stands for the ultimate encounter of man and God, in the form of the two experiences of limit, that of mystical Revelation and that of death, [which] is the metaphorical representation of the Redemption."[27] Rosenzweig states:

> Just as the structure of the face is dominated by the forehead, so its life, all that surrounds the eyes and shines forth from the eyes is gathered in the mouth. The mouth is consummator and fulfiller of all expression of which the countenance is capable, both in speech as, at last, in the silence behind which speech retreats: in the kiss. It is in the eyes that the eternal countenance shines for man; it is the mouth by whose words man lives…God sealed [Moses'] completed life with a kiss of his mouth. Thus does God seal and so too does man.[28]

Thus, Rosenzweig sees the star as symbolic of the face that is both the revelation of God's countenance and the reflection of God's countenance in the face of the human Other. Stéphane Mosès describes the groundedness of this metaphor when he says, "There can only be a vision of the 'face of God' through the appearance of the face of man."[29] Divine Truth reveals itself in the human face. To look into the face of the Other is to see God's countenance blazing through, as Karl Wolfskehl experienced in his meeting with Rosenzweig, when he recalled, "The moment our eyes met his, community was established." Even in his physical entombment, Rosenzweig enabled the poet to see God's countenance shining through his face, and he thus established the ground of dialogue with the Other. Rosenzweig wrote:

> The irreversibility of the truth can only be enunciated in the image of a living being. For in the living being, an Above and a Below are already designated by nature prior to all theory or regulation. And of living beings in turn there, where self-consciousness is awake to this designation: in man. Man has an above and below in his own corporeality. And just as the truth which gave itself configuration in the Star, is in turn assigned within the Star to God as whole truth, and not to man or the world, so too the Star must once more mirror itself in that which, within the corporeality, is again the Upper: the countenance. Thus it is not human illusion if Scripture speaks of God's countenance and even of his separate bodily parts. There is no other way to express the Truth. Only when we see the Star as countenance do we transcend every possibility and simply see.[30]

Thus, "star-seeing" is simultaneously receptive and outgoing, as a person can both look at the Other and receive the experience of the Other through the same perceptual operation—that of seeing, the star-seeing of Wolfskehl's epiphany. Buber's failure to experience star-seeing occurred when he allowed an unworldly mystical experience to cloud his experiential encounter with Mehe, concealing from Buber the primary immanence of God's material countenance as mediated through the physical organs of sense. Rosenzweig showed us how an inter-subjective space is created when one engages in speech-thinking. This inter-subjective space is the in-between that opens up in one's encounter of the Other. It is a form of dialogue. The element of time gives us the space for a surprise within the dialogic encounter.

Unlike Rosenzweig, who argued that we need time as an element in order to encounter the Other, Buber takes the opposite stand. He argues that to have a direct encounter with the Other, we need to break out of the time-space continuum. Time and space outside of ourselves ground us to an object, which blocks our direct experience of the present. The I–It relationship is grounded in the past. When we experience something from the past, we objectify our experience. As Buber explains,

> The *I* of the primary word *I–It*, that is, the *I* faced by no *Thou*, but surrounded by a multitude of "contents," has no present, only the past. Put in another way, in so far as man rests satisfied with the things he experiences and uses, he lives in the past, and his moment has no present content. He has nothing but objects. But object subsist in time that has been.[31]

The recipe to break out of this restriction to the I–It objectified relationship to the world is to experience a direct I–Thou, which is always in the present. "The present is not fugitive and transient, but continually present and enduring. The object is not duration, but cessation, suspension, a breaking off and cutting clear and hardening, absence of relation and of present being."[32] Rosenzweig viewed the element of time in a direct encounter as a duration that is a moment of waiting for a response. Buber, on the other hand, shows that the I–Thou relationship requires one to let go of relating to nature, a person, or art as an object. One needs to have no sense of being connected to an object when entering the I–Thou relation. This means letting go of the past. In order to experience the I–Thou there has to be "No-thing" in the way of the encounter with the Other. When there is No-thing, then the inter-subjective space is created. Thus, we need to stop seeing time and space outside of ourselves in order to have an I–Thou relationship. Buber explains:

> And just as prayer is not in time but time in prayer, sacrifice not in space but space in sacrifice, and to reverse the relation is to abolish the reality, so with the man to whom I say *Thou*. I do not meet with him at some time and place or other. I can set him in a particular time and place; I must continually do it: but I set only a *He* or a *She*, that is an *It*, no longer my *Thou*.[33]

Buber notes that we can only have this inter-subjective space when we enter into the I–Thou relationship. The I–Thou erupts with an openness that lets us truly encounter the Other. In the I–Thou relationship, we are present and not distracted by our own connection to an I–It and to experiencing the Other as an object, as had Buber in his encounter with Mehe. Buber was not present for Mehe in the encounter; he was wrapped up in his own mystical experience, which blocked him from experiencing Mehe as a Thou instead of an object. Yet Buber describes what a human being is not: "Thus Human being is not *He* or *She*, bounded from every other *He* and *She*, a specific point in space and time within the net of the world; nor is he a nature able to be experienced and described, a loose bundle of named qualities."[34]

If Buber had disengaged from his mystical experience, he could have been there for Mehe and engaged him in an I–Thou dialogue, but he did not. Instead, he saw Mehe as a He, a loose bundle of qualities, not as a Thou. Even contemplating something from our past in the same moment when we engage in dialogue with the Other disrupts our potential to experience the other as a Thou. We are only in an I–Thou relationship with the Other when we are not bound to someone as an object, when we are not blocked. Buber remarks, "True beings are lived in the present, the life of objects is in the past."[35]

Hence Buber begins his philosophy of the Other with the concept of relationship. Buber suggests that when a primary word is spoken, the speaker enters the world and takes his or her stand in it. In the primary word of the I–It, the It is bound to time and space as an object. Buber writes:

> [But] once the I–Thou is spoken, the speaker has no-thing for his or her object. For where there is a thing there is another thing. Every "It" is bounded by the Others. It exists only through being bounded by others. But when Thou is spoken there is no thing. "Thou" has no bounds. When Thou is spoken, the speaker has no thing: he has indeed nothing but he takes his stand in relation.[36]

For Buber, being in the world means not only having experience of an object but being in "relation." Having No-thing gives us the inter-subjective space to be in relation to another Thou. Experiencing the It is outside the bounds of an I–Thou relationship. Experiencing the It tells us only about the qualities of things, not about the Other. It is an epistemological relationship. Yet we can only encounter the Other through the dynamics of the I–Thou relationship. For Buber, as we have seen, this conclusion holds not only for human–human relationships, but also for human encounters with art, nature, animals, or spiritual beings.

We are reminded here of Rosenzweig's discovery that the old ontologically based philosophy, devoid of the experience of relationships, would always be incomplete. It was through speech-thinking, the very grammar of relationships, that Rosenzweig discovered the Other. And it was the dynamic of the present moment that would reveal the I–Thou moment to Buber. Buber postulates that it is in the relationship to the Thou of the Other that we can have a relationship to the Eternal Thou. He writes:

> Here language is consummated as a sequence, in speech and counter-speech. Here alone does the word that is formed in language meet its response. Only here does the primary word go backwards and forwards in the same form, the word of address and the word of response live in the one language, *I and Thou* take their stand not merely in relation, but also in the solid give-and-take of talk. The moments of relation are here, and only here, bound together by means of the element of the speech in which they are immersed. Here what confronts us has blossomed into the full reality of the *Thou*. Here alone, then, as reality that cannot be lost, are gazing and being gazed upon, knowing and being known, loving and being loved.[37]

There is a striking similarity between Rosenzweig's description of revelation as being in the cohortative tense and Buber's description of the relationship to the Thou. Buber shows us that ultimately, when we are in the I–Thou relation, we are in the form of dialogue. For Buber, the Other is addressed in a similar way to that in which, for Rosenzweig, the Other is invoked in the present tense. There is a speech and counter-speech, a back-and-forth as the I and Thou take their stand in the solid give-and-take of talk. Rosenzweig emphasizes the waiting for a response to the invocation, and Buber points out the immediacy of the standing-in-relation of the I and Thou.

Buber explains that when we are present to the Other, we are able to look at the Thou in the eyes of the other and see the Eternal Thou: "He who loves a woman, and brings her life to present realisation in his, is able to look in the *Thou* of her eyes into a beam of the eternal *Thou*. But he who eagerly desires 'ever new subjugation'—do you wish to hold out to his desire a phantom of the Eternal?"[38] It is interesting that Buber uses the example of the love of a woman to demonstrate an understanding of the Eternal Thou. In other words, if a man falls in love with a woman and tries to possess her, he is subjugating her. He is treating her as an object in an I–It relationship. But, if he is able to be present to her and with her, then he is not trying to grasp or subjugate her. He is in an I–Thou relationship and can, in that moment, experience and see the Eternal Thou. Such a man looks into the eyes of a woman to see the Eternal Thou.[39] Conversely, if a man subjugates a woman, he also subjugates the Eternal. Levinas, like Buber, describes the encounter of the Other as a gazing into the face, and, he too uses the metaphor of the Feminine to describe the Other.

Levinas

Emmanuel Levinas was already an accomplished scholar and philosopher when he was drafted into the French army in World War II. As an officer, when he was captured, he was held as a POW and not sent to a concentration camp with his fellow Jews. While he was a POW, his parents, who were still in Ukraine, were killed in the concentration camps, and his wife and daughter survived only by hiding in a monastery in France. Levinas was born in Kovono, Lithuania and emigrated from Ukraine to Paris in 1923 at the age of seventeen to pursue his studies. He had been a student of Husserl and Heidegger. He identified strongly as a Jew and once stated, "to be Jewish was as natural as having eyes and ears."[40] The effects of the war show up not only in Levinas' ethical philosophy of the Other but also in the examples he uses to demonstrate his points. In one example, he discusses the power to kill and asks what stops the soldier from killing. His response is, "the gaze into the face of the Other."

We can better understand Levinas' views of the Other by reading his work through the prism of Rosenzweig's methodology of speech-thinking. Levinas himself acknowledges Rosenzweig's influence in his *Totality and Infinity* (1961). Even earlier, in his essay "Is Ontology Fundamental?" (1951), Levinas stated:

> The relation with the other (*autrui*) is not therefore ontology. This tie to the other (*autrui*), which does not reduce itself to the representation of the Other (*autrui*) but rather to his invocation, where invocation is not preceded by comprehension, we call *religion*. The essence of discourse is prayer. What distinguishes thought aiming at an object from the tie with a person is that the latter is articulated in the vocative; what is named is at the same time that which is called.[41]

We can compare this invocation to revelation as Rosenzweig describes it. When God asks the human, "Where art thou?" and the human responds, "Here I am," the human and the Other are mutually and reciprocally invoked. This reciprocity is the essence of the *Sprachendenken* method. The Other is invoked using the present tense and a proper name, grammatically the vocative, and commands in the grammatical imperative. This invocation is not a projection. It is utter presence. Levinas goes one step further. He emphasizes the ethical significance of our responsibility towards the Other, invoking the shocking language of murder:

> At the very moment when my power to kill realizes itself, the other (*autrui*) has escaped me. I can, for sure, in killing *attain* a goal; I can kill as I hunt or slaughter animals, or as I fell trees. But when I have grasped the other (*autrui*) in the opening of being in general, as an element of the world where I stand, where I have seen him *on the horizon*, I have not looked at him in the face, I have not encountered his face. The temptation of total negation, measuring the infinity of this attempt and its impossibility—this is the presence of the face. To be in relation with the other (*autrui*) face to face is to be unable to kill. It is also the situation of discourse.[42]

Finally, Levinas, using a negative or reductive argument, sees in the face the same sensibility that Rosenzweig allegorized by the star. To negate the immanence of the face-to-face experience is to grasp power over the Other, and is thus tantamount to murder. This notion inserts a fundamental ethical concern for life into the I–Thou of speech-thinking:

> The face resists possession, resists my powers. In its epiphany, in expression, the sensible, still graspable, turns into total resistance to the grasp. This mutation can only occur by the opening of a new dimension. For the resistance to the grasp is not produced as an insurmountable resistance, like the hardness of rock against which the effort of the hand comes to naught, like the remoteness of a star in the immensity of space. The expression the face introduces into the world does not defy the feebleness of my powers, but my ability for power. The face, still a thing among things, breaks through the form that nevertheless delimits it. This means concretely: the face speaks to me and thereby invites me to a relation incommensurate with a power exercised, be it enjoyment or knowledge.[43]

Rosenzweig demands that we wait for a response in order to encounter the Other without objectifying her. This waiting is the duration of time. Buber states we must enter into the I–Thou relationship, which is not located in time–space but is instead total presence with no attachment to anything. The I–Thou relationship is No-thing. Levinas, like Rosenzweig and Buber, shows that it is only when we are not grasping, when we are not possessing, that we can face up to the Other and gaze into her eyes. This gaze happens when there is a sense of the future in the present.

What Levinas means is that when we are in the present moment, the future is embedded in it. The future is something that is ungraspable. We do not know what will happen in the future or how we will respond to future events. Levinas compares the concept of the future to the situation of death. We do not know what death is; it is a mystery that is ungraspable. It is only when we have faced death that we can begin to experience the Other. Levinas, as a soldier in the French army during World War II, had faced death just as Rosenzweig had during World War 1. "Consequently," Levinas wrote, "only a being whose solitude has reached a crispation through suffering, and in relation with death, takes its place on a ground where the relationship with the other becomes possible."[44] The future is a mystery that we cannot know or anticipate. This not-knowing creates an element of surprise, and it is in surprise that we can experience the face of the Other. The experience of the Other is outside of ourselves and our ego. It is a radical alterity. As Levinas explains in *Time and the Other*:

> But it is possible to infer from this situation of death, where the subject no longer has any possibility of grasping, another characteristic of existence with the other. The future is what is in no way grasped. The exteriority of the future is totally different from spatial exteriority precisely through the fact that the future is absolutely surprising. …the future is what is not grasped, what befalls us and lays hold of us. The other is the future. The very relationship with the other is the relationship with the future.[45]

Levinas, like Buber, describes the relationship to the Other in erotic terms, and he identifies the Other as feminine.[46] Just as the Other as future is a mystery, so the Other as feminine is ungraspable and easily slips away. Levinas uses the term feminine because to him it implies mystery, something that is hidden and modest. He writes:

> Hiding is the way of existing of the feminine, and this fact of hiding is precisely modesty. So this feminine alterity does not consist in the object's simple exteriority. Neither is it made up of an opposition of wills. The Other is not a being we encounter that menaces us or wants to lay hold of us. The feat of being refractory to our power is not a power greater than ours. Alterity makes for all its power. Its mystery constitutes its alterity.[47]

Levinas argues that the face-to-face meeting with the Other is the place where the future is felt in the present. He writes, "Relationship with the future, the presence of the future in the present, seems all the same accomplished in the face-to-face with the Other. The situation of the face-to-face would be the very accomplishment of time; the encroachment of the present on the future is not the feat of the subject alone, but the inter-subjective relationship."[48] Once we have this face-to-face encounter, which can only happen when the future is embedded in the present, there is a total ethical dependence of the Other on us. This ethical dependence is where we see the face of God in the Other. Richard Cohen points out that God for Levinas is "encountered in the alterity of the other person. God Himself 'comes to the idea' in proximity, in the non-in-difference of one to the another. The wholly other, God, shines in the face of the Other."[49] To see the face of God in the face of the Other is "[t]hus to care for one's neighbor more than oneself, to take on responsibility for the Other, ethics, and to take on the Other's responsibilities..."[50]

As we have seen, Rosenzweig views the relationship to the Other in opposite terms; it is we who are totally dependent on the Other. Rosenzweig and Levinas thus describe the encounter as two different forms of dependence of one person on the Other. Levinas demonstrates the ethical necessity of this dependence, and Rosenzweig shows the necessity of waiting. For Buber the encounter is simply mutual; we have no attachments to things when we have an immediate experience of the Other. For all three philosophers, God is ultimately experienced through the encounter of the Other. Arendt, in contrast, does not describe seeing God in the Other. Writing from a political rather than a theological perspective, she shows how the encounter reveals the Other's uniqueness, and she describes the horrific consequences (namely violence and genocide) of failing to encounter the Other as a unique individual. The first three thinkers show us the possibility of Divinity within the Other, while Arendt stresses the uniqueness of the Other within a political context.

Arendt

The fourth philosopher, who rounds out this essay on the immanence of the Other, is Hannah Arendt, who fled Germany for Paris and Paris for the United States, thus removing herself from the war zone during World War II.[51] Arendt was born in 1906 in Königsburg, East Prussia, and studied with Heidegger and Jaspers. While in Paris in the 1930s, she worked with Youth Aliyah, helping young Jews immigrate to Palestine to escape the impending doom.[52] She herself was interned in the prison camp at Gurs for being a German national. She was one of the last of the German Jewish intellectuals to escape the Holocaust in Europe when she arrived in New York in 1941. She was a vehement critic of totalitarianism in any form. Action, for her, spoke louder than words, and she went so far as to accuse Eastern European Jews of "collaboration" for their lack of radical action to oppose the Nazis.[53]

Arendt is relevant to this essay on the Other in two important ways. One is that she focuses on speech and action in the public space, which is the space of appearance and inter-subjectivity, and the stage upon which we discover the Other. The second is that she demonstrates how through the space of appearance we come to know the Other as a unique individual. The Other is presented to us through her speech and action taken together, which show us her own unique distinctness and individuality. In fact, her Otherness is what makes her human. For Arendt the critical quality of the Other is to be unique, yet she recognizes the paradox of uniqueness and commonality when she says: "In man [sic], otherness, which he shares with everything that is, and distinctness, which he shares with everything alive, become uniqueness, and human plurality is the paradoxical plurality of unique beings."[54]

In other words, when unique individuals are in a group, the collective or human plurality, this fact does not erase their individual uniqueness. Human plurality is paradoxical because the individual can be recognized for the person she is while at the same time being part of a group. The analogy of a melody demonstrates this paradox. A musical note sounding alone is unique, and even when it is simultaneously part of a melody, its unique sound is not erased. It is when this uniqueness is not encountered, acknowledged, or recognized that human plurality in the Arendtian sense becomes a notion of grand universals such as the concept of nation. The individual's uniqueness is erased.

The individual's uniqueness is revealed to us through her speech and action in the public space. Arendt writes:

> Speech and action reveal this unique distinctness. Through them, men distinguish themselves instead of being merely distinct; they are the modes in which human beings appear to each other, not indeed as physical objects, but *qua* men. This appearance, as distinguished from mere bodily existence, rests on initiative, but it is an initiative from which no human being can refrain and still be human.[55]

Arendt's concept of uniqueness rests on a human being's initiative, or her ability to insert herself into the world through speech and action. Such action is a form of birthing, of making a new beginning in the world. Each time a human reveals herself by her initiative of action and speech, she begins anew. Arendt uses the term natality to describe this new beginning. She writes:

> Action has the closest connection with the human condition of natality: the new beginning inherent in birth can make itself felt in the world only because the newcomer possesses the capacity of beginning something anew, that is, of acting. In this sense of initiative, an element of action, and therefore of natality, is inherent in all human activities. Moreover, since action is the political activity par excellence, natality, and not mortality, may be the central category of political, as distinguished from metaphysical, thought.[56]

The root of human action is initiative, which leads to a new beginning; hence her term natality. Action, like speech, depends upon the element of time; initiative takes place not only in bounded time but also space. This action, beginning, or sense of exteriority in Levinas' sense, throws us into the world. Arendt writes, "With word and deed we insert ourselves into the human world, and this insertion is like a second birth, in which we confirm and take upon ourselves the naked fact of our original physical appearance."[57]

Arendt makes the important point that action and natality are categories of the political, not the metaphysical. Rosenzweig demonstrated that we cannot gain any knowledge from metaphysical thought about the three elements of God, World, and Man. We can only come to know the relationship between these three elements. Buber pointed out that we can only come to know the Other by entering into an I–Thou relationship. Levinas also rejected ontology in favor of relating to the Other through invocation and gazing into her face. Arendt says that we can only know the Other through natality. The Other inserts herself into the world by acting and appearing before us.

Arendt feels very strongly about the importance of the Other's uniqueness and her ability to show it through her insertion into the world by speech and action. Hence, the idea of a nation or a people erases for Arendt the notion of a plurality of unique individuals. It excludes the possibility for a person to insert herself into the world as a distinct, unique individual. Arendt, in her own personal life, concretely asserts her philosophical and moral stance. She points out the political implication of grand universal schemes both in her book *The Origins of Totalitarianism*[58] and in an exchange of letters to Gershom Scholem about her book *Eichmann in Jerusalem: A Report on the Banality of Evil*.[59] The Jewish community was outraged at Arendt for accusing Jews of going to the gas chamber without resistance and of cooperating with the Nazis in the deportations. Gershom Sholem writes to her, in response to *Eichmann in Jerusalem*, that she does not have a love for her own people, the Jewish people. Arendt agrees with Sholem's contention that she lacks any love for her people. This, to her, is a philosophical issue. She feels that one can never love a mass or a group but only individuals, that in one's personal life one can relate only to particulars, not universals. She writes back to Sholem,

> You are quite right—I am not moved by any "love" of this sort and for two reasons: I have never in my life "loved" any people or collective—neither the German people, nor the French, nor the American nor the working class or anything of that sort. I indeed love "only" my friends and the only kind of love I know of and believe in is the love of persons.[60]

This issue is critical for her, for the Nazis' mistake was their worship of the Aryan people. Arendt was a person of principles, and it worried her that when people believed in groups of people (the Aryan Race, the Jewish people), they lost their perspective and could end up treating such groups as an excess population, which could lead to genocide. The group was a human plurality no longer.

Arendt thus goes a step beyond Levinas. Levinas argued that if we cannot see the face of the Other, we can kill her. Arendt shows us that if we cannot encounter the uniqueness of the Other as expressed through her own initiative in the world, we can commit genocide. The subjugation of human initiative is the blocking of the element of surprise. Surprise is grounded in the unexpected and in not being able to anticipate. When surprise is gone from the relationship to the Other, then violence is possible.

Arendt demonstrates in *The Origins of Totalitarianism* that what made genocide possible was the ability of governments to believe in the superfluousness of populations and to annihilate the individual. The masses were viewed as a problem of excess population, which meant that murderers like the Nazis could solve the problem of excess population by genocide without feeling guilt. The manipulators of this system believed in their own superfluousness as much as in that of all others, not caring if they themselves were alive or dead.

In other words, totalitarianism has the effect of erasing the value of life itself. Arendt's main point to Sholem is that when a people only believe in themselves as a people, they can believe in even their own superfluousness and totally lose their ability to honor the uniqueness of each person. The possibility for the person to insert herself into the world through her own initiative is erased. There is no longer a sense of surprise because when we think of a universal concept of a group, the individuals in it are stereotyped and no longer display their individuality. Arendt writes, "After murder of the moral person and annihilation of the judicial person, the destruction of the individuality is almost always successful.... For to destroy individuality is to destroy spontaneity, man's power to begin something new out of his own resources, something that cannot be explained on the basis of reactions to environment and events." [61]

The consequence of not encountering the Other, of not seeing the face of the Other is more than the ability to kill the individual. We are able to kill masses of people, to commit genocide, as witnessed many times in the course of the 20th century. Not only is it an imperative to see the face of the Other, it is a fundamental necessity. When we lose our sense of surprise, we end up with death of masses of people. Surprise and natality create unlimited possibilities, but without surprise we have no possibilities other than violence, death, and destruction. Arendt thus demonstrates the broader implications of not facing the Other. She shows us the web of consequences.

Levinas described the face of the Other, but neither Levinas nor Buber nor Rosenzweig referred to the physical appearance of the Other. Arendt, on the other hand, states that "initiative may be stimulated by the presence of others whose company we may wish to join, but it is never conditioned by them; action may spring from beings and objects in the world to which we were born, but our response is always the beginning of something new, something that comes from our own initiative. To act, therefore, in its most general sense, is to take an initiative to begin or set something in motion."[62]

Rosenzweig showed in the new-thinking methodology that to speak is also to have a conversation, and conversation contains uncertainty in that we can never know what the Other will say, or how we will respond. Arendt furthers this premise by arguing that:

> It is in the nature of beginning that something new is started which cannot be expected from whatever may have happened before. This character of startling unexpectedness is inherent in all beginnings and in all origins.... The new always happens against the overwhelming odds of statistical laws and their probability, which for all practical, everyday purposes amounts to certainty; the new therefore always appears in the guise of a miracle. The fact that man is capable of actions means that the unexpected can be expected from him, that he is able to perform what is infinitely improbable. And this again is possible only because each man is unique, so that with each birth something uniquely new comes into the world.[63]

Karl Wolfskehl stated that when one entered Rosenzweig's room, "the incredible became the norm." In Arendtian terms, Rosenzweig chose to take initiative and insert himself into the world. Rosenzweig was literally reborn—having a second birth by coming up with a new way to be in the world and creating the space to be with others. He devised a way to present himself, despite the crude interface of pecking at a keyboard and depending on his wife for interpretation, by looking directly into the face of the Other, by listening, and by responding. As Arendt describes the beginning as miraculous, and as I use the term surprise, Rosenzweig's Other expresses herself against overwhelming odds. Yet for Arendt, every speech or action is a new beginning. She writes:

> With respect to this somebody who is unique it can be truly said that nobody was there before. If action as beginning corresponds to the fact of birth, if it is

the actualization of the human condition of natality, then speech corresponds to the fact of distinctness and is the actualization of the human condition of plurality, that is of living as a distinct and unique being among equals. Action and speech are so closely related because the primordial and specifically human act must at the same time contain the answer to the question asked of every newcomer: "Who are you?" This disclosure of who somebody is, is implicit in both his words and his deeds; yet obviously the affinity between speech and revelation is much closer than that between action and revelation.[64]

Arendt develops a concept of speech as action that goes beyond speech-thinking. Both Arendt's and Rosenzweig's methods are based on observations of the Other and encounters with them. For Arendt, we must ask "who" we come to know, and we come to know this "who" through her revelation of herself in speech and action. Arendt is interested in "who" the person in, not "what" her qualities are. She writes:

> In acting and speaking, men show who they are, reveal actively their unique personal identities and thus make their appearance in the human world, while their physical identities appear without any activity of their own in the unique shape of the body and sound of the voice. The disclosure of "who" in contradistinction to "what" somebody is—his qualities, gifts, talents, and shortcomings, which he may display or hide—is implicit in everything somebody says and does. It can be hidden only in complete silence and perfect passivity, but its disclosure can almost never be achieved as a willful purpose, as though one possessed and could dispose of this "who" in the same manner he has and can dispose of his qualities.[65]

Arendt says that there is an immanence of the Other which the Other herself does not even know, but which is revealed through her acts and deeds in the world. For Rosenzweig, God reveals herself to Man just as for Arendt humans reveal themselves to each other by reason of the unique, distinct, and individual actions of each person. Rosenzweig recognizes this individuality when he says that God, World, and Man are irreducible, and cannot be known to each other or to the Other. Speaking of the first volume of *The Star,* he says that it wants "to teach nothing more than that none of these three great basic concepts of philosophical thinking can be reduced to one of the others."[66] In this way they are able to interact with each other and show us how they form a triangle, each side of which depends on the others.

This triangle is the "who" from the Arendtian perspective, as she suggests when she points out that the revelatory quality of speech and action comes forth when people are with others but not for or against others. She says that through speech and action there is a space of inter-subjectivity, which is the space of appearance where the Other can begin something unexpected. For Rosenzweig, in contrast, it is the being dependent on time that creates the space of inter-subjectivity.

Arendt labels the space where being, action, and space interact "the web of human relationships."⁶⁷ Rosenzweig showed how speech and dialogue are connected to time, and how the time lag associated with waiting for the surprise makes us dependent on the Other. Arendt deepens this insight by arguing that this period in which we wait, the in-between, happens between people only when they are speaking to each other. She says:

> Since this disclosure of the subject is an integral part of all, even the most "objective" intercourse, the physical, worldly in-between along with its interests is overlaid and, as it were, overgrown with an altogether different in-between which consists of deeds and words and owes its origin exclusively to men's acting and speaking directly *to* one another.⁶⁸

Arendt's use of this metaphor of the in-between considerably expands the horizon from the previous three thinkers. They embrace the Other in a one-to-one correspondence without taking into consideration either the impact the encounter has beyond the space of the one-on-one encounter or the space itself. Arendt's web, like the spider's web in nature, begins in the middle and weaves outward, including in its design the spaces created between points of connection. An actor enacting speech-action metaphorically does the same when she reveals herself to the world. Arendt writes:

> The disclosure of the "who" through speech, and the setting of a new beginning through action, always fall into an already existing web where their immediate consequences can be felt. Together they start a new process which eventually emerges as the unique life story of the newcomer, affecting uniquely the life stories of all those with whom he comes into contact.⁶⁹

The uniqueness that emerges through the individual's action in the world has a direct impact on the observer. The actor's otherness and the actor's uniqueness affect those around her and forces them to reengage and rebirth their own uniqueness. The observer is no longer an observer, but in the process of responding to the Other's disclosures and actions, she reveals who she is through her own speech and deeds. The result is a surprise. The observer is unaware of her own uniqueness until she becomes engaged with the Other. Arendt calls the moment of surprise a miracle. Action, speech, and initiative are miraculous because something unexpected happens, something improbable. Using scientific terminology, Arendt describes the miracle as the "infinite improbability which occurs regularly."[70] As Karl Wolfskehl stated about his visit to Rosenzweig, the "improbable became the norm." Their encounter illustrates the concept of natality according to Arendt. Natality makes human plurality possible because each time someone inserts herself into the world, there is a new beginning and the improbable happens. All these new beginnings create a web-like effect. And each new beginning reveals a surprise. As we have seen, this surprise appeared in the acts towards the Other during the recent historical moment of September 11, 2001.

Epilogue

March 13, 2002

As I sit here doing another rewrite of this paper on the Other, the Israelis have taken Ramallah, the center of Palestine, by storm. The pictures of Palestinian men between the ages of 14 and 45 being rounded up, blindfolded, handcuffed, and marked with numbers like cattle take me back to another time and place. The Nazis burst into people's homes in a rampage just as the Israeli soldiers are doing to the Palestinians. The numbers written on the arms are all too haunting. How can one not think of Jewish prisoners in concentration camps having the numbers seared into their flesh as though they were cattle? The mainstream Jewish community would scream at me for making this comparison, but it is the truth. As Arendt teaches, once we lose hold of the unique person and start thinking in terms of a group with no particular individual identity, we can easily commit acts of genocide. This is one of the main moral lessons of the Shoah. The numbers scrawled on the heads and arms of Palestinian men who are fathers, brothers, husbands, and sons are sickening. They are a tactic to disengage the soldiers from thinking of these men as unique individuals with families. Are we acting out the Shoah on the Palestinians? Is this what we have learned? To treat the Palestinians as a people is to release the soldiers from moral responsibility. Once a soldier can stop thinking of his victim as a human, then he can kill him. Levinas teaches that if we look into the face of the Other, then we cannot shoot her. Both Levinas and Arendt, as survivors of the Nazi period, knew all too well what happens when we forget the Other.

April 6, 2002

Ten days have passed since the Passover suicide bombing in Netanya and the Israeli invasion of Palestine. Horror and nausea take over my being as the eyewitness accounts of the siege are transmitted to the outside world. The horrors are unspeakable: Israeli soldiers razing houses to the ground with people inside them; crushing Palestinians to the bone without giving them a chance to escape; bulldozing a mass grave for human corpses. Does the Sharon government think that these actions will stop the suicide bombings? Maybe they will, for the brief period of the invasion, but they will also produce a whole new stream of people volunteering to be martyrs. Israel will be assaulted by many more suicide bombers than they can imagine over the course of time.

The United States is not untouched by what is going on in Israel and Palestine. For the first time since the beginning of the Al-Aqsa Intifada, I again feel pulled into the swirling vortex of intense anger and desire for revenge. First my rage was directed at the suicide bombers and the groups that sponsored them, then at the people who encourage and support suicide bombers, now at the Israeli Defense Force soldiers and the Sharon government. As I read the e-mails of Palestinians who are under siege in Ramallah, Bethlehem, Jenin, Nablus, and other West Bank cities and towns, pleading for help from the international community, the shock and horror of their plight numbs my heart. I am stunned that the IDF is perpetrating on the Palestinian civilians the same acts that were committed against Jews during years of pogroms. I am outraged that women, children, and the elderly are not treated as humans but are left to die in cold blood while their relatives are helpless. No ambulances are allowed to take wounded Palestinians to the hospital. Where is the moral code of war? Why are war crimes being committed by Israeli soldiers?

The IDF prides itself on being an army of morally sophisticated soldiers that are allowed to question what is going on and, if they object to a situation, refuse to participate in it. When I asked a relative and a friend who are reserve medics in the IDF about the code of the medic, they replied that she is to help anyone who is wounded, whether Palestinian or Israeli. What has happened? Where are the Israeli medics that are attached to each unit? Is Palestinian blood different from Jewish blood? Is Jewish blood redder?

After the Shoah, somehow I had hoped that a Jewish army would be different. Sharon is a war criminal who is attempting to terrify the Palestinian civilian population into leaving, going into exile as they did in 1948. I feel that 2000 years of Jewish suffering and oppression are being taken out on the Palestinian civilian population. Two thousand years of being forced into exile, expelled from many countries, and then tortured and finally gassed are playing in the minds of Sharon and his government.

How can the mainstream Jewish community not see the perspective of the ordinary Palestinian who has lived under oppression for thirty-five years? I hear in my head the voices and arguments that will be thrown back at me. The Arab countries never took in the Palestinians; they do not care for their people. They left them in refugee camps because their goal is to eradicate Israel and push her into the sea. The latest quote sent to me, "We will have peace with the Arabs when they love their children more than they hate us," is a quote by Golda Meir. Then the response of the liberal Jewish community is, "Why do they raise their children to be suicide bombers? Why can they not demonstrate their resistance like Gandhi, put themselves in front of the Israeli tanks and die non-violently? This would be a stronger statement of their commitment to establishing a state and throwing out their occupiers."

The situation breeds a desire for total revenge, a mentality of taking down as many as you can. The voices of the Palestinian people tell a different story. They are under siege and ransacked and left to die in their own blood. How is it that young men who are somebody's sons, brothers, or fathers can do these things? How can they let human beings who are not a threat to them die in their own blood? Everything that I know about the Jewish tradition has lost its meaning. It is the death of the Judaism if Jewish soldiers can do these things. Yet I have realized that my feelings of rage will not help create dialogue or peace.

April 10, 2002

Yesterday was Yom Hashoah, Holocaust Remembrance Day, and the IDF may have massacred hundreds of Palestinians in the Jenin refugee camp. How the world weeps, except for the United States. We should not only be remembering our dead, the Jewish dead of the Shoah, but the Palestinian dead killed by our own people. Today my worst fears are fully realized. The IDF is committing war crimes with the full support of the Sharon government. We have become our own worst enemy. I cannot believe I have lived to see such a terrible day in Jewish history. The solution is not hard—just pull back to the 1967 borders and give the Palestinians their own state. Then the suicide bombings will end. We have fallen deep into the dark abyss of no return. The scars of the Palestinians will now take generations to heal. Anti-Semitism is rising around the world, and Ariel Sharon has brought it on his people.

April 21, 2002

On April 17 and 18, there were two bomb scares at my children's school. Luckily not too many children were there, just parents and teachers. Someone called the front desk and said there was a bomb in the school. Everyone was evacuated. The police came and investigated. They found a lunch box on the school roof that turned out to have a cheese sandwich in it. Then again on Friday morning someone called the school claiming there was a bomb. Again, the school was evacuated. The police came with their search dogs and investigated. Nothing turned up. My children go to a Jewish school, so it is a target for anyone with feelings of hatred toward Jews. We do not know who pulled this prank, but it brings home, in a mild way, what Israelis and Palestinians are experiencing at every moment. It seems as if the reality of the Israeli-Palestinian conflict is right here in my own back yard. I ponder all the questions that a concerned parent must. Is it all right for me to send my children to school? Should I refuse to leave San Francisco so I can be readily accessible to my children and others if there is another bomb scare? Should I go to school with my children? Should I pull them out of school and homeschool them? Should I send them to a school that is a less obvious target? I have chosen to keep their lives and my own as normal as possible. I will send them to their school, and I will travel out of San Francisco.

As the violence continues to rage relentlessly and endlessly, we need to reexamine our concept and relationship to the Other. War crimes are being committed against the Palestinians by the Israeli government and armed forces. Crimes against humanity are being committed against the Israelis by the suicide bombers. We need to understand how it happens that neither side can see the face of the Other. How has the Other been so demonized that these crimes can be committed? Reflecting on these four Jewish thinkers' view of the Other helps to shed light on this issue. For Rosenzweig, Buber, Levinas, and Arendt lived during dark times, just as we do now.

The horror of the Israeli-Palestinian conflict is that there is no willingness on the part of either the Israeli government or the suicide bombers to engage in dialogue. There is no willingness to invoke the enemy and call out to her by name. There is a refusal to wait in, Rosenzweig's sense, to hear what the Other has to respond. There is a refusal to enter into an I–Thou relationship with the Other and to stop having an I–It relationship, as Buber teaches. There is a failure to see the face of the Other and fulfill her needs as Levinas commands us. There is a failure to recognize "who" the Other is in the web of human relations, but instead each side demonizes her by ascribing qualities to her, by viewing her as "what" she is. Let us now heed the call of these four thinkers who lived in very dark times and apply what they learned from their terrible circumstances. The violence has to end. A political discourse has to replace the violent one. It is only when the Israelis recognize the Palestinians as human—as the Other—and give them their human rights to be free in their own state that there will be peace. Who knows what surprises can erupt when the Israeli government recognizes the Palestinians and the suicide bombings cease. Peace is the infinite possibility of *surprise*!

Notes

1. Maurice Friedman, *Martin Buber's Life and Work: The Early Years, 1878–1923* (London: Search, 1982), 201.
2. Nahum Glatzer, "Introduction," in *Franz Rosenzweig: His Life and Thought*, by Franz Rosenzweig (New York: Schocken Books, 1953/1961), xxxiii–iv.
3. Ibid., xxxiv.
4. Emmanuel Levinas, *Totality and Infinity: An Essay on Exteriority*, trans. Alphonso Lingis (Pittsburgh: Duquense University Press, 1969), 28. See also Franz Rosenzweig, *The New Thinking*, ed. and trans. Alan Urdoff and Barbara E. Galli (Syracuse, NY: Syracuse University Press, l999), especially 70–86.
5. Rosenzweig, *New Thinking*, 70.
6. Ibid., 75.
7. Ibid., 82.
8. Ibid., 84.
9. Ibid., 85.
10. Ibid., 85–86.
11. Robert Gibbs, *Correlations in Rosenzweig and Levinas* (Princeton: Princeton University Press, 1992), 67.
12. Emmanuel Levinas, *Outside the Subject,* trans. Michael B. Smith (Stanford, CA: Stanford University Press, 1994), 57.
13. Else-Rahel Freund, *Franz Rosenzweig's Philosophy of Existence: An Analysis of* The Star of Redemption, trans. Stephen L. Weinstein and Robert Israel (The Hague: M. Nijhoff, 1979), 155.
14. Franz Rosenzweig, *The Star of Redemption*, trans. William H. Hallo, (Notre Dame: University of Notre Dame Press, 1985), 81, quoted in Freund, *Analysis*, 155.
15. Freund, *Analysis*, 155.
16. Rosenzweig, *New Thinking*, 86.
17. Ibid., 86–87.
18. Ibid., 87.
19. Ibid., 87.

20. Ibid., 88.
21. Friedman, *Early Years*, 181.
22. Ibid., 184.
23. Ibid., 184.
24. Cited in Friedman, *Early Years*, 186.
25. Cited in Friedman, *Early Years*, 188.
26. Cited in Friedman, *Early Years*, 190.
27. Stéphane Mosès, *System and Revelation: The Philosophy of Franz Rosenzweig*, trans. Catherine Tihanyi (Detroit: Wayne State University Press, 1992), 285.
28. Rosenzweig, *The Star*, 423.
29. Mosès, *System*, 285.
30. Rosenzweig, *The Star*, 422.
31. Martin Buber, *I and Thou* (New York: Charles Scribner's Sons, 1958), 12–13.
32. Ibid., 13.
33. Ibid., 9.
34. Ibid., 8.
35. Ibid., 13.
36. See Martin Buber, *I and Thou*, 5ff.
37. Ibid., 102–3.
38. Ibid., 106.
39. I wonder if it is possible from Buber's perspective to turn the metaphor around. Can a woman bring a man into her life? Would this conceptual change alter his metaphor? Is he making a point that he does not realize about the categories of Man and Woman? Does he imply that Man is active and Woman passive? A feminist reading and deconstruction of Buber would be an interesting pursuit. Was Buber thinking that Woman only entered the discourse when Man desired her?
40. Cited in Emmanuel Levinas, *Nine Talmudic Readings*, trans. Annette Aronowicz (Indianapolis: Indiana University Press, 1994), x. For more on Levinas' dual identity, see Aronowicz's introduction.
41. Emmanuel Levinas, *Emmanuel Levinas: Basic Philosophical Writings*, eds. Adriaan T. Peperzak, Simon Critchley, Robert Bernasconi, (Bloomington: University of Indiana Press, 1996), 7–8.
42. Levinas, *Basic Philosophical Writings*, 9.
43. Levinas, *Totality and Infinity*, 197–98.
44. Emmanuel Levinas. *Time and the Other*, trans. Richard A. Cohen (Pittsburgh: Duquesne University Press, 1987), 76.
45. Levinas, *Time and the Other*, 76–77.
46. Simone de Beauvoir in *The Second Sex* (1949) calls Levinas' reference to the Feminine as Other sexist. I agree with Richard Cohen's commentary on this matter. He states, "De Beauvoir takes Levinas to task for allegedly assigning a secondary,

derivative status to women: subject (he) as absolute, woman as other. The issue is important but certainly not as simple as de Beauvoir, in this instance, makes it out to be, because for Levinas the other has a priority over the subject." See Levinas, *Time and the Other*, 69ff. Actually, Levinas has a more sophisticated application of the feminine as a category than Buber. Buber just assumes that Man brings Woman into his presence. He is unaware of how he is being sexist, even as he points out that a woman can only be brought into the relationship when she is not subjugated. Levinas notes what he is doing and how he is using the category of the feminine. He goes a step farther than Buber in describing the Man–Woman relationship. Levinas' reading of the concept of the feminine is very nuanced. He states that the encounter of the Other is a radical alterity, which is a type of mystery. Levinas writes, "I am thus describing a category that falls neither into the being-nothingness opposition, nor into the notion of the existent. The existent is accomplished in the 'subjective' and in 'consciousness'; alterity is accomplished in the feminine... The feminine is not accomplished as a being [*étant*] in a transcendence toward light, but in modesty." (*Time and the Other*, 88) In other words, the feminine for Levinas describes the paradoxical encounter of the Other. It is a form of humbleness that does not penetrate. It is simply there. Levinas writes, "One must recognize its exceptional place among relationships. It is a relationship with alterity, with mystery—that is to say with the future, with what (in a world where there is everything) is never there, with what cannot be there when everything is there-not with a being that is not there, but with the very dimension of alterity." (*Time and the Other*, 88).

47 Levinas, *Time and the Other*, 86–87.
48 Ibid., 79.
49 Ibid., 23.
50 Ibid., 24.
51 See her essay "We Refugees" in *The Menorah Journal*, January 1943, 69–77.
52 Although she was a Zionist in the 1930s in Paris, Arendt later became an anti-Zionist during the War because of the way the Jewish state had become a nationalistic, chauvinist political agent. The state refused to recognize the rights of the Palestinian people. See her articles "Zionism Reconsidered," *The Menorah Journal*, October 1944, 162–96 and "To Save the Jewish Homeland," The American Jewish Committee, Harcourt Brace Jovanovich, 1948. Her writings and opinions of over fifty years ago are prophetic about the problems of Israel today. She always identified as a Jew even though she was an anti-Zionist, which got her into major trouble with the American and Israeli Jewish communities. She lived her life on her own terms as a conscious "Jewish pariah." Her politics demonstrated her views of how we should interact with the Other.
53 See Hannah Arendt, *Eichmann in Jerusalem: A Report on the Banality of Evil* (New York: Viking Press, 1963).
54 Hannah Arendt, *The Human Condition* (Chicago: University of Chicago Press, 1958),176.
55 Arendt, *The Human Condition*, 176.

56 Arendt, *The Human Condition*, 9.
57 Arendt, *The Human Condition*, 176–77.
58 Hannah Arendt, *The Origins of Totalitarianism* (New York: Harcourt Brace Jovanovich, 1951).
59 Arendt, *Eichmann in Jerusalem*.
60 For more discussion of this issue, see unpublished paper by Emily Leah Silverman, "What is Ahavat Yisrael? The Jewish Community's Reaction to Hannah Arendt's Book *Eichmann in Jerusalem*" (1989), 9. This paper was presented at WESCOR (Now known as the Western Region American Academy of Religion) at University of the Redlands, Redlands, California 1995
61 Arendt, *The Origins of Totalitarianism*, 455. For a more in-depth discussion of the murder of the individual see the chapter "Totalitarianism and power."
62 Arendt, *The Human Condition*, 177.
63 Ibid., 177–78.
64 Ibid., 178.
65 Ibid., 179.
66 Rosenzweig, *New Thinking*, 75.
67 Arendt, *The Human Condition*.
68 Ibid., 182–83.
69 Ibid., 184.
70 Ibid., 246.

References

Arendt, Hannah, *Eichmann in Jerusalem: A Report on the Banality of Evil*. New York: Viking Press, 1963.

———. *The Human Condition*. Chicago: University of Chicago Press, 1958.

———. *The Origins of Totalitarianism*. New York: Harcourt Brace Jovanovich, 1951.

Buber, Martin. *I and Thou*. New York: Charles Scribner's Sons, 1958.

Freund, Else-Rahel. *Franz Rosenzweig's Philosophy of Existence: An Analysis of The Star of Redemption*. Translated by Stephen L. Weinstein and Robert Israel. The Hague: M. Nijhoff, 1979.

Friedman, Maurice. *Martin Buber's Life and Work: The Early Years, 1878–1923*. London: Search, 1982.

Gibbs, Robert. *Correlations in Rosenzweig and Levinas*. Princeton: Princeton University Press, 1992.

Glatzer, Nahum. "Introduction." In *Franz Rosenzweig: His Life and Thought*, by Franz Rosenzweig, xxxiii–iv. New York: Schocken Books, 1953/1961.

Levinas, Emmanuel. *Emmanuel Levinas: Basic Philosophical Writings.* Edited by Adriaan T. Peperzak, Simon Critchley, and Robert Bernasconi. Bloomington: University of Indiana Press, 1996.

———. *Nine Talmudic Readings.* Translated by Annette Aronowicz. Indianapolis: Indiana University Press, 1994.

———. *Outside the Subject.* Translated by Michael B. Smith. Stanford, CA: Stanford University Press, 1994.

———. *Time and the Other.* Translated by Richard A. Cohen. Pittsburgh: Duquesne University Press, 1987.

———. *Totality and Infinity: An Essay on Exteriority.* Translated by Alphonso Lingis. Pittsburgh: Duquense University Press, 1969.

Mosès, Stéphane. *System and Revelation: The Philosophy of Franz Rosenzweig.* Translated by Catherine Tihanyi. Detroit: Wayne State University Press, 1992.

Rosenzweig, Franz. *The New Thinking.* Edited and translated by Alan Urdoff and Barbara E. Galli. Syracuse, NY: Syracuse University Press, 1999.

———. *The Star of Redemption.* Translated by William H. Hallo. Notre Dame: University of Notre Dame Press, 1985.

About the Author

Kohenet, Dr. Emily Leah Silverman is a Visiting Scholar at The Graduate Theological Union. Berkeley, CA. She received Smicha (ordination) from the Hebrew Priestess Institute and is recent Past President of American Academy of Religion Western Region. Silverman has developed the field study of Feminist Theology of Spiritual Resistance. Her current research is on the Feminist theology of Spiritual Resilience and Resistance of Jewish Women during the Nazi Holocaust. She most recently was an invited lecturer at University of Wales and was formerly a lecturer at San Jose State University and taught at Graduate Theological Union. Dr. Silverman also investigates the reclaiming and retrieval of Hebrew Priestess lineage, their 12 spiritual pathways and practice. Dr. Silverman was the organizer of Rosemary Radford Ruether Frestschrift and co-edited with Dirk Von der Horst and Whitney Bauman *Voices of Feminist Liberation: Writing in Celebrations of Rosemary Ruether.* Silverman has also published *Edith Stein and Regina Jonas: Religious Visionaries of the Death Camps.* Silverman is a sought after invited speaker. She holds a Master of Divinity from Harvard Divinity School and Ph.D. from the Graduate Theological Union.

7 Religion, Values and the Claims of Value Free Education: An Examination of My Teaching and Publications over Fifty Years*

Rosemary Radford Ruether

Value-free education and its methodology of research and knowledge represents (ironically) a "value" seen as foundational to objective or scientific knowledge. Those who claim to pursue "value-free" knowledge and education see "values" as subjective biases that prevent the discovery of truth, of reality, of what is or has been actually the case. This is often seen as what is "reality" everywhere, in all times and places, not biased by particular cultures. Physical sciences have been seen as the model of this reality that can be known objectively in all times and places. Thus, the physical components of water are the same East and West, yesterday, today and tomorrow. To obtain authentic knowledge of any reality, one must use this scientific methodology.

It is presumed that this same method applies to the study of any culture, society or particular history. Objective knowledge means finding out what is or has been the case, what exists or existed, by finding adequate empirical evidence for this reality. It is claimed that no value questions motivate or flow out of such knowledge. Knowledge begins and ends in discovering what is or has been the case. Having found out what water is, one does not need to then explore how water might be polluted in some contexts, causing illness in people or animals, or whether water might be insufficient in some contexts, causing drought and lack of capacity to grow adequate food for humans and animals. Having discovered what kind of culture shaped thirteenth century France, one need not explore how this culture furthered justice and well-being for some people and injustice and poverty for others. These questions are not a part of knowledge.

The teaching of religion seems to fall outside the realm of this value-free knowledge since religion seems preeminently to be about values. Some who

---
*2014 American Academy of Religion Western Region Plenary Address

are dedicated to scientific knowledge would simply exclude religion from educational institutions. Others would say religion can be included by being impartial and value-free in discussing it. One discusses a particular religion or, preferably, several religions by finding out what the religion has been historically, what it has taught, how it has functioned, but not to raise questions of whether the way it has functioned or what it has taught is good or bad, promotes justice or injustice, love or hate. On this basis the teaching of religion or religions can be included in university education on the same basis as any other human or natural activity.

This idea of value-free knowledge as the norm of education has gained credence in Western culture and spread around the world in recent centuries due to a rebellion against the domination of Western or European schools in the medieval and modern world by the Christian Church and religion, as well as by other religious institutions in some contexts. Schools owned or controlled by the Church built the truth and value claims of Christianity into education. It was assumed that God is the source of truth and wellbeing. God is truly known only by believing in Jesus as the Christ and the Savior of humans. The aim of human development is redemption in heaven beyond this earth, available only through belief in Christ as Savior.

Medieval schools were not devoid of scientific knowledge, but science was constructed within this religious framework of cosmology and redemption. The movement in Europe that came to be understood as "modernization" sought to free knowledge from this framework of Christian redemption. Scientific knowledge as a method of knowing what is physically the case came to be seen as the method of freeing knowledge from Christian norms. The human quest for knowledge was thus freed from control by the Church and opened to a quest for understanding what is the case anywhere, in any time and place, apart from Christian norms of ultimate hope and wellbeing, or any other value system.

There have been several stages in this process of freeing education from the Church. Emmanuel Kant in the late eighteenth century sought to free moral values from a specific Christian context by universalizing it as a good will that would be good in all times and places. By contrast, John Dewey in his 1939 book *Theory of Valuation* adopted an empirical approach that rejects values as intrinsic to reality. Values are not an inherent property of things, but arise through our human valuative activity as purposeful beings, which we then impose on particular things, claiming that something is good in itself, rather than being valued for how we use or don't use the thing. For Dewey, values belong to the context of use of things.

But those who hold up value-free education often go beyond this empirical context of values and assert in practice that since values are always part of particular contexts and purposes, in order to free knowledge from any bias of context or culture, one should not discuss values at all. Knowledge is simply an empirical method of finding out what is or has been the case, not whether it is good or bad. But this means ignoring the purposive meaning of human activity. Thus, in studying agriculture, one can ask what are the methodologies for producing food, but not questions such as "how do we produce enough food so that all the people in a given region will have access to a well-balanced diet and social and ecological stability will be maintained?"

By cutting off the valuative questions about what we do and why we do it, education engages in what Allan Bloom (1987) called "The Closing of the American Mind." This "closing of the mind" in education involves shutting out the whole person in his or her purposive context from being involved in questions. This not only closes the mind, but also closes "the heart." One can ask only "how" to do something, but not why to do it; or how is this activity affecting human individuals and communities for good or ill. This emasculates education, cutting off the exploration of the purpose and meaning of human activity.

This criticism does not deny the value of the scientific method of knowledge. The methodology of objective knowledge which seeks to accumulate the empirical evidence to understand what has been the case has its place in every field of education. This includes religion, as much as the physical sciences, sociology or history. But it should not be cut off from the valuative questions, which ask the "why" questions; why was this done and how has it enhanced or lessened human and natural wellbeing? Education should be a rich interaction between both these questions, the "what" questions and the "why" questions.

Looking back over my own teaching, research and writing over the last fifty years or more, it is evident to me that I and the scholars I have been working with have been deeply engaged in the interaction between these two questions. I have been writing for publication since 1953. In 1953–4 I was editor for my high school newspaper in La Jolla, California where I produced an editorial every week and encouraged a group of fellow writers who contributed to the newspaper to probe the questions of truth and justice that concerned us. Our newspaper gained sufficient notoriety that a retired admiral in our town contacted the high school principal and complained that our paper was "un-American," since we were questioning American righteousness and justice. The principal called us in to tell us of this complaint, but fortunately did so only to reaffirm the integrity of our writing.

I went on to college at Scripps College in Claremont, California and then to the M.A. and Ph.D. at the Claremont Graduate University from 1954 to 1965. I then began my first college teaching at the Immaculate Heart College in Los Angeles, which was under pressure for its liberalism from the Archdiocese of Los Angeles. I then moved on to teach for ten years at the Howard University Graduate School of Religion in Washington, D.C. By the end of this time (in 1975) most of the themes of my ongoing writing had developed.

In 1972 I read the Club of Rome report on the ecological and economic "limits to growth" and became committed to the questions of ecological sustainability and justice. The rights of women to participate as equals in society and education also emerged as integral to my social context and became a permanent part of my concerns. Racial justice was also a major part of my context at a Black university in Washington, D.C., as well as my earlier work in racial justice in Mississippi in 1965. Liberation theology was developing in Latin America in this period as well, and articulated for me the global context of these questions of class and racial justice. The issue of Christian anti-Semitism was an early concern for me, sparked by my relation to my Jewish uncle and childhood mentor. The Israel–Palestine conflict emerged somewhat later, after a trip to Israel in 1980. For me, both these issues, Christian anti-Semitism and Israeli injustice to Palestinians are expressions of the injustice of dominant societies to their subjugated minorities. In my writings over the last fifty years, I have continually worked on variant aspects of all of these issues, individually and in their interconnections.

From 1963 to the present, I have published forty-eight books, not counting their appearance in different languages, as well as many hundreds of articles in magazines, journals and as chapters in books. The dominant theme running through the majority of these books and articles is "women," that is, sexism; the bias of the Christian tradition and Western culture against the women and how to overcome it. Much of this work has to do with recovering the actual history of women, the accomplishments of key women thinkers and writers hitherto silenced by a history that had ignored them and their work. This was the major agenda of the collaborative work that I and Rosemary Skinner Keller did together over 1980–2006 in which we edited the three volumes of *Women and Religion in America*. We began in volume one with the recovery of women's work in the United States in the nineteenth century, in movements, such as revivalism, utopian communities, Catholic women's religious orders, women's preaching, Jewish women's movements, and social reform movements. In volume two we moved back to the colonial and Revolutionary War periods, and then in volume three turned to the twentieth century in the period of 1900 to 1968. A fourth volume, published in

1995, collected together the main lines of all three of these earlier volumes, as well as new areas beyond them, with chapters on Catholic women, Protestant laywomen, Jewish women, African-American women, Evangelical Protestant women, social reform movements, women and the struggle for ordination across all these traditions, utopian communities, American Indian women and new dialogue among women in religions.

The 1,300-page, three volume *Encyclopedia of Women and Religion in North America*, published by Indiana University Press, emerged in 2006. This covered a multiplicity of chapters in such areas as women in Catholicism, in a variety of Protestantisms, in Judaism, Islam, Buddhism, Hinduism, new religious movements, women's education, and reform movements. Although the work of women in religion in North America has hardly been exhausted by these seven volumes, we opened this largely silenced history with these major contributions, as a basis on which additional research can build.

In addition to this work on documenting women's work in religion in North America, which I did with Rosemary Keller, I have published more than another twenty volumes, primarily developing feminist theology and women's history in Christianity from the New Testament era to modern times. These include such volumes as *Sexism and God-talk: Toward a Feminist Theology* (1983 and a second edition in 1993), *Women and Redemption, A Theological History* (1998, 2012) and the history of "goddesses" or female images of the divine in Western religion (2005).

Although issues of women, sexism and feminist thought dominate my writings over the years, I also have published numerous books that discuss other areas of concern. Liberation theologies, church reform, anti-Semitism, the Israeli–Palestinian conflict, ecology, the history of the family, and mental illness are among the areas that I have written both book length volumes and many articles.

The purposes of this canvasing of my many areas of writing, which are also areas of my teaching, is not to provide a bibliography for this gathering, but to lay the basis for discussing the question of values in research and teaching. My research, writing and teaching has always been driven by values, and are incomprehensible to me apart from these driving values. This also means I have never done any research or writing based on the need for academic preferment. The term "publish or perish" was unknown to me as a phrase or an idea in the first twenty-five years of my post-graduate academic work, and when I first heard it, it mystified and amused me. Far from being lauded for my many publications, on several occasions I have been put down or negated because I was seen as having too many publications, that is, more than most of my academic colleagues, and this was seen as threatening.

But my purpose has never been to compete one way or the other with my colleagues, but to make available to readers and colleagues suppressed or hitherto unknown knowledge. For me, this knowledge needed to be known, not to make for me a mark as having been published, but because critical values had been denied or suppressed and needed to be made available.

What is this value? Basically, I would sum up this value that has driven my research and writing, as well as my teaching, simply as "justice." For me, the fact that women have been largely absent from theological education, Catholic, Protestant, as well as Jewish and Muslim and other religions, has been a deep injustice. Once some women began to be present in theological education, the fact that they had little or no material to study written by women and which documented the work of women in religion through the ages was another deep injustice. When some women became present in education, they were likely to be white and of privileged class. If there was anything written by women and about women, again it was likely to be by and about white women, of privileged class. To help more women participate in such education is the first step to overcome this injustice. To help women of marginalized races and classes to do so as well takes another step toward further justice. To reclaim materials written by women and to further seek out work by and about women of marginalized classes and races goes several steps farther on the road of justice. The aim is not to reverse patriarchy and make women dominate, but simply to work toward making more women equal. It is to rectify the long history of women's silence and absence, doubly so for marginalized classes and races of women.

This is what my scholarship has been about. When I hear a student say, "I took your Matristics class, and as a result I discovered this great fourteenth century woman who has really enhanced my understanding of the meaning of life…" – this is music to my ears.

Yet I too stand on the shoulders of many earlier researchers, men and women, who have found and reclaimed women writers. The pathways by which women thinkers and writers of the past have been made available to us today is often very complex and haphazard. In the Greek and Latin patristic period of the Christian church from the first to the sixth centuries, hardly any writings from women have been preserved. There is a small handful: a few Montanist oracles by women prophets; Egeria's "Diary" of her Pilgrimage; a few letters by women preserved by Jerome.

Yet we know many more women from this period whose lives and thoughts we can reconstruct, thanks to their men friends who valued them and preserved their memory. Gregory Nyssa saw his sister Macrina as his mentor and preserved her thought in his writing. Jerome does so for several of his women friends. Yet the dogma of the church fathers, declared by Jerome himself, that women are not authorities in their own right and so their writings cannot be made public, caused their writings not to be preserved by the patristic church, despite these relationships.

The medieval church is much richer in the survival of the actual writings by women, largely through the development of women's religious communities that copied and preserved manuscripts by women and became the means of survival of such writings. Yet the pathway to their survival is often tenuous. The vital reflections of Julian of Norwich, so valuable for feminist theology, was written down by her and preserved by the fourteenth century male religious community that supported her. But at the Reformation this writing would have been lost if this male religious community had not fled England for continental Europe, taking this work with them.

There it was discovered many centuries later and published for modern reading. Since women's writings have no clear lineage to support their preservation, as was the case with revered male leaders, the pathway to their survival is itself a study in accidental and fortuitous events. Generations of women and men have intervened through the ages to preserve women's writings and thus make it possible for researchers like myself to build on this work and make such writings available today in publications and in classes.

For me, teaching, research and writing have always been deeply interconnected. What I have researched and written about has generally emerged from teaching classes on the subject and thereby developing the sources and themes for later writing. Having produced a book on a subject, I continue to teach about it, with the published book now becoming the textbook for the course. A textbook for my course on ecofeminism is my book, *Gaia and God: An Ecofeminist Theology of Earthhealing* (1992). Having taught this course several times at the Theological Union in Berkeley, California, I developed a second book, titled *Integrating Ecofeminism, Globalization and World Religions* (2005) which I now use as a second textbook in my more recent teaching of this course.

But these are of course not the only textbooks. I incorporate several others, reflecting both other thinkers and more recent developments. Bill McKibben's 2010 book, *Eaarth: Making a Life on a Tough New Planet* was a key text when I taught this course in 2011. I will teach it again this spring of 2014 and will use his new 2013 work *Oil and Honey*, on his ecological social organizing of the last two years. This continual updating through new work means my own work also will need updating and perhaps appear in a new edition in the future. Knowledge tied to justice cannot be static, but continually developed.

Today I am in the pleasant position of being semi-retired and thus able to teach on a part-time basis those courses which are most interesting to me. At the Claremont School of Theology, Lincoln University and the Claremont Graduate University I am able to offer one course a semester over a two-year period. So, I can teach my four favorite courses: Feminist Theology in North America; Third World Feminist Theology in Asia, Africa and Latin America; Ecofeminism; and Matristics: Women Writings from the Second to the Seventeenth Centuries. My students are M.A. and Ph.D. students who are not required to take any of these courses, but take them because they are interested in them and are well prepared scholars: a great boon for a teacher.

I will discuss briefly something of the value issues I see as integral to these four courses. Clearly justice is an integral value that underlines all four of these classes. In the Ecofeminist course two crucial justice issues interconnect. There is the question of ecology, that is, how our modern economic system is debilitating the natural world around us and causing a crisis to planetary health itself and how this debilitation of the natural world has been built on the ideology and practice of the domination of women, enforced by racist and classist domination. The purpose of the course is both to understand this system, but also to commit ourselves to changing it and to creating a more just and sustainable world system, although how each student decides to do this is up to them. In other words, the value questions that underline my courses are finally questions for each student to grapple with in free conscience. They are implied in the context of the issues, but not dogmatized as demands.

The underlying justice issue of the Matristics course is simply to make available to the students, women and men, the great variety to women thinkers and writers that actually have existed in patristic and Western European history from the second to the seventeenth centuries. But there is no dogma in this material that assumes that these women were uniformly oppressed or liberated. Rather we seek simply to discover how they actually functioned or made choices of meaning in complex and ambiguous contexts.

The course Feminist Theology in North America brings the issues of feminism, or an affirmation of the equal value of women's lives, into the context of the historical culture of the students taking the course. There is of course no pre-requirement that students be feminist to take this course. Theoretically students might take it who are personally averse to the idea of women's equal value with men as human beings. However, since the course is offered as a free choice, and not a requirement in the curriculum, and to advanced level theological students in a liberal setting, the students who have taken this course, women and men, have always assumed that feminism was a value they affirmed. Many were deeply and overtly involved in struggling with how to become more feminist in their own lives and how to testify to this in their relations to others, especially in the church.

The last time I taught this class, in the Fall of 2013, I had twenty-five students, M.Div. and Ph.D. levels, a third of them males. Since the school where I teach is moving to become interfaith, several of the students, male and female, were Muslim, and one female student was Jewish. Many students of Christian background were struggling with what Christianity meant for them. The issue of feminism thus related to each student in a variety of contexts. One Muslim male student was eager to testify to the feminist potential of Islam, while a Muslim female student testified to her disgust with the lack of affirmation of women as equal with men in the local mosques she knew and why she could no longer attend them, although still identifying herself as a Muslim.

Several men of Christian background in this course were deeply involved in how to support women's equality in the church and the difficulties this commitment had created for them, while several Christian women testified to their suffering from sexism in the church, but also their difficulties with moving further in incorporating feminism in their own theology. In short, feminism as a value implied in the content of the course was picked up and affirmed by each student in their own context and way, making for a rich and lively dynamic.

The fourth course that I teach on feminist theology in the Third World makes available to mainly North American students the development of feminist thinkers in Latin America, Africa and several areas of Asia, broadening their understanding of these issues on a global perspective. But perhaps this also allows them to be less personally impacted than the course on feminist theology in North America. This course also brings in third world feminist thinkers who are Muslim, Jewish and Buddhist, although the majority of the readings are about third world Christians.

A new challenge in teaching these courses, or others at the Claremont schools today, has to do with the movement toward becoming interfaith, and no longer almost exclusively Christian. As more students in these courses are Muslim, Jewish, Buddhist or perhaps Jain or Sikh, the cultural context of what is presented needs to evolve. We need to develop ways of presenting theological material that draws on the comparative visions of the religious traditions that are now represented in our schools and classrooms. We need to draw on the experience in religious life of the range of students in our classes. This is an exciting challenge.

In conclusion, I want to reemphasize that objective analysis of realties and grappling with values are not mutually exclusive. Properly, they are dynamically interrelated. In my research, writing and teaching, the two interconnect. I am drawn to research and to teach on certain issues because of commitment to value concerns, such as justice for women and for racial minorities and commitment to ecological sustainability. But in discovering what is actually the case, for example, in how women functioned in the medieval world, or what women are doing in the third world, I do empirical research to find out what was actually going on in these contexts, in the same way as any other historical or scientific research. Yet in gathering and analyzing this research, my work flows out into ongoing value commitments, into making knowledge of women available to women students today and developing commitments to ecologically sustainable ways of living. These two dimensions of knowledge and value are not in contradiction but dynamically interdependent. Without objective research and knowledge our work loses it factual basis, and without value and purpose it would lose it meaning.

References

Bloom, Allan. *The Closing of the American Mind.* New York City: Simon and Schuster, 1987.

Dewey, John. *Theory of Valuation.* Chicago: University of Chicago Press, 1939.

McKibben, Bill. *Eaarth: Making a Life on a Tough New Planet.* New York City: Times Books, Henry Holt and Company, 2010.

———. *Oil and Honey: The Education of an Unlikely Activist.* New York City: Times Books, Henry Holt and Company, 2013.

Ruether, Rosemary Radford and Keller, Rosemary Skinner, editors. *Encyclopedia of Women and Religion in North America.* 3 vols. Bloomington, IN: Indiana University Press, 2006.

———. *Women and Religion in America.* 4 vols. San Francisco: Harper & Row, 1981–1995.

Ruether, Rosemary Radford. *Gaia and God: An Ecofeminist Theology of Earth Healing.* San Francisco: HarperSanFrancisco, 1992.

———. *Goddesses and the Divine Feminine: A Western Religious History.* Los Angeles: University of California Press, 2005.

———. *Integrating Ecofeminism, Globalization, and World Religions.* New York: Rowman & Littlefield Publishers, Inc., 2005.

———. *Sexism and God-Talk: Toward a Feminist Theology.* 2nd edition. Boston: Beacon Press, 1993.

———. *Women and Redemption, A Theological History*. 2nd edition. Minneapolis, MN: Fortress Press, 2012.

About the Author

Rosemary Radford Ruether was a pioneering feminist theologian who received her doctorate in classics and patristics from Claremont School of Theology in 1965. Her illustrious career included positions at Howard University and several visiting lectureships including at Harvard Divinity School and Princeton Theological Seminary. Ruether spent almost 30 years as the Georgia Harkness Professor of Applied Theology at the Garrett-Evangelical Theological Seminary. After retiring from there she became the Carpenter Professor of Feminist Theology at the Pacific School of Religion and Graduate Theological Union. She was also the recipient of fourteen honorary doctorate degrees from esteemed institutions all over the world. Ruether authored or edited dozens of books, including *Sexism and God Talk: Toward a Feminist Theology* (1983) as well as hundreds of articles and chapters. She passed away in 2022 at the age of 85. Rosemary Radford Ruether is remembered as a scholar-activist committed to civil rights and ecofeminism with a passion for anti-racism, battling poverty, and advocating for progressive values and liberation in the Catholic Church.

PART III

Solidarity and Activism

8 Intersectionality, Solidarity, and Ultimately Flourishing

Sarah E. Robinson

One St. Patrick's Day, in the late 1990s, I went to choir rehearsal with the Oakland Interfaith Gospel Choir, festively in green. I thought of Minty McCoy, one of my Irish ancestors, realizing she is only the tip of the iceberg of ancestors whose names, backgrounds, and identities I may never know. I asked one of my choir friends if she had Irish ancestry, and she replied tersely, "Not by choice." My cheeks colored crimson and I probably apologized. Her European or Irish American ancestors, she implied, had taken her African American ancestors by force, thus her having no reason to celebrate part of her ancestry through this holiday.[1] As her ancestors had reason to mistrust my ancestors, this awkward moment brought to light the work needed by people like me, whose privilege includes a kind of blindness, which I call privilege blindness.

I begin with this example in order to echo and amplify the concern of many writers that good intent is not enough. Revising and reframing epistemology can be crucial, but remains incomplete without concrete activity to match it. Myriad scholars assert methods for addressing systemic, epistemological, pedagogical, social, political, and environmental issues. I develop two at the nexus of such scholarship, intersectionality and solidarity. Innumerable threads connect contemporary, intersectional concerns with the field of religious studies, producing a need to generate academic tools relevant for this historical moment. Solidarity and intersectionality provide method and means for navigating critical issues in religious studies toward greater community flourishing.

Context in Specific Social Location and Organization: Women's Caucus Example

In order to more fully encompass the work at hand—beyond ephemeral words as marks on paper, pigmented pixels on a screen, or sounds passing momentarily through shared air—I begin and end with organizational grounding, first in the work of a scholarly Women's Caucus and completing the chapter with specific stories from biographical narrative and classroom solidarity building. These touchpoints provide opportunities to render more concretely the analysis on solidarity and intersectionality, the goal of which is, ultimately, flourishing.[2]

To begin, the intent of the Women's Caucus of the American Academy of Religion, Western Region, is encapsulated in its mission:

> The mission of the Women's Caucus is to provide a forum where women, their allies and those they are allied to can support and encourage one another as we create dialogue, honor difference, listen and learn, challenge and be challenged, and discover together what justice we can create.
>
> We are dedicated to the advancement of women inside and outside of the academy, giving special attention to women's voices in the field of religion and the challenges diverse women of our region face.
>
> Towards these ends, the Women's Caucus hosts a pre-conference event each year at the AARWR Annual Meeting and a business meeting. We are currently working to create more opportunities for ongoing participation and collaboration within the caucus.[3]

The Women's Caucus spans the focused needs of our various disciplines and our complexities as scholars and human beings, together facing the work ahead in this particular historical moment.

As chair of the Women's Caucus in spring 2017, I considered various speakers to invite to provide valuable perspective or a balm in the wake of a divisive and derisive Presidential campaign, election, and inauguration of Donald Trump as the 45th President of the United States. I thought of panels representing people pained by politics, bringing together leaders, faculty, independent scholars, laypeople, or students facing discrimination of various kinds. I considered inviting scholars famous for their contributions to conversations by, for, and about "others." Recognizing that the term "women" becomes problematic when coded to represent only women of European descent, I thought of the various kinds of inclusion I hoped to represent.

To be most relevant for the group, it was not possible to proceed in a so-called "color-blind" way, nor through tokenizing gestures that can further commodify others, including women of color or non-binary people. In this particularly challenging historical moment, a variety of voices rose to reassert courage and dignity for all by prioritizing the marginalized, the suffering, the oppressed, the forgotten, the omitted. During 2016 to 2017, multifarious people experienced abject fear and shock in response to divisive rhetoric and destructive actions from the highest echelons of U.S. political influence to localities worldwide where transparency, accountability, and truth-telling were destabilized. This historical moment has enabled the unspeakable that must be named, challenging truth-telling among all educators in our fundamental capacities to do work with integrity, facing limits on academic freedom when that freedom is most crucial. I observed the fear-based silences echoing through educational, political, and other institutional hallways, undermining the principles of good governance that, paradoxically, the U.S. has exported around the world.

To serve this regional group that keeps women's voices central, I asked myself various questions about representation and privilege: How many times are people of color deputized to address issues of racism, while white folks stand aside? How many times are women and LGBTQI+ people given responsibility for talking about gender and sexism, while cis men stand aside? How many people lack the political voice to speak for themselves? How might the recipients of "unearned privileges"[4] represent "others" in partial, but crucial attempts to give voice to the wholeness of those whom they seek to understand? Who is served when a "we" becomes another "us" versus "them"? As a chaotic barrage of new national policies lead on a path of greater uncertainty, destabilization, and vulnerability, problematic "tribal" identity politics have arisen as a band-aid to soothe societal ills, reinforced by confirmation bias on social media.[5] Yet even as people of a myriad of backgrounds and identities need soothing, connection, and local places of meaning, such temporary solutions may slide a slippery slope toward manifesting a dystopian politic between mutually dehumanized and dehumanizing groups.

Further questions arose: How many people sharpen lines between distinct identities—mine versus yours—while neglecting or rejecting the value of coalitions across lines of difference? Would slavery have ended if some privileged Euro-Americans had not worked to ensure the full, legal humanity of enslaved human beings? Would women have won the vote if particular men had not stood with them, exercising their privilege to acknowledge women's full citizenship, predicated on their full humanity? In this historical moment, how are religious and non-religious communities providing sanctuary to one another, to Jewish people whose children play at Jewish Community Centers subject to bomb threats, to Muslim Americans who wish to travel home to visit aging parents, but do not know if they will be able to return to the U.S., to all the bodies whose border-crossings now are scrutinized unconstitutionally. And the list goes on.

I hold a particular responsibility as a white, middle class, female human being in North America at the start of the 3rd millennium when anthropogenic climate weirding affects us all, but disrupts, destroys, and displaces the most vulnerable, and when U.S. policies in the first quarter of 2017 have served to increase the number of marginalized and vulnerable people across the planet and close to home. Attending to disruptions to human dignity, ecological wellbeing, and their interconnected wholeness cannot be left only to the most vulnerable and the so-called victims. If so, the "voiceless" natural world would continue to speak only in perilous floods, droughts, and extreme weather events. Those people whose ancestors set the stage for exploiting nature and marginalized human beings, including some of my ancestors and perhaps some of yours, must also answer the call to transform. Also, we recognize that our own ancestries contain multiplicities: decider/disenfranchised, oppressor/oppressed, urban/rural, master/servant, national leader/locally influential voice, media amplified voice/silenced, but not voiceless. To see each group as internally diverse is helpful for understanding religious groups, as well as identity groupings, particularly when considering the work ahead in addressing multiple oppressions in effective ways, such as through intersectionality and solidarity.

The Rise of Intersectionality and Its Application for Religious Studies

Intersectionality theories arose across a span of interdisciplinary work in the 1980s and 1990s, further popularized in the 2000s and 2010s. Legal scholar Kimberlé Crenshaw coined the term intersectionality in 1989, and sociologist Patricia Hill Collins, among others, further theorized the interlocking structure of compound oppressions.[6] Intersectionality has been intellectually popular in the 2000s and early 2010s, amplified by wider popular usage in the #MeToo movement. The social movement #MeToo integrated intersectionality, recognizing how race, class, gender, and other oppress-able categories combine into both potentially more intensely oppressive conditions and into identities that resist disentangling. A person cannot separate age, race, religion, and gender when walking into a room, down a nighttime street, or into the D.M.V. A Ph.D. does not shield recipients from discrimination in the workplace, the grocery store, or the airport. Intersectionality names the confluence of varieties of oppression, marginalization, and silencing via various "-isms." Despite distinct ways that particular categories take on meaning historically and geographically, intersectionality names the inseparability of categories of race, class, gender, sexuality, ability, age, religious affiliation or non-affiliation, and more, both in individuals and in community groups facing marginalization. These myriad facets of any person in community become key defining features for religious self-understanding and affiliation.

Born from experiences of Black women in the U.S., intersectionality asserts multiplicity, internal diversity, and simultaneous identities inextricably connected for each person. Scholars use the term for feminist, critical race, Black, African American, postcolonial, multicultural, indigenous, "Third World," and multiracial feminisms, as well as womanism.[7] Intellectual intersections go beyond these conversations, as a moniker for any conjunction, and the term intersection has become more diffusely used as it has become popularized. Yet, scholarly and activist uses of intersectionality highlight the confluence of factors at work in oppressive situations, the multiple dimensions in any social location, and the at times contradictory or fluid boundary of status and identity positionality amidst changing circumstances. For the study and teaching of religion, an intersectional understanding of religious groups assists in recognizing internal diversity, avoiding homogenizing generalities that silence or further marginalize minority voices.

In the intellectual history of Black feminism, intersectionality arises from late 20th and early 21st century social movements toward alleviating oppression with deeper roots in American popular conscience. Rooted in the work of many unsung and unremembered Black women of the colonial and early American periods, intersectionality concurs with Sojourner Truth's 1851 speech prior to the Civil War and emancipation, "Ain't I a Woman," naming the tension between her experience and the public imaginary of womanhood as elite and Anglo-American.[8] In 1977, the Combahee River Collective issued a statement applying Marx to the "specific economic situation as Black women."[9] In 1983, activist Angela Davis published her book *Women, Race, and Class*, and Black feminist scholar Barbara Smith wrote of the "simultaneity of oppression" faced by Black feminists as "one of the most significant ideological contributions of Black feminist thought."[10] Thus, when Crenshaw wrote fluidly of intersectionality, some of the intellectual foundation had been cast already:

> Consider an analogy to traffic in an intersection, coming and going in all four directions. Discrimination, like traffic through an intersection, may flow in one direction, and it may flow in another. If an accident happens in an intersection, it can be caused by cars traveling from any number of directions and, sometimes, from all of them. Similarly, if a Black woman is harmed because she is in an intersection, her injury could result from sex discrimination or race discrimination. ... But it is not always easy to reconstruct an accident: Sometimes the skid marks and the injuries simply indicate that they occurred simultaneously, frustrating efforts to determine which driver caused the harm.[11]

The imagery of the intersection becomes clearer from this passage, as the issue of reconstructing responsibility can challenge even careful legal scholars like Crenshaw. Collins continues and further popularizes this notion of intersectionality in her sociological studies, which fuel some sociologists of religion.[12]

Additional contemporary voices confirm the value of thinking intersectionally. Cultural critic, bell hooks, alludes to this need for intersectionality as she writes, "The moment anybody black moves out into the world somewhere, away from segregation, we always have to think about the ways that race matters, sometimes more than gender, sometimes the same as gender, but always in convergence and collusion."[13] Womanist theologian Karen Baker-Fletcher writes, "Environmental abuse, racism, sexism, and classism are interlocking forms of oppression and evil. They inaugurate a cruel dance of dispensability. The assumption seems to be that some of us are expendable, a drain on government resources like the pollutants imposed upon us."[14] Baker-Fletcher interprets intersectional analysis as elucidating a purist willingness to sacrifice marginalized people's health and dignity amid environmental injustice.[15]

Applying Intersectionality to the Study of Religion

In 1996, sociologists Maxine Baca Zinn and Bonnie Thornton Dill identified six main components to multiracial feminisms relevant to intersectionality theory. First, categories like race and gender do not represent essential, naturalized, individual traits, but rather socially defined structures with context-specific meanings. Second, a conglomerative category, such as "women," is not unified, homogenous, or static, but rather commonality and solidarity must be made through social analysis and practice within dynamic historical conditions, recognizing social hierarchies. Third, inequalities of many sorts are interlocking and do not function in isolation. Fourth, human agency functions alongside social structures, such that social change, interrelatedness, and complicated positionalities exist amidst oppressive conditions. Fifth, no unitary theory encompasses the methodological diversity helpful for theorizing intersectionality, but attention to complex, lived experience in marginal locations assists theory building. Sixth and finally, analysis must derive from specific, local, historical conditions in order to address interlocking oppressions, highlighting the value of comparative analysis.[16]

Baca Zinn and Thornton Dill's list applies to the study of religion in terms of intersectional feminist studies of religion and beyond. First, specific social contexts shape experiences of meaning in ways that some people may attribute, questionably, to natural or essential realities. To address this issue, when religious studies naturalizes socially constructed meaning, responsible scholars must recognize and interrogate this misrepresentation. Second, religious communities are not entirely homogenous or fixed, thus a lens conglomerating millions or billions of people into an ahistorical framework becomes intellectually troubling.

Recognizing subjugated voices of history, dynamism in frameworks of meaning, and the urge to reinforce unity out of historical memory, scholars of religion may identify oversimplifying frameworks, seeking the granularity of inclusive complexity. Third, when framing dominant or subjugated discourses in religious studies, scholars might consider multiple frames to recognize interlocking systems of meaning production. Fourth, and perhaps most importantly, scholars can avoid repeating discourses that normalize victimization by asserting and reinforcing agential capacities within social, historical conditions that include, but are not encompassed by, oppression. Fifth and sixth, theorizing religion intersectionally requires attention to local specifics, found in various methods, such as case study analysis, lived religion, comparative religious ethics, womanist ethics, Black theologies, and myriad methods employed by members of communities facing oppressive conditions, though not all.

Intersectionality brings attention from singularly defined identity categories to the interconnected meanings of multiplicity; but ultimately intersectionality leads back to placing value on lives neglected by those with more social power. This methodological turn reflects a hunger for human decency and a desire to ground ideals in concrete, lived experience. Through truth-telling and engagement toward universal dignity, these methods begin with those who suffer oppression and subsequently engage unearned privilege in the work of solidarity.

Generating Solidarity among Intersectional Locations

Solidarity is a religiously and secularly significant term, naming the ability of people to stand with those who face suffering, marginalization, oppression, violence, and intimidation.

Solidarity is a tool for spanning differences, while recognizing spaces of social power that can be harnessed for the good of "others." Solidarity is relevant for political, religious, and other social spaces of inequality. From Catholic liberation theology to intersectional feminism to contemporary political philosophy, solidarity arises as a means to transform current suffering and correct historical wrongs, at both individual and structural levels. Because solidarity is a term of widespread use, I will keep my definition consistent with theologian Rosemary Radford Ruether, a beloved mentor and prominent figure in late 20th and early 21st century religious studies.

In her autobiography (2013), Ruether writes about her first experiences of living a commitment to solidarity in the U.S. civil rights movement in 1965. She describes her summer in a Mississippi town where, the prior year, locals had shot other out-of-towners working for civil rights. She defined solidarity as an activity not without vulnerability:

> The thought occurred to me that I too might get killed. It was the first moment in my life that I remember thinking about dying. I had three young children and was in no way eager to become a martyr. It was an important moment as I weighed the possibility of death against doing the right thing. I determined that I must go on.[17]

Ruether clearly explains her active engagement with solidarity, living among, listening to, and endeavoring to serve the self-expressed needs of Black Mississippians during the 1960s civil rights struggle. She "got a glimpse of what White America looked and felt like from the side of Black people.... You only begin to glimpse the full reality of a society if you locate yourself in the disadvantaged sector and look at it from that context."[18] Her sense of solidarity fueled ongoing work in Israel-Palestine, Nicaragua, South Africa, the U.S., and elsewhere.[19] In these movements, her presence did not make the movement tick, but she chose to accept the invitation into unfamiliar spaces, in order to understand directly and work toward the well-being of others. Her epistemology of solidarity was shaped by the act of being physically present in a space occupied primarily by others, combined with her willingness to learn through empathy and reflection on those experiences. Although the language and theorizing on intersectional analysis was absent from the mid- to-late 20th century, Ruether engaged the complex field of race, class, gender, and other simultaneous, yet non-static, dynamic aspects of identity for herself and those with whom she stood in solidarity.

From 1965 Mississippi to the present, Ruether gained prominence as a leading theologian of the 20th century. Thirty years later, in 1996, Ruether published and framed a set of essays in a book *Women Healing Earth*.[20] This publication represents another example of solidarity, providing a means for communication between women in Africa, Asia, and Latin and South America. Representing religiously significant work by women in non-profit organizations, universities, and local communities, Ruether made concrete in book form her commitment to amplify the voices of those marginalized from the "centers" of discourse.

In the U.S. in the late 2010s, despite bullying, intimidation, vandalism, and outright violence littering the country and the press, as a scholar and human being, I endeavored to locate antitheses. In fall 2016, I taught a first-year undergraduate course on Climate Change and Religion, which focused on cultivating solidarity toward climate justice and intergenerational ethics. Through specific case studies, scientific literacy, and religious pluralism education, students increasingly recognized that current marginalized groups and future lives may suffer undue oppression based on the decisions of contemporary power brokers. Although some students seemed to equate solidarity with altruism or with simply being friendly, I endeavored to impart another level of solidarity, which recognizes social power imbalances. For this reason, solidarity must continue less theoretically or discursively, and more practically, through seeking to lift up the oppressed, using whatever social power a person might have. Incorporating intersectional analysis into the study of religion for early undergraduates, the course developed and named examples of internal complexity for religious locations, emphasizing pluralistic human diversity, while appreciating the need to see difference, make value judgments, build justice, and engage in solidarity with unfamiliar and familiar others.

To conclude, intersectionality provides epistemological ground for acts of solidarity, which have always been relevant, but are particularly urgent in this historical moment. Solidarity emerges in a variety of spaces, but here I highlight the epistemological requirement to consider intersectionality in the work of solidarity. The current era has provided ample opportunities to engage with solidarity, particularly as divisive language has eroded the pluralistic fabric of American inter-religious community understanding and identities. People of distinct politics, ethnicities, and religions share a potential for further pluralistic encounter, which is enhanced when recognizing the dynamically changing, discriminatory interweaving of various politics of exclusion. To build greater solidarity, understanding intersectionality then supports fuller encounter with "others" in a pluralistic setting. Further, the intent of solidarity, certainly, involves the hard work of collective struggle, but the longer horizon for these theoretical and practical projects is to generate greater potential for flourishing, ultimately.[21]

Notes

1 Although some claim that Irish people were enslaved alongside Africans during the American period of chattel slavery, this has been debunked as a myth, which a variety of scholarly voices called "racist ahistorical propaganda" in an open letter on the subject. Such false claims blur the lines between time-limited indentured servitude for Irish inhabitants of the Americas with the "racialized perpetual hereditary chattel slavery" to which African inhabitants of the Americas were subjected. Liam Hogan, "Open Letter to Irish Central, Irish Examiner and Scientific American about their 'Irish Slaves' Disinformation," Available online: https://medium.com/@Limerick1914/

open-letter-to-irish-central-irish-examiner-and-scientific-american-about-their-irish-slaves-3f6cf23b8d7f#.tb66klcft; Internet; accessed 5 July 2017.

2 This chapter has been adapted from two American Academy of Religion presentations, one for the national Graduate Student Committee and one for the regional Women's Caucus, thus these concepts have been tested in real communities. "Humility, Solidarity, and Mutuality: Three Holistic Methodological Goals for Comparative Religious Study," American Academy of Religion (AAR) National, Graduate Student Roundtable, November 23, 2015. "Intersectionality, Solidarity, and Mindful Attention: A Presentation and Discussion about Dehumanization, Dignity, Community Sustainability, and Ultimately Flourishing," AAR-Western Region Women's Caucus Pre-conference Event, March 17, 2017.

3 "AARWR Women's Caucus Mission," Women's Caucus, American Academy of Religion, Western Region. Available online: https://www.aarwr.com/womens-caucus.html; Internet; accessed 15 March 2019.

4 Peggy McIntosh, "White Privilege and Male Privilege: A Personal Account of Coming to See Correspondences Through Work in Women's Studies," working paper 189, Wellesley College Center for Research on Women, Wellesley, Mass., 1988.

5 Here, the term "tribal" does not refer derisively to indigenous peoples, but rather to the term's problematics regarding small groups of like-minded people who fail to recognize the full humanity of others outside the self- defined "tribe." This use of the term tribalism involves in-group identification and out-group dehumanization, such as that described in Paolo Freire, *Pedagogy of the Oppressed* (New York: Continuum, 2000).

6 Kimberlé Crenshaw, "Demarginalizing the Intersection of Race and Sex: A Black Feminist Critique of Antidiscrimination Doctrine, Feminist Theory, and Antiracist Politics," *University of Chicago Legal Forum*, 1989, 139–67. Patricia Hill Collins, *Black Feminist Thought: Knowledge, Consciousness, and the Politics of Empowerment*, second edition (New York: Routledge, 2001).

7 Cynthia Fabrizio Pelak. *The Blackwell Encyclopedia of Sociology, Vol. V*, ed. George Ritzer (Malden, Mass.: Blackwell Publishing, 2007), 2395.

8 Sojourner Truth, "Ain't I a Woman?" Women's Convention, Akron, Ohio, May 28–29, 1851.

9 The Combahee River Collective, April 1977. Quoted, for example, in Beverly Guy-Sheftall, ed., *Words of Fire: An Anthology of African-American Feminist Thought* (New York: The New Press, 1995), 235. The statement is available online at www.circuitous.org/scraps/combahee.html. Cited in Sharon Smith, "Black Feminism and Intersectionality," *International Socialist Review 91*, Winter 2013–14 Web resource: http://isreview.org/issue/91/black-feminism-and-intersectionality; Internet; accessed 15 March 2017.

10 Angela Y. Davis, *Women, Race, and Class* (New York: Vintage, 1983). Barbara Smith, ed., *Home Girls: A Black Feminist Anthology* (New Brunswick: Rutgers University Press, 2000), xxxiv.

11 Crenshaw, "Demarginalizing the Intersection of Race and Sex," 149.

12 Collins, *Black Feminist Thought*.

13 bell hooks, *Wounds of Passion* (New York: MacMillan, 1999).
14 Karen Baker-Fletcher, *Sisters of Dust, Sisters of Spirit* (Minneapolis: Fortress Press, 1998), 62.
15 Womanist voices, including Baker-Fletcher, are relevant to this discussion, but will not be expanded upon here due to space limitations. Womanism draws from the literary genre as a source of historical and cultural memory, particularly drawing on the fiction and non-fiction writings of Alice Walker. In theological work, womanist theologians span from Delores Williams' *Sisters in the Wilderness* to more recent ecowomanists like Melanie Harris. See also: Panashe Chigumadzi, "Intersectionality and Womanism: A Brand of Feminism Relevant for a Young Black Woman," *Vanguard Magazine*, 19 August 2014. Available online: http://vanguardmagazine.co.za/intersectionality-and-womanism-a-brand-of-feminism-relevant-for-a-young-black-woman; Internet; accessed March 2017.
16 Baca Zinn, Maxine and Bonnie Thornton Dill, "Theorizing Difference from Multiracial Feminisms." *Feminist Studies* 22 (1996): 321–331, in Pelak (2007).
17 Rosemary Radford Ruether, *My Quests for Hope and Meaning: An Autobiography* (Eugene, Or.: Cascade Books/Wipf and Stock, 2013), 11.
18 Ruether, *My Quests for Hope and Meaning*, 14.
19 Ibid., 14.
20 Rosemary Radford Ruether, ed., *Women Healing Earth: Third World Women on Ecology, Feminism, and Religion* (Maryknoll, N.Y.: Orbis Press, 1996).
21 For a comparative study of flourishing, please see Laura M. Hartman, ed. *That All May Flourish: Comparative Religious Environmental Ethics* (New York: Oxford University Press, 2018).

References

Baca Zinn, Maxine and Thornton Dill, Bonnie. "Theorizing Difference from Multiracial Feminisms," *Feminist Studies* 22: 321–331, 1996, in Pelak, Cynthia Fabrizio. *The Blackwell Encyclopedia of Sociology, Vol. V*, edited by George Ritzer. Malden, Mass.: Blackwell Publishing, 2007, 2395–2398.

Baker-Fletcher, Karen. *Sisters of Dust, Sisters of Spirit*. Minneapolis: Fortress Press, 1998.

Chigumadzi, Panashe. "Intersectionality and Womanism: A Brand of Feminism Relevant for a Young Black Woman," *Vanguard Magazine*, 19 August 2014. Available online: http://vanguardmagazine.co.za/intersectionality-and-womanism-a-brand-of-feminism-relevant-for-a-young-black-woman/; Internet; accessed March 2017.

Collins, Patricia Hill. *Black Feminist Thought: Knowledge, Consciousness, and the Politics of Empowerment*, 2nd ed. New York: Routledge, 2000/2009.

The Combahee River Collective Statement, April 1977. Available online at www.circuitous.org/scraps/combahee.html; Internet; accessed July 2017.

Crenshaw, Kimberlé. "Demarginalizing the Intersection of Race and Sex: A Black Feminist Critique of Antidiscrimination Doctrine, Feminist Theory, and Antiracist Politics," *University of Chicago Legal Forum*, 1989: 139–67.

Crenshaw, Kimberlé W. "Race, Reform, and Retrenchment." In *Theories of Race and Racism: A Reader*, edited by Les Back & John Solomos, 549–560. New York: Routledge, 2000/2003.

Davis, Angela Y. *Women, Race, and Class*. New York: Vintage, 1983.

Donaldson, Laura. "The Breasts of Columbus." In *Postcolonialism, Feminism, and Religious Discourse*, edited by Laura E. Donaldson and Kwok Pui-Lan, 41–61. New York: Routledge, 2002.

Freire, Paolo. *Pedagogy of the Oppressed*. New York: Continuum, 2000.

Guy-Sheftall, Beverly, editor. *Words of Fire: An Anthology of African-American Feminist Thought*. New York: The New Press, 1995.

Hartman, Laura M., editor. *That All May Flourish: Comparative Religious Environmental Ethics*. New York: Oxford University Press, 2018.

Hogan, Liam. "Open Letter to Irish Central, Irish Examiner and Scientific American about their 'Irish Slaves' Disinformation," Available online: https://medium.com/@Limerick1914/open-letter-to-irish-central-irish-examiner-and-scientific-american-about-their-irish-slaves-3f6cf23b8d7f#.tb66klcft; Internet; accessed 5 July 2017.

hooks, bell. *Wounds of Passion*. New York: Macmillan, 1999.

McIntosh, Peggy. "White Privilege and Male Privilege: A Personal Account of Coming to See Correspondences Through Work in Women's Studies," working paper 189, Wellesley College Center for Research on Women, Wellesley, Mass., 1988.

Moe-Lobeda, Cynthia. *Resisting Structural Evil: Love as Ecological-Economic Vocation*. Minneapolis: Fortress Press, 2013.

Pelak, Cynthia Fabrizio. *The Blackwell Encyclopedia of Sociology, Vol. V*, edited by George Ritzer, 2395–2398. Malden, Mass.: Blackwell Publishing, 2007.

Ruether, Rosemary Radford, editor. *Women Healing Earth: Third World Women on Ecology, Feminism, and Religion*. Maryknoll, N.Y.: Orbis Press, 1996.

Ruether, Rosemary Radford. *My Quests for Hope and Meaning, An Autobiography*. Eugene, Or.: Cascade Books/Wipf and Stock, 2013.

Smith, Barbara, editor. *Home Girls: A Black Feminist Anthology*. New Brunswick: Rutgers University Press, 2000.

Smith, Sharon. "Black Feminism and Intersectionality," *International Socialist Review 91*, (Winter 2013–14). Web resource: http://isreview.org/issue/91/black-feminism-and-intersectionality; Internet; accessed 15 March 2017.

Spivak, Gayatri Chakravorty. *A Critique of Postcolonial Reason: Toward a History of the Vanishing Present*. Cambridge, Massachusetts: Harvard University Press, 1999.

Truth, Sojourner. "Ain't I a Woman?" Women's Convention, Akron, Oh., May 28–29, 1851.

About the Author

Sarah E. Robinson, also Robinson-Bertoni, is a critical-constructive scholar of religion, environment, and social justice. She is a professor at Pacific Lutheran University and Santa Clara University, teaching courses in environment, social justice, women's and gender studies, and religion, supported by research in Buddhist, Christian, and Muslim communities. In 1999, she completed a BA in American Studies with a minor in Conservation and Resource Studies at the University of California, Berkeley. After graduation, her work in religious, arts, and environmental non-profit organizations included managing the first summer youth jobs program in 2001 for California Youth Energy Services, a project of Rising Sun Center for Opportunity, which provides "green house calls" and has trained over 2000 youth and adult energy specialists, served over 52,000 homes, saved nearly a trillion gallons of water, and offset over 117,500 tons of carbon dioxide. Robinson received an MA in History from the Graduate Theological Union in 2005, researching historical contexts for varying documents deriving from the early Jesus movement. At Claremont Graduate University, she earned a PhD in Religion in 2015, employing comparative religious ethics and qualitative research methods to study three sustainable agriculture projects in religious contexts. Robinson serves the American Academy of Religion in the Steering Committee for the Religion and Food unit. She has served the American Academy of Religion, Western Region, as conference manager, Women's Caucus liaison to the Board, Regional Student Director to national-level Student Committee, and as unit chair for Ecology and Religion, Graduate Student Professional Development, and Women and Religion. Select essays appear in the Springer Encyclopedia of Food and Agricultural Ethics ("Islam and Food"), Columbia University Press' Religion, Food, and Eating in North America ("Refreshing the Concept of Halal Meat: Resistance and Religiosity in Chicago's Taqwa Eco-food Cooperative"), Oxford University Press' Flourishing: Comparative Religious Environmental Ethics ("All God's Creatures Are Communities Like You (Qur'an 6:38): Precedents for Eco-halal Meat in Muslim Traditions"), Routledge's Key Thinkers on the Environment ("Seyyed Hossein Nasr"), and the journal Religions ("Re-territorializing Religiosity in Wholesome Muslim Praxis"). Her 2021 co-edited book Valuing Lives, Healing Earth: Religion, Gender, and Life on Earth highlights narratives of global women striving for community health and religious integrity in justice-seeking ways. Her teaching and scholarship focus on lived religion, religion and food, comparative religious ethics, women's studies in religion, and ecology and religion.

9 #OrlandoStrong: Yes, Baby, the Gay Bar is Still Our Church—Still Our Religion[1]

Marie Cartier

The worst gun massacre in United States history happened in a gay bar, PULSE, Sunday, June 12, 2016 in Orlando, CA.[2]

It happened during Pride month in the United States, which commemorates the Stonewall riots of June 1969. The Stonewall riot was the first televised riot over a period of time (approximately one week), allowing members and supporters of the LGBTQ community to join the protests against police violence and harassment.[3]

Today's many social media platforms allow us to respond more quickly than they were able to in 1969. By the eve of June 12, 2016 memorials and vigils were happening around the country. I attended one in Long Beach, California, at which a couple hundred folks lit candles, sang, and mourned. By the following evening I was at a vigil for Orlando in Los Angeles attended by many thousands at which, in Los Angeles style, the reading of the victims' names began with an emotional tribute to the victims by Lady Gaga.[4]

In Pagan traditions, especially that in which I am ordained (Temple of Isis/Fellowship of Isis), we chant for our loved ones who have passed, "Say their names so we remember them." Often in the week following this massacre, these 49 names were chanted—*say their names so we remember them*:

Stanley Almodovar III, 23 years old
Amanda L. Alvear, 25 years old
Oscar A. Aracena Montero, 26 years old
Rodolfo Ayala Ayala, 33 years old
Antonio Davon Brown, 29 years old
Darryl Roman Burt II, 29 years old
Angel Candelario-Padro, 28 years old
Juan Chavez Martinez, 25 years old
Luis Daniel Conde, 39 years old
Cory James Connell, 21 years old

Tevin Eugene Crosby, 25 years old
Deonka Deidra Drayton, 32 years old
Simón Adrian Carrillo Fernández, 31 years old
Leroy Valentin Fernandez, 25 years old
Mercedez Marisol Flores, 26 years old
Peter Ommy Gonzalez Cruz, 22 years old
Juan Ramon Guerrero, 22 years old
Paul Terrell Henry, 41 years old
Frank Hernandez, 27 years old
Miguel Angel Honorato, 30 years old
Javier Jorge Reyes, 40 years old
Jason Benjamin Josaphat, 19 years old
Eddie Jamoldroy Justice, 30 years old
Anthony Luis Laureano Disla, 25 years old
Christopher Andrew Leinonen, 32 years old
Alejandro Barrios Martinez, 21 years old
Brenda Marquez McCool, 49 years old
Gilberto R. Silva Menendez, 25 years old
Kimberly Jean Morris, 37 years old
Akyra Monet Murray, 18 years old
Luis Omar Ocasio Capo, 20 years old
Geraldo A. Ortiz Jimenez, 25 years old
Eric Ivan Ortiz-Rivera, 36 years old
Joel Rayon Paniagua, 32 years old
Jean Carlos Mendez Perez, 35 years old
Enrique L. Rios, Jr., 25 years old
Jean Carlos Nieves Rodríguez, 27 years old
Xavier Emmanuel Serrano-Rosado, 35 years old
Christopher Joseph Sanfeliz, 24 years old
Yilmary Rodríguez Solivan, 24 years old
Edward Sotomayor Jr., 34 years old
Shane Evan Tomlinson, 33 years old
Martin Benitez Torres, 33 years old
Jonathan A. Camuy Vega, 24 years old
Juan Pablo Rivera Velázquez, 37 years old
Luis Sergio Vielma, 22 years old
Franky Jimmy DeJesus Velázquez, 50 years old
Luis Daniel Wilson-Leon, 37 years old
Jerald Arthur Wright, 31 years old[5]

The Gay Bar

I reposted a meme on Facebook that was circulating asking "Where was your first gay bar?" Within the first hour, over a hundred people had not just liked it, but responded with memories of "their first." The responses came back from all over the United States, from East and West and also abroad from several countries, among them Australia, England, and Belgium. It seemed, like their first love, everyone could remember "their first" gay bar.

It mattered—that first gay bar. Why?

In my book, *Baby, You Are My Religion: Women, Gay Bars, and Theology Before Stonewall* (*BYAMR*), I was the first to say that the gay bar was more than a bar—it was sacred space.[6] For the book, I interviewed over 100 people, primarily pre-Stonewall gay women and lesbians. The thesis of *BYAMR* is that the gay bar was "the only place" (as so named by all of the informants for my book). The gay bar was an alternative church space, I postulate, for those who were exiled from all other churches—and all other public spaces, major and minor. The gay bars were a sanctuary. And, as we saw with Orlando, they often still are.

How important is the gay bar to LGBTQ people? President Obama said, in the wake of Orlando, that the gay bar is a place of "solidarity and empowerment."[7] Yes. It is nothing less than the cauldron of possibility for birth into selfhood. The place where you can see yourself reflected in the eyes of another and experience, as Judith Butler phrases it, the transformative nature of the gaze, or as I name it in *BYAMR*, baptism. It is when someone sees you for the first time as not the sinner, outcast, mentally ill, felon, deviant, nation's highest security risk—which were all "gazes" suffered by the queer population pre-Stonewall and often still today. When you are seen with this radically new gaze you have not experienced before, you birthed yourself into community with this person, into a self which is "not" just that sinner—but is something else. Something radically different than what society has us believe of gay folk. When this happens, we become wanted community members, friends, lovers, protectors, creators, and activists for the claiming of public space. This was true for what could happen in gay bars pre-Stonewall and true today.

One of the maxims I repeat in *BYAMR* is that *we as queer people have to be proud of the history we have, and not create a history to be proud of.* The main reason I wrote *BYAMR* as my doctoral dissertation and then published it as a book is that I wanted to claim the pride of the gay bar history. Yes, I come from a people birthed in the fire of gay bars—literally the fire. I come from a people who claimed public space on the edges of cities, in dangerous passageways of geography and physical lives, crossroads they had to traverse and coalitions they had to make work based on their need for survival. I am proud of a lineage of people that survived despite the hatred, harassment, beatings, rape, and arrests. My people continued to claim these spaces—these often dirty, scary, dangerous gay bar spaces—not because they were bar flies (necessarily), or alcoholics (necessarily), but because they were forging, with grit, the real estate of public space and community from which would arise gay liberation. This is our LGBTQ history. And we get to claim it without apology.

Gay bar attendance as an act of courage

Gay bar attendance is an act of activism, love and support. We often chant in the streets, "Out of the bars and into the streets." But I want to remind my community that first we had to have the courage to go *into* the bars. Our first initial chant was to ourselves as we began the arduous task of "coming out." Most of us had to chant to ourselves, repeatedly, "go into the bar." Go into that cauldron of possibility, stir the pot and see if you can find yourself reflected.

The gay bar was central to community pre-Stonewall and the book could have been called "The Only Place" because there *literally* was no other public space for queer folks to go. Anyone's birthday, anniversary, sacred union (in lieu of the legal weddings that would come decades later), comforting after a break-up, make up session in a dark but public corner, or any coming into community had to happen in a gay bar because it was the only space the community had. Because there weren't the gay centers, queer studies programs (in which I now teach), LGBTQ sanctioned "safe spaces," women's centers, etc. These spaces had not yet been invented. During this time, even feminism had yet to get a foothold strong enough to acquire community real estate. And gay liberation as a public force would come after Stonewall.

So gay bars for these folks were the public space—the space of coming into community of "solidarity and empowerment." And, post Orlando, we are recognizing that they still are. The gay bar is where you figure out who you are as a gay person. Are you in fact gay? Is this a place you finally fit with all of your conflicting feelings that don't make sense anywhere else? Often you parked blocks away, circled the block, could not come in that first time and had to come back a second, third, fourth, or more time before you got the courage to go in. Maybe it took you years to get up the courage.

A recent Twitter meme celebrating the gay bar post-Orlando was retweeted thousands of times, proclaiming that, "If you've never been afraid to hold hands with someone you love, you don't understand how important it is to be inside a gay bar."

What we see with Orlando is that the gay bar is just as important as it always has been in creating our communities. The tragedy that is Orlando has allowed us, as an LGBTQQIAA population (lesbian, gay, bisexual, transgender, intersex, allied, asexual, queer and questioning—did I miss anyone?) to stand in solidarity with gay bar culture and with the folks in the PULSE bar. We empathize with those who were there discovering themselves—because that is where *we* discovered ourselves.

Gay bars saved our queer lives. And this wasn't just true for pre-Stonewall folk who had nowhere else to go. Gay bars are our sanctuaries still. And they are *still* the only place for many queer folks to go.

In Florida, where you can still be fired based on your sexuality (even though you can legally marry), a gay bar is a sanctuary where you can expose feelings and behavior that would get you fired if displayed in another public arena—behavior that marks you as "gay." The conversations surrounding gay bars post-Orlando celebrate them almost as queer colleges: Where did you go? What year? We are alumni searching for our classmates who were there when we figured out our identities, those who helped us by also claiming that contested public space to form our first community.

A gay bar is the place where you often also figure out not just that you can have friends, but that you can be a friend. That someone would want you as a friend—you, the gay person so often reviled as sinner, mentally ill, deviant, etc. in the wider world. Today we stand with Orlando. The Facebook meme that quickly became a profile frame allowed you to put your picture into activism framing your profile with the words "We Are Orlando." Meaning we, our queer tribe, is Orlando—we are the kids going to the gay bar. The mother wanting to celebrate with her son. The young underage kid getting in with a false ID. We are that community; that was us. And is still us. We are Orlando. We are embracing our gay bar history when we say, "Of course they were in a gay bar. Gay people go to gay bars. We still go there." *It is history we can be proud of.*

Gay people and allies who were "outed" because of the massacre, because they were inside the PULSE nightclub and survived, may have survived only to find out that they have lost their jobs. You can still lose your job, your children, your church affiliation, your residence because you are gay. These kinds of discrimination are not just awful but still legal in many places. The gay bar becomes a dangerous but necessary breathing space between a rock and a hard place—still. You can still be classified as mentally ill as a minor and be sent for reparative therapy. This is only beginning to be illegal and is still legal in many states. The gay bar then is—and constantly becomes again—the only place, that dangerous but accepting place.

You take your body to a gay bar so you can talk, dance, look, feel—be. My favorite meme of the post-Orlando blast on social media was of two men dancing proudly with stylized crowns on their heads, proclaiming, "In celebration of all those who just wanted to dance." One of the reasons Stonewall was targeted in 1969 was that it was one of the only New York clubs where you could "touch dance." Touching a person of the same sex was illegal activity pre-Stonewall, and still dangerous today.

A history we can be proud of—in celebration of all those who just wanted to dance. The last chapter of my book begins with lines from the "last call" dance at many gay clubs, "Last dance. Last chance for love. This is my last dance…last chance for love."[8] I open the book with a list of those informants' names who passed before my book was published and wrote after their names, "May the last dance always be a sweet one."

Today I add the names of the Orlando victims to my litany and pray for them, in whatever gay bar they are dancing in now. Not "rest in peace," but my own sweet, gay prayer, "May the last dance…may the last dance…may the last dance…always be a sweet one."

Notes

1 A version of this work was originally published in the online blog "Feminism and Religion" (FAR) on June 24, 2016. https://feminismandreligion.com/2016/06/24/orlandostrong-yes-baby-the-gay-bar-is-still-our-church-still-our-religion-by-marie-cartier/

2 "Orlando Nightclub Massacre," *NBC News*, https://www.nbcnews.com/storyline/orlando-nightclub-massacre, (accessed March 18, 2019).

3 "1969, The Stonewall Riots Begin," This Day in History: June 28, accessed March 18, 2019, https://www.history.com/this-day-in-history/the-stonewall-riot

4 Marie Cartier, "Los Angeles Pulse Vigil…reading the names of the victims," Facebook, June 14, 2016, https://www.facebook.com/marie.cartier.7/videos/vb.597556673/10153575964476674/?type=3&theater.

5 "Victims' Names," City of Orlando, June 12, 2016, accessed March 18 2019, http://www.cityoforlando.net/blog/victims/.

6 Marie Cartier, *Baby, You Are My Religion: Women, Gay Bars, and Theology Before Stonewall*, (New York: Routledge, 2013).

7 Barack Obama, "President Obama delivers a statement" (speech, Washington, DC, June 12, 2016), President Obama on the Tragic Shooting in Orlando, https://obamawhitehouse.archives.gov/blog/2016/06/12/president-obama-tragic-shooting-orlando.

8 Donna Summer, "Last Dance," track A4 on *Thank God It's Friday (The Original Motion Picture Soundtrack)*, Casablanca Records, 1978, vinyl.

References

Cartier, Marie. *Baby, You Are My Religion: Women, Gay Bars, and Theology Before Stonewall*. New York: Routledge, 2013.

———. "Los Angeles Pulse Vigil…reading the names of the victims." Facebook, June 14, 2016. https://www.facebook.com/marie.cartier.7/videos/vb.597556673/10153575964476674/?type=3&theater.

City of Orlando. "Victims' Names," June 12, 2016. Accessed March 18 2019. http://www.cityoforlando.net/blog/victims/.

Obama, Barack. "President Obama delivers a statement." Speech, Washington, DC, June 14, 2016. https://www.facebook.com/marie.cartier.7/videos/vb.597556673/10153575964476 674/?type=3&theater.

"Orlando Nightclub Massacre." *NBC News*. https://www.nbcnews.com/storyline/orlando-nightclub-massacre. Accessed March 18, 2019.

Summer, Donna. "Last Dance," track A4 on *Thank God It's Friday (The Original Motion Picture Soundtrack)*. Casablanca Records, 1978, vinyl.

This Day in History: June 28. "1969, The Stonewall Riots Begin." Accessed March 18, 2019. https://www.history.com/this-day-in-history/the-stonewall-riot

About the Author

Marie Cartier has a PhD in Religion with an emphasis on Women and Religion from Claremont Graduate University. She is the author of the critically acclaimed book *Baby, You Are My Religion: Women, Gay Bars, and Theology Before Stonewall* (Routledge 2013, second edition going to press in 2026). She is a senior lecturer in Gender and Women's Studies and Queer Studies at California State University Northridge, and in Film Studies at University of California Irvine. She is also a published poet and playwright, accomplished performance artist, scholar, and social change activist. Cartier holds a BA in Communications from the University of New Hampshire; an MA in English/Poetry from Colorado State University; an MFA in Theatre Arts (Playwriting) and an MFA in Film and TV (Screenwriting), both from UCLA; and an MFA in Visual Art (Painting/Sculpture) from Claremont Graduate University. She is co-chair of the Lesbian-Feminisms and Religion session of the national American Academy of Religion and co-chair at the regional level of the Queer Studies in Religion session, founder of the western region's Queer Caucus, and a perma-blogger for Feminism and Religion. She is also a first-degree black belt in karate, Shorin-Ryu Shi-Do-Kan Kobayashi style, and a 500-hour Yoga Alliance certified Hatha Yoga teacher.

10 Bodies of Evidence and Why Thanxgrieving?*¹

Ibrahim Abdurrahman Farajajé

I greet the Four Directions of the universe and ask permission of our First Nations relatives of all genders, the First People, to gather on their soil, near their waters. I also call upon all of those who have gone before us, all of those whom we have lost to HIV, and ask them to be present here with us today, to bring us the strength and resilience of their spirits and to ask them to remind us today and every day of our lives the crucial importance of the work in which we are engaged. Without them, we cannot exist and if we do not do what we are challenged to do, then perhaps there will be no tomorrow.

I come to the task of doing HIV the@logies with an intense passion. It is my firm belief that "theology," as we know it, has been radically changed by the HIV pandemic. We can no longer continue with business as usual. HIV the@logies are indeed grassroots, subversive the@logies, for they arise from the lives, dreams, struggles, fears, and triumphs of people living with HIV and those who love them and make community with them. These HIV the@logies challenge the complacency of "theology" in the face of the HIV disease and also force us to look at the role that "theology" has played in fostering the kinds of conditions that allow HIV to be where it is today in this country and elsewhere, especially amongst those whom the dominating culture considers "disposable people."

I have been arrested several times for committing acts of civil disobedience connected to HIV-related issues. In 1992, I lost my heart-brother, Zawadi-Lazarus, to HIV. By the end of that year, most of my circle of friends had died of HIV-related complications. I am the foster-father of a 23-year-old who is living with HIV. For the last 15 years, my community has been the HIV community. I worked in HIV first in Switzerland and from 1986 until the present here in the United States. I have worked as an HIV-test counselor/educator, and as a "safer sex" activist I have also taught a course on HIV the@

---

* AIDS and Religion in America Conference, Atlanta, Georgia, 1998

logies in seminaries since the late 1980s. The course is about how to develop grassroots the@logies and practices out of the multiple intersecting contexts of people living with HIV. The only requirement for this course was that one be trained as a "safer sex" educator, an HIV-educator, a test counselor, etc., and be directly involved in HIV work. As part of this class, people have been tested and then reported back on their different experiences with test counselors and clinics and the ways in which they were received based on the assumptions that the counselors made about them, about who they were. This is helpful in getting people in religious/spiritual leadership to understand that often their work in regards to HIV might be the work of advocacy and agitation. One of the most important theoretical parts of the course was looking at religious attitudes towards the Plague and particularly the role of the poor during the Plague.

Chrystos, that great Native American (Menominee)/Two-Spirit/lesbian poet and critical thinker, activist for queer rights, First Nations' land and treaties rights; and prisoners' rights, says in her poem, "From the Other World":

> The dead call to me singing in voices I barely remember...
> We are a people for whom death is common as colds
> We stagger under grief not even able to lean on one another
> because no one stays rooted in a hurricane
> Rain comes from the south blowing hard
> the grass lies down until it is over
> We hardly speak of the deaths for we know we have years more to carry
> The hatred we have had to withstand storms on
> There is little pity for us in the hearts we live among as we face time with no shelter...[2]

How do we create new ways of facing time "with shelter?" In 1851, Sojourner Truth gave her great "Ain't I a Woman?" speech, in which she makes it very clear to us that there is nothing "essential" (as we would say today) or fixed in stone about gender identity/gender expression, any more than there is anything immutable or fixed in stone about race, class, sexuality, or the right to self-definition and self-determination. Sojourner Truth, that great escaped slave, abolitionist, womanist, the@logian, traveling orator, preacher, gender-outlaw and over-all paradigm subverter, points to the intersections of race and class in the construction of gender/gender expression. Sojourner is my shero, because, instead of trying to adapt herself to the societally-accepted definition of *woman* of her time, she challenged both the definition and the standards that had created it. Her speech, but more importantly her life, exposed the concepts of "woman" and "man" as being socially constructed and therefore, like notions of race, class, sexuality, or self-determination, subject to change according to social, political, geographical, historical, ideological, economic, etc. factors and circumstances. Sojourner Truth deconstructed with her words *and with her body.*

For her, there was no conflict between Sojourner Truth the abolitionist and Sojourner Truth the women's rights activist. The one informed the other, for the same power of white male supremacy substood both. And the example of Sojourner Truth leads us to look at HIV as we know it today as being at the intersection of many different issues that we have to begin to address simultaneously.

HIV is pushing us to move beyond either/or thinking. This is what I call "HIV-in-intersection." At the end of the 20th century and facing the beginning of the 21st century, HIV-in-intersection means acknowledging the particular issues of women of color with HIV in their struggles against multiple oppressions. HIV-in-intersection means acknowledging that it is impossible to understand these issues without a class-analysis of the socio-political economic factors contributing to sexism (understood as systemic oppression perpetuated by a process of socio-sexual power relations which reflect and reproduce male dominance) as compounded by white supremacy (not just "bad" white people).

Without sexism, gender oppression, cis-gender-heterosexism (the systemic display of cis-gender-heterosexual male power and privilege), ableism, classism, racism, erotophobia (the fear of the erotic and of its power), etc. coming together to shape and inform religious and societal discourses, the response to HIV in this country could have been profoundly different. So, HIV-in-intersection means also being a Muslim transgender woman lesbian of color single mother with HIV living right here in Atlanta who risks losing custody of her children for a whole host of reasons.

HIV-in-intersection means acknowledging that race, class, gender, gender expression, disability, sexuality, and spirituality are not monolithic, distinct categories. It means creating a space where we all can come to an understanding of race that must include an understanding of the elements of class, gender/gender expression, disability, sexualities, geographies, etc. that go into shaping notions of race. How race, gender/gender expression, disability, sexualities, and geography go into shaping notions of class; how race, class, gender/gender expression, disability, geography, and religion are factors and facets in the shaping of sexualities; how race, class, disability, sexuality, geography, and religion are factors in the shaping of notions of gender/gender expression; how racism, fear and hatred of women, erotophobia, homo-hatred, fear of the Earth, and HIV-phobia/aparth-AIDS all came together so that now we can see how the war against women and their bodies, from the Inquisition until the beginning of the dismantling of women's reproductive rights, is connected to the masculinization and the industrialization of healing; which is connected to the hardening of Western Christian religious dogma in Northern Europe; which is connected to the driving out of all feminine manifestations of the Divine; which is connected to the expulsion of the Other, of Muslims and Jews from Spain; which is connected to the African slave trade and the invasions of the Americas, Asia, and the Pacific Islands, where Indigenous Peoples, Africans, and Asians were enslaved and massacred because they were considered to be "like women." Incarnations of evil, unbridled lust, too connected to the body and sex, too filled with disease (like HIV), too connected to the earth, the black and red earth which, like women, was to be destroyed because, like women, it was considered to be wild and needing to be dominated; like dark-skinned peoples, it too needed to be dominated and controlled. We cannot understand or effectively struggle against HIV in all of our communities if we do not attempt to grasp the complex ways in which HIV and the problems surrounding it are all inextricably bound-up together.

In *Birth of a Clinic: An Archaeology of Medical Perception*, Michel Foucault writes:

> Doctor and patient are caught up in an ever-greater proximity, bound together, the doctor by an ever-more attentive, more insistent, more penetrating gaze, the patient by all the silent, irreplaceable qualities that, in him, betray—that is, reveal and conceal—the clearly ordered forms of the disease.... Let us call tertiary spatialization all the gestures by which, in a given society, a disease is circumscribed, medically invested, isolated, divided up into closed, privileged, regions, or distributed throughout cure centers, arranged in the most favorable way...it brings into play a system of options that reveals the way in which a group, in order to protect itself, practises exclusions, establishes the forms of assistance, and reacts to poverty and to the fear of death.[2]

Why does it sometimes seem that HIV prevention and education efforts have not been able to do what they set out to do? The deeper issue, again from the perspective of tertiary spatialization, is that HIV is not a separate, isolated issue. It cannot be seen in isolation from other issues such as the prison industrial complex (in which people of color are grossly disproportionately present), sexism, ableism, heterosexism, sexphobia, racism, and classism, just to name a few. Especially in communities of color, HIV represents an entire complex of issues. We have consistently avoided dealing with these issues, and that is why it often seems that we are back at the starting point. In order to move wisely into the future, the interconnectedness of these issues will have to be constantly addressed. This might mean that we will have to develop much more complex and complicated approaches to prevention, education and health-care, but is there really any other solution?

According to an article entitled, "The Death Penalty: AIDS and Medical Care in California Prisons," the California Department of Corrections held more than 165,000 prisoners in its system as of 1997.[3] It also identifies only 1,500 prisoners with HIV/AIDS. However, according to Judy Greenspan, the chair of the HIV in Prison Committee of California Prison Focus, even the Department of Corrections' own studies conducted with the state Department of Health Services revealed a seroprevalence rate of about 3%, which equals approximately 4,000 HIV-positive prisoners. There are, however, according to Greenspan's findings, approximately 10,000 prisoners living with HIV. Needless to say, they receive absolutely substandard medical care.

Prisoners relate how they are deprived of their HIV medications when prison doctors feel that their attitudes are too negative. One doctor at Corcoran has been known to refuse to give vitamins to an HIV positive prisoner. Furthermore, pain medications are often systematically denied to prisoners of all genders with HIV since it is believed that they are all drug-users. HIV-positive prisoners state that when they are relocated from one prison to another, their medications are stopped when they enter a new prison. This seems to be especially the case when it comes to combination therapies including protease inhibitors; this, of course, creates the context for HIV to develop resistance to these particular medications. Others state that those prisoners who are on combination therapies are often subjected to seven- to fourteen-day prescription delays when they run out of their medications. They are required to request a new prescription every time they have exhausted their supply of medications. This, of course, creates the kind of context that leads to HIV developing drug resistance, as well. Prisoners who try to create hidden supplies of HIV medications so that they will not run out are punished. Four to six week waits to get medical attention are not unusual.

The situation for women prisoners with HIV is even more grim: according to Greenspan, at the Central California Women's Facility, the only on-call physician is a retired pediatrician whose information about HIV/AIDS is limited to what he has learned from the prisoners.[4] Guards with minimal medical training do triage; this means that women prisoners with HIV are often misdiagnosed and opportunistic infections go untreated. Some prisoners die simply because their medical complaints are ignored; they are often sent back from the infirmary with their problem never having been addressed. Women prisoners in California are basically in a system where there is no medical care. At the Central California Women's Facility and the Valley State Prison for Women, the one and only infectious disease physician does not do medical exams. Women hardly ever (if at all) get to see a gynecologist; this is particularly dangerous since many of the HIV-related complications in women impact their uterine system. Being in prison should not mean that one is subjected to substandard health care; being in prison with HIV can become its own death sentence. And the problems are magnified when it comes to issues of transgender prisoners living with HIV.

If the conditions that foster the development of HIV strains that are drug resistant are allowed to persist in prisons, then we are actually facing new forms of the death penalty. And this will have an effect on how HIV will develop in the general population. Foucault, in the above-mentioned work, does point out that in the history of medicine, it was understood (for example, in post-revolutionary France) that the first task of the healer (be that healer religious worker/social worker/cultural worker/healthcare worker) was political: "The struggle against disease must begin with a war against bad government."[5]

We live in a world of fluid constructions of sexualities, desires, and genders, where there are many people who have sex with all genders in varying and dazzling relational configurations. This should shape the ways in which we see the many faces and facets of HIV prevention and education. HIV is not a separate and isolated issue; community development and empowerment are part of HIV prevention and education. HIV cannot be seen in isolation from other issues such as anti-immigration, erotophobia, racism, classism, ableism, ageism, domestic violence, lesbiphobia, biphobia, transphobia, etc. It means that we must move beyond a way of thinking rooted in binary oppositions (either/or thinking) so that we can understand how injectable drug users might also be lesbian/gay/bisexual/transgender/intersex/queer/questioning; where women with HIV also means lesbian/bisexual/transgender/intersex/queer/questioning women; where erotophobia hampers prevention and education strategies by not letting us talk openly about sex (it cost surgeon-general Elders her job[6]). When we talk about HIV in prisons we are not only talking about, but also talking about lesbian/gay/bisexual/transgender/intersex/queer/questioning people in prison, not just situationally, but who went in that way and will come out that way.

HIV-in-intersection provides ways for us to say that boundaries are blurred, that erotophobia, the fear of the power and uses of the erotic, sets us up to be dominated and controlled and kept in neat, monolithic categories. Part of our colonized mentality has made us think that if we deny the centrality of sexuality in our context, in our experiences, in our lives, in our thought, in our creativity, if we trivialize it, then we will be more acceptable.

Erotophobia is rooted in hatred of the body and anything that reminds us of it. So, since this society fears and hates women, it depicts them as temptress/seductress, as the very incarnation of the body, as the very incarnation of the libido, sex, the dirty. So, you cannot separate erotophobia from the fear and hatred of women. Erotophobia and racism intersect in the investment of people of color as the exotic/erotic Other, people who are seen as the very incarnations of the erotic (all women of color considered to be "available") and the libido (and therefore, of evil) and who need, like women, to be dominated because of being dangerous, disease-filled, but inferior.

Erotophobia keeps shame around rape to silence those who are believed to just be asking for "it." Poor people of all colors are to stay controlled because they are too erotic and just "reproduce" for poor people. The propaganda of anti-Muslim, anti-Jewish and anti-Earth-based religions spreads images of Muslims, Jews and practitioners of Earth-based religions as being too erotic and therefore needing to be annihilated. Just as desire is to be policed and women's bodies are to be controlled for profit by men, and people of color controlled by white people (who are pure and virtuous by definition), so is the environment to be controlled.

Instead of acknowledging the ways in which women in the sex industry have taken leadership in teaching and practicing safer sex in the context of commercial sex work, erotophobia perpetuates images of them as carriers and spreaders of disease. Erotophobia keeps us from talking about safer sex in terms that are unmistakably clear, keeps us from distributing dental dams, needles, or condoms; leads us to exclusively advocate abstinence. Yet, at the same time, the marketing industry makes fortunes using sex and pleasure, or at least the illusion of them, to sell everything from underwear to whiskey. This has greatly impeded us from talking about all that goes into our sexualities and the expression of our desires. It has led to a desexualizing of AIDS that sends a double, and definitely negative message, especially to those of us who are lesbian/gay/bisexual/transgender/intersex/queer/questioning people.

The work of creating and fostering the conditions for safer sex goes back much further than just telling people to use condoms. What are the psycho-spiritual conditions of people who have been told that they can only have sex involving latex barriers for the rest of their lives? What about those who, after fifteen years or more of being HIV-positive, decide to have latex-free sex with other HIV-positive persons? How are HIV the@logies present to them?

Erotophobia keeps us from talking about sexualities of young people because they are not supposed to have sex; nor are older people. We never say that we have another way of viewing sexualities and bodies and health and illness because we know that *our bodies* blur the personal/political split. When your body is always on the line, you know that you are transgressing the public/private split by your very existence. When you can be arrested because of your body, skin, color, height, hair (or lack thereof), what's on your skin, perceived health condition, gender expression, clothes (or lack thereof), etc., then you know that your body is political and that it does matter. When the power apparatus of this country expends incredible amounts of time, money, and energy to legislate on controlling and policing our bodies and the ways in which we decide to use them, but does not spend equal amounts of money on housing, feeding, educating, healing, nurturing those very same bodies, then you know that your body is political and that it really does matter. And this brings us back to the primacy of the body and the centrality of our sexualities.

Bodies matter; in the ways in which the dominating culture has organized its meaning and conferred and confirmed identities, we have been led to believe that just rich, white, male, cisgender, heterosexual, temporarily able-bodied bodies matter (or those that resemble them the most closely); that these are the *perfect bodies*, bodies that really matter. But all bodies matter; not numbers, not statistics. *Bodies matter*: not ball-gowned and tuxedoed and academically-attired bodies matter, but just plain old bodies matter.

> Dead bodies matter,
> dying bodies matter,
> infected bodies matter,
> disabled bodies matter,
> decolonizing bodies matter,
> decolonized bodies matter,
> bones-and-braces bodies matter,
> reservation bodies matter,
> wheelchair bodies matter,
> deaf bodies matter,
> blind bodies matter,
> poor bodies matter,
> injectable drug-using bodies matter,
> commercial sex-worker bodies matter,
> ghetto bodies matter,

projects bodies matter,
trailer-park bodies matter,
lesbian/gay/bisexual/transgender/intersex/queer/questioning bodies matter,
FTM bodies matter
MTF bodies matter
genderqueer bodies matter
two-spirit bodies matter
colored bodies matter,
working-class bodies matter,
children's bodies matter,
women's bodies matter,
mental health bodies matter,
imprisoned bodies matter,
mixed heritage bodies matter,
public assistance bodies matter,
addiction bodies matter,
immigrants' bodies matter,
prisoners' bodies matter,
bodies that speak languages other than English matter,
HIV bodies matter,
cervical cancer bodies matter,
breast cancer bodies matter,
changing bodies matter
hypertension bodies matter,
sickle-cell bodies matter,
prostate cancer bodies matter,
diabetes bodies matter,
depression bodies matter,
homeless bodies matter,
refugee bodies matter,
Muslim bodies matter,
Earth's body matters:
Bodies matter,
All bodies matter!

For us, HIV-in-intersection is about recognizing the intersectionality of our very own bodies and minds. We should be able to take cognizance of a rich, variety of possibilities of existence, of wholeness, of life. HIV-in-intersection challenges us to understand that disability does not mean incompleteness; that the tendency to equate disability with tragedy keeps us from struggling together for justice. Disability makes us confront issues of access and accessibility which are issues for all of us, in many differing contexts. Disability makes us address its social aspects such as poverty, class, isolation, alienation, social erasure, marginalization; it makes us understand that bodies are not just flesh-and-bones bodies, but that they are also bones-and-braces bodies, bones-and-wheelchair bodies, deaf bodies, blind bodies. The refusal to address the concerns of people living with disabilities is to reinscribe oppressive notions of the *perfect body* and to perpetuate marginalization, exclusion, discrimination, and annihilation. HIV-in-intersection also forces us to acknowledge the issues of youth with HIV, as well as those of elders with HIV. These people, as well as all others living with HIV, must be allowed to advocate for themselves.

In the years to come, the struggle against HIV must be continually rooted in a war against all those structures that do not facilitate this process of liberation of the whole being. The HIV-in-intersection perspective of our HIV the@logies leads us to acknowledge the following fact: We are fighting for all of our lives. Our bodies do matter.

Why Thanxgrieving?[7]

Every day is Ashura, every place is Karbala: Reflections on Thanxgrieving/Thanksgiving in a time of Ashura.

November 21, 2012 at 4:35pm
Dedicated to the memory of Jon Paul Hammond, Freedom-Fighter July 19, 1960 – November 5, 2010

> "Je dirais que le plus dur n'est peut-être pas de mourir; le plus dur c'est de rester vivant et de se sentir étranger à son propre pays…" ("I would say that dying is not the most difficult thing; I'd say rather that the most difficult thing is living and feeling like a foreigner in one's own country.")[8]—Jean-Marie Tjıbaou, cultural, spiritual and political leader of the Kanak struggle for independence

> "Always depend upon the Creator, not the creation. Love all, serve all, pray for all. Help ever, hurt never."— Hz Moinuddin Chishti, Gharib Nawaz, friend of the destitute, the marginalized, the poor

Those of you who have known us since the 1990s remember the off-the-chizain Thanxgrieving parties that started back in those days in the occupied territory known as the District of Columbia, moving from Brookland to 13th

Street and continued in the land of Tonantzin in Alta California in the Tree House until we left for Morocco in 2005. Someone asked "Why Thanxgrieving?" Why not just leave Thanksgiving as it is?

As a historian of religions/ritual artist/technician of the sacred/guerrilla theologian/cultural studies/gender theorist, etc., I follow closely how ritual practices start, develop, morph, transform, grow, stabilize, gradually disappear, become even larger, etc. An example of ritual developing in response to a particular crisis: the memorial service as now practiced in the US owes its existence to memorial services developed by communities surrounding people who had died from HIV-related complications. Many of those people could not be buried by their spiritual communities of origin because those communities did not want to acknowledge them in life, let alone in death. And some families of origin didn't want to acknowledge them, either. Sometimes, there was no one to bury them.

Some families that did bury their dead didn't want anyone to know that the person had died from HIV-related complications or that they had lived happy lives in a world beyond the borders of heteronormativity. Life-partners were not recognized as chief mourners, life-narratives were re-written, and their artistic creations were destroyed, denying the world their gifts after death. The person who was buried was not the same person who had lived and died in the struggle with HIV.

But people began to come together to create meaningful rituals to celebrate the lives of their beloveds, thereby challenging the hegemony of the funeral industry. They told the narratives as they had experienced the lives, challenging the newspapers who would only print obituaries written in a certain way and would not mention certain things. One learned to be a "Law and Order" medical examiner, piecing together who had died from HIV-related complications on the basis of what little was said in the paper. Little by little, this began to change. If you read obituaries in the *San Francisco Chronicle* today you will see that they are very different from how they were written in the 1990s. The impact of communities taking back their dead and memorializing and commemorating them and not letting them be "disappeared," even in death, soon spread around the US and gave birth to new forms.

Part of ritual is the telling of its history, of its story. And every year as we gathered for Thanxgrieving ritual and celebration, I would tell the story of how we came to say Thanxgrieving instead of Thanksgiving. Not that everyone had to do it, or that we looked askance at others who did not say it, but we just simply explained why we called it what we called it and how we celebrated it.

And, just keeping it real, I know that some people get pretty upset when you mess with their holidays. A few years ago, I forwarded to a friend some emails written by a white anti-racism activist in which he talked about how he was troubled by the intensely racist messages and images of repetitive and divergent languages of "whiteness" in everything surrounding Christmas. I was having one of those years where I was all about building alliances and I had really, personally, had about all I could take of the fake snow, the "white Christmas," and the troubling undercurrents in how "Christmas" was constructed and perceived in certain worlds. I thought that the white anti-racist activist who had written the mails was right on point. The person to whom I sent them chastised me very strongly and never had any more contact with me. So, I know that people don't like having people mess with their holidays. As someone once said (not to me), "You are not going to ruin my vacation!"

In 1995, I had a child and my whole world changed. In a few years, my child was saying "Thanxgrieving" and inviting friends from his Berkeley pre-school to come to his house for Thanxgrieving! And, he wanted to know why we called that day by a different name and even celebrated it on a different day!

Why Thanxgrieving? For years, I had a hard time conceptually giving thanks on a holiday when the major players in the holiday had been massacred and their lands had been invaded and occupied; whoa! How to give thanks for that, dude? I mean, just sit with that for a moment: if you look at it from that perspective, other than commemorating it so that no one would forget what had happened, would you really want to celebrate that day? I'm just saying, looking at it from that perspective, from that place, from that location, from being those people....I mean, I could be grateful to the earth for the blessings bestowed on us; I could thank ar-Razzaq, the Bestower of Sustenance, for the gifts of life, but did I need that one day a year to do it if I strived to do it every day? To make life a multicolored, multitextured, multimedia, multidimensional of *shukr*, of gratitude, of *shukru bil qalb*, gratitude in the heart, wishing the best for all of creation and working for that, expressing gratitude, and using the divinely-given gifts for all of creation? *Shukr*/gratitude, the twin of *sabr*/patience: gratitude and patience in the unfolding of life. That one day was a good reminder though, but how to hold that gratitude in the face of the prison-industrial complex, homelessness, no universal healthcare, abuse and destruction of the earth, denial of First Nations/Native American sovereignty rights, the intersecting oppressions that keep us all from the fulness of life?

Why Thanxgrieving? My partner and I, having lived most of our lives far away from our family of origin, made family of choice with people with whom our lives intersected, with whom we struggled for the transformation of the world. But since we were far from having family of origin holiday obligations, since we were usually on the other side of the world, we were particularly aware of the lives of people who were cut off from their families of origin because those families had decided they no longer belonged. So, since we didn't "have" to do anything with anyone, we decided to raucously sing Rumi's song. We sang to whomever would hear,

> "Come, come whoever you are. Wanderer, worshipper, lover of leaving."[9]
> Vegan, vegetarian, omnivore, pescatarian;
> Non-defined, fluid/non-fluid, poly,
> Post/pre-whatever:
> Come! Come! Ours is no caravan of despair.
> Come, yet again come!

So, we've got a house full of people to overflowing every year, a house of people who sometimes would have had nowhere else to go. Everybody was grateful to be together. And, we had amazing food grounded in attempting to recognize the global implications of our celebrations.

It also became an important time for invoking the presence of ancestors who had died in the preceding year, ancestors fallen in the harshest years of the HIV pandemic at that time. In Roman Catholic tradition, November was already a month for praying for the dead. As good residents of Alta California, we followed the Mexican traditions of Día de los Muertos. By the time we got to the Thanxgrieving celebrations, our memorial tables and altars were already dressed, the orange marigolds in vases, the copal smoke wafting, the white candles in glass whose light reflected on the frames of photos of the ancestors, new and old; the ritual foods on the ancestors' table, this table like the table of Prophet Ibrahim Khalilullah, there to feed all, the peoples of all worlds. "It's the blood of the ancients that runs through our veins. And the forms pass but the circle of life remains."[10] "Those who have gone before us, rise up and call their names!" Blessed water was flying in every direction and we sang and wept and laughed and wondered when and if we would eat. And we laughed...

There were children who grew up with these celebrations and they helped pour the libations and lead the chants and tell the story of Thanxgrieving. and they still talk about it today...

Part of my main purpose in writing "Why Thanxgrieving?" is that doing this is part of my assignment in the world to remember the "forgotten," especially those who lost their lives in the HIV pandemic. Many people whom we knew and loved were radical social transformers, creating revolutionary beauty with every gesture. And, although people talked about them for a few years, as time went by, they were mentioned less and less. It has always been my assignment to keep their memories alive, to keep them present.

My best friend at that time, Craig Gerard Joachim Harris, HIV pioneer, pro-feminist/pro-womanist writer extraordinaire and fellow Vassar alum (Vassar: Represent!) was one of the first to challenge African-descent communities to become educated about HIV and to be communities of inclusion. Craig had just died days before Thanksgiving 1991, and he always threw a legendary feast, long before people were calling themselves "foodies" and blogging about it, he used the phone! That shifted things and added great urgency to how we would "celebrate." Craig had made me promise that I would lead his funeral services and I was terrified at the thought of having to bury my best friend in front of everyone who was anyone in the world of HIV, the arts, activism of every sort. It was bad enough to have to bury my best friend, but with that kind of audience in New York City? So, how to do Thanksgiving? Acknowledging the ancestors was very central to our expressions of gratitude. One of those ancestors is one of the very new ancestors, Jon Paul Hammond, who was the person who gave to me the word Thanxgrieving. I did not invent the word; it came to me from JP and I want that to be known. I want him to be acknowledged as the source of this word, at least as it came to me. This is important to me, because I really dislike when people get erased and other people get credit for their work: it makes me profoundly sad. Let me tell a little bit about the history of how and why we started using the word. Hint: it was during the very bleak years of the HIV pandemic.

I met Jon Paul Hammond at an ACT/UP action in D.C. in fall of 1991. We had friends in common and therefore knew about each other, but we had never met in this world. Since there were not that many dreadlocked men of color visible at ACT/UP actions, we bumped into each other at the end of the day. ACT/UP came to our anarchist house in Brookland—northeast D.C.—before going back to Philly. It was sealed: JP and I were friends, long-lost cousins reunited in our work to allow people to have life and to have it more abundantly. It was clear that we had known each other in the world of the souls, so we had some catching up to do! JP and his partner, Wende Elizabeth Marshall, one of the fiercest theologians whom I had ever met, were soon to become close members of our family; in fact, our families soon overlapped completely. When Craig Harris, may his memory be as a blessing to all generations, died, I had to call JP to tell him and to have someone with whom I could talk about Craig. Craig had died just days before Thanksgiving. How in the world were we going to make it through a holy day meal that afternoon?

We struggled as we prepared our beautiful organic veggies and organic turkey and made Craig's mac and cheese; we worked as though anesthetized.

Zawadi Baba, Rahmatullahi Aleyhi, was weaker and weaker and we were forever getting phone calls about someone or other going to the hospital or almost dying or dying. Here was our dilemma: gratitude for all that ar-Rahman had given us; gratitude for the gifts of our Mother, the Earth. Sorrow for the dead and those dying. Anger at a government's inaction in face of the HIV pandemic, anger at how racism, classism, economic injustice, immigration policies, lack of health care, sexism, prison-industrial complex, militarism, lack of housing, imperialism, erotophobia, disappearing people with disabilities, transphobia, homophobia, continued abuse of First Nations/Native American sovereignty rights, AIDSphobia, aparthAIDS, etc., conspired to make it OK for the most incredible people to die without anyone seeming to really care. And our beloved Zawadi Baba, Rahmatullahi Aleyhi, the original whirling dervish, was dying. Another friend would die shortly after Craig's funeral. And the other ancestors? What about all of those "forgotten" (they were never really forgotten) people who built up the Americas, indigenous people, brown people from all over the earth, poor white people? This was not just a seminar-induced dilemma; this was a real-life problem! How was it spiritually possible to hold these things together?

So, JP and I talked about this and cried and laughed and cried and laughed. We were tempted to just cancel the dinner, but it seems that JP whispered into my ear the word that held it all: Thanxgrieving! We give thanks for our multiple blessings; we express our gratitude for all things and we grieve land stolen from people, not being in right relationship with the earth, living in intersecting oppressions, etc., but we were going to draw strength from the Friends of the Beloved, our ancestors, new and old. We got on the phone and called people and told them the meal was on; it might be a bit subdued since we were in major mourning, with the understanding that we were just entering into a long season of mourning. But we were going to keep on moving because there was civil disobedience to be done, actions to be held, memorial services to perform.

I'll never forget that first Thanxgrieving. We acknowledged the Friends of the Beloved, our ancestors and, in particular our new ancestor, Craig. We ate his food and told his stories and laughed and the phone rang non-stop. And when it was all over, we prepared to go to New York so that I could perform Craig's funeral. Wow. And JP and Wende drove down from Philly to D.C. to be there for what they knew would be a difficult first Thanxgrieving. We made music and danced and JP did his wild-jungle-bird calls. And thus, Thanxgrieving was born.

We were actually able to really celebrate. We received strength from honoring our dead; we experienced deep *gratitude* and in brilliant darkness we experienced profound joy. The Friends of the Beloved are living. The love flowing from and towards the Friends of the Beloved absolutely transformed everything and everyone beyond our wildest imaginations. Acknowledging the ancestors might sound morose and weird to some people, but for us it was accompanied by lots of singing and noise-makers, and water flying in all directions, good smells and an atmosphere of celebration grounded in the pain of separation and loss and the acknowledgement that the "circle of Life remains," as the song says. There's nothing like hearing little children drumming and chanting, "those who have gone before us, rise up and call their names!"

Soon, people were asking already in summer, "Is there going to be a Thanxgrieving celebration in November? I know what I what to bring; I know what I want to do!" It brought healing and joy, wholeness and fun! The celebration became so popular that people were getting upset because they had family obligations and couldn't come and would therefore have to miss it! So, we moved our celebration from Thursday to early Friday afternoon so that everyone could come; sometimes it flowed right into Kabbalat Shabbat!

Why Thanxgrieving? So, once again, people will come together and meditate and celebrate, *Insha'Allah*; let us commit to resist our lives becoming someone else's occupied territories. I would like to return to where we started when we asked Why Thanxgrieving? by sharing these words, written in 1998 by Standing Deer, aka Robert Hugh Wilson, at the time a 65-year-old Choctaw man incarcerated in the "control unit" at Estelle Unit prison in Huntsville, Texas, USA. Standing Deer was a tireless prison activist.[11]

WHAT IS IN YOUR HEART THEY CANNOT TAKE.

DO THEY FORBID YOU TO HAVE A SWEAT LODGE? YOU ARE SITTING IN ONE EVERY DAY. THE ROOF OF YOUR PRISON IS THE SACRED COVERING: THE BARS THE SACRED WILLOW; THE STONE FLOOR IS YOUR MOTHER; THE SACRED ROCKS ARE HEATED IN THE FIRE OF YOUR INDIAN HEART. TAKE THE WATER FROM THE SINK IN YOUR CELL AND POUR IT OVER YOUR HEAD AND YOU SHALL BE PURIFIED.

DO THEY TAKE AWAY YOUR PIPE, YOUR FEATHERS, YOUR MEDICINE, OR YOUR PRIVILEGES? WHO CAN TAKE YOUR POWER? WHO CAN TAKE YOUR DREAM? WHO TAKES YOUR VISIONS? YOUR PIPE IS YOUR SOUL. IT HAS NO FORM. YET, LOOK AT YOUR BROTHER. DO

YOU SEE THE LIVING PIPE? YOU HAVE NO FEATHERS? THEY ARE INVISIBLE. YET WAKAN TANKA KNOWS YOU WEAR THEM AND PRAY WITH THEM. YOUR HOLY MEDICINE IS YOUR TEARS. IT IS GOOD TO CRY LIKE A MAN FOR WISDOM. WHEN YOU SEE YOUR BROTHER CRYING, GO TO HIM AND LICK THE TEARS FROM HIS CHEEKS AND YOU SHALL HAVE MEDICINE. THESE ARE YOUR PRIVILEGES.

YOUR POWER IS TO RESIST THROUGH YOUR WILL. STRENGTHEN YOUR WILL. WITH EVERY TEAR YOU GROW STRONGER BECAUSE THEY FEAR YOUR WILL TO ENDURE. THEY ARE ALREADY DEFEATED BECAUSE THEY ABUSE WHAT THEY CANNOT CONQUER. YOUR LIFE IS THEIR DEFEAT.

Notes

1. Adapted from Ibrahim Abdurrahman Farajajé, "Bodies of Evidence/Atlanta 1998," *Khalvatdaranjuman* (blog), April 17, 2015, https://tmblr.co/Zyys0y1ibyvuM.
2. Michel Foucault, *Birth of a Clinic: An Archaeology of Medical Perception*, trans. A. M. Sheridan, (New York: Routledge, 1989), 15–16.
3. Tim Kingston, "The Death Penalty: AIDS and Medical Care in California Prisons," *San Francisco Frontiers*, Aug 13, 1998.
4. Ibid.
5. Foucault, *Birth of a Clinic*, 38.
6. Jocelyn Elders, Surgeon General of the United States from 1993–1994, was forced to resign from the Clinton administration due to remarks she made about sex education and contraception.
7. Adapted from Ibrahim Abdurrahman Farajajé, "why thanxgrieving?" *Khalvatdaranjuman* (blog), November 26, 2014, https://tmblr.co/Zyys0y1WWJx8d.
8. Jean-Marie Tjibaou, *La Présence Kanak* (Paris: Odile Jacob, 1996), 138.
9. Jalaluddin Rumi, "Come, Come, Whoever You Are," All Poetry. https://allpoetry.com/Come,-Come,-Whoever-You-Are.
10. Charlie Murphy and Jami Sieber (vocalists), "Blood of the Ancients," by Ellen Klaver (lyricist), track 3, on *Canticles of Light* (Serpentine Music), 1997.
11. I was going to work on the language to make it more inclusive, but I felt deeply called to leave it as it is. I am in no way going to alter the voice of an incarcerated First Nations holy person! This poem follows a letter that you can read by going to this link: http://www.nativeweb.org/pages/legal/sdeer-poem.html

References

Farajajé, Ibrahim Abdurrahman. "Bodies of Evidence/Atlanta 1998." *Khalvatdaranjuman* (blog), April 17, 2015. https://tmblr.co/Zyys0y1ibyvuM

———. "why thanxgrieving?" *Khalvatdaranjuman* (blog). November 26, 2014. https://tmblr.co/Zyys0y1WWJx8d

Foucault, Michel. *Birth of a Clinic: An Archaeology of Medical Perception*, translated by A. M. Sheridan. New York: Routledge, 1989.

Kingston, Tim. "The Death Penalty: AIDS and Medical Care in California Prisons." *San Francisco Frontiers*, Aug 13, 1998.

Murphy, Charlie and Jami Sieber, vocalists. *Canticles of Light*. Serpentine Music, 1997.

Rumi, Jalaluddin. "Come, Come, Whoever You Are." All Poetry. https://allpoetry.com/Come,-Come,-Whoever-You-Are

Standing Deer (Robert Hugh Wilson). "What Is In your Heart They Cannot Take." February 1998. http://www.nativeweb.org/pages/legal/sdeer-poem.html

Tjibaou, Jean-Marie. *La Présence Kanak*. Paris: Odile Jacob, 1996.

About the Author

Ibrahim Abdurrahman Farajajé was a scholar, activist, queer theologian, artist, and Sufi spiritual leader. He received his bachelor's degree in religion at Vassar and went on to earn an M.Div. from St. Vladimir's Eastern Orthodox Seminary in New York. Following this, Farajajé, then known as Elias Farajajé-Jones, earned his doctorate in theology from the University of Bern in Switzerland. Throughout his life, Farajajé was a prominent HIV/AIDS activist. Among his notable work, Farajajé published *In Search of Zion: The Spiritual Significance of Africa in Black Religious Movements* in 1990. He taught for ten years at Howard University School of Divinity and then joined the Starr King School for the Ministry where he remained for twenty-one years. He was fondly known as "Ibrahim Baba" and was the provost and a professor of cultural and Islamic Studies when he passed away in 2016.

11 Moayyad

Shiraz Abdullahi Gallab

I remember first meeting Moayyad when I was eight years old. He must have been eleven or twelve, close to my sister's age probably. He had a raspy voice and an infectious laugh back then, and he was always eager to speak with me and my siblings in English. Moayyad's English was impressive. Most of my other cousins only knew how to ask, "how are you?" and respond, "fine, thank you," but Moayyad held lengthy conversations with us. He was one of the few cousins I spoke to in English exclusively, even after learning Arabic and speaking it every day, and I think we both preferred this.

We always spoke to each other in English, but Moayyad taught me things about myself that I couldn't properly access in America. He helped me understand Sudanese customs and traditions that aren't valued or even recognized in the West: how and why we gather around communal and congregational spaces, engage in regular prayer, and serve tea so often throughout the day. In exchange, I shared insights on American pop culture, fast food, and other things that feel frivolous now.

Moayyad and I translated ourselves with a shared interest in learning something new and bridging our differences, which, in hindsight, weren't that different from each other. And as I look back and reflect, I don't think I've known anyone with Moayyad's courage and curiosity. Just by talking to me and making himself available with consistency, he made me feel like anything was possible … like the connections we built were something to be cherished and sustained and honored with each new conversation, like this perpetual honoring could lead to virtually anything we envisioned for ourselves. I didn't always understand this as a little kid, because I was shy and socially awkward, and because I grew up in a country where people are expected to function in isolation. But I think I understand now.

Moayyad Ibrahim Mohammad Musa passed away in late July of 2023. He was stuck in Halfa, a city nestled at the border between Egypt and Sudan, where he spent three months waiting for visa clearance to enter Egypt. He spent three months desperately trying to escape the bloody conflict between our country's military and paramilitary forces. He spent three months telling his parents, siblings, and relatives that he'd see them soon, and alhamdulillah, he is doing fine. Like many others who are still waiting at the border, Moayyad slept on hot floors in masjids and relied on strangers for food and basic necessities. He most definitely was not alone, but I'm sure he felt isolated.

Sudanese relationships tend to hinge on an interdependent framework that falls apart when separation and siloes are made apparent, or even implied, in a dynamic. We don't do well on our own; we're much better off when we can call on folks to lend a hand or simply listen to us when we need to talk. My parents and I keep asking ourselves if we could have done something to protect Moayyad from feeling so isolated, and while it may not be healthy to indulge in this line of questioning, I can't stop myself from posing, asking, wondering.

Moayyad, if I could turn back time, I'd be there with you and reassure you that you aren't alone. I'd ask your parents and mine about alternatives and insist that we take a bus to Port Sudan, because I've never been. I'd distract you from your legitimate frustrations by playing up my American traits, which have always been a source of entertainment for you. I'd ask you about your goals and dreams. I'd ask about your favorite song. If I could turn back time, Moayyad, I'd tear down this wall that is both impenetrable and suffocating and make it known that you aren't alone, just as you did for me.

About the Author

Shiraz Abdullahi Gallab is a designer, educator, and publisher who was born but not raised in Khartoum, Sudan. She is interested in language, form, and specificity, alongside media, Black studies, and popular culture. Shiraz holds a BA in Public Policy Studies from the University of Chicago and an MFA in 2D Design from Cranbrook Academy of Art. She has taught and lectured at California College of the Arts, Virginia Commonwealth University, Yale School of Art, Purchase College, Otis College of Art and Design, Rhode Island School of Design, Rutgers University, and the University of Illinois at Chicago. Her work has been featured in *IDEA Magazine*, *Amalgam*, *Spine Magazine*, and *AIGA Eye on Design*, and in 2022, she contributed an essay to Geoff Kaplan's *After the Bauhaus, Before the Internet: A History of Graphic Design Pedagogy*. Shiraz is a book design and production specialist at the University of Michigan Press, where she designs books on subjects that include political science, music and performance, disability studies, sexuality studies, and poetry.

Index

Abduh, Muhammed, 54, 58, 62
ableism, 179, 180, 182
abolitionism, 178, 179
Abu Bakra, 67
activism, 3, 4, 6, 14, 16, 22, 25, 26, 52, 53, 54, 60, 65, 69, 161, 172, 173, 174, 177, 178, 179, 188, 190, 192
Adam, 35–36
Aflatun, Inge, 64
Africa, 13, 23–24, 53, 150, 151
ageism, 182
Ahmed, Leila, 57–59, 60, 62
'Aisha (wife of the Prophet), 67
Alfonso X, king of Castile, 35
Allison, Dorothy, 20
alterity, ethics of, 5, 77–78, 79, 80, 81, 83–84, 126–27
Amin, Qasim, 54–60, 62
ancestors, 13, 14, 20, 157, 160, 189, 190, 191, 192
anthropocentrism, 77, 83
anti-Semitism, 136, 146, 147
Anzaldua, Gloria, 15–16
Al-Aqsa Intifada, 135
Arab Feminist Union (AFU), 52, 61, 62
Arendt, Hannah, 5, 108–109, 110, 111, 127–34, 137
Aristotle, 94
Arora, Alka, 15
al-'Asqalani, Ibn Hajar, 67
animism, 84
atheism, 77

Baca Zinn, Maxine, 162
Badawi, Abdel-Rahman, 99–100
Baghdad, 92, 97
Baker-Fletcher, Karen, 162
al-Banna, Hasan, 62
Baring, Evelyn, earl of Cromer, 55, 58–59
al-Bashir, Omar, 2

Batinites, 95
beauty, standards of, 3, 17, 22
Beauvoir, Simone de, 77, 78
Berry, Thomas, 80
biphobia, 182
al-Bistami, Bayazid, 5, 91, 92, 98, 99, 100
Bjerre, Poul, 117
Bloom, Allan, 145
Bodhisattva Vow, 25
Borbon, Angelita, 18
Borel, Henri, 117
boycotts, 24
Buber, Martin, 5, 108, 109, 110, 111, 117–23, 125, 126, 127, 129, 131, 137
Buddhism, 25, 32, 81, 147, 151, 169
al-Bukhari, 66, 67, 68
Butch (identity), 17, 47
Butler, Judith, 172

Casey, Edward, 5, 83
childbirth, 23
Christianity, 20, 24, 59, 63, 79, 84, 112, 117, 144, 146, 147, 148, 151, 169, 180
Chrystos, 178
cis-gender, 17, 159, 179, 184
civil rights movement, 164
classism, 78, 150, 162, 179, 180, 182, 191
climate change, 2, 80, 82, 83, 84, 164–65
climate weirding, 159
Collins, Patricia Hill, 160, 162
colonialism, 24, 58–60, 61, 79
colonization, 2, 24, 25, 79, 80, 81, 182
Combahee River Collective, 161
companion species, 80, 81, 82
complementarity, 24
condoms, 183
contemplation, 25
Crenshaw, Kimberlé, 6, 160, 161, 162

Dalit people, 20

Dante Alighieri, 58
Darfur, Sudan, 3
Davis, Angela, 161
Davis, Doris, 20
decolonization, 16, 184
deconstruction, 77, 82, 179
deities, 13, 19, 21
Derrida, Jacques, 5, 77, 80, 83–84
Dewey, John, 144
Día de los Muertos, 189
dialectic, 111
Din, 40, 42, 47, 48
disability, 7, 16, 17, 19, 179, 184, 185–86, 191, 196
'divinanimality', 80
divorce, 20, 58, 61, 69
domestic violence, 182
domination, logic of, 78–79, 82, 144, 150

'Earth Others', 5, 79, 84
eco-deconstruction, 5
ecophenomenology, 5, 77, 83
ecofeminism, 5, 77, 78, 79, 149, 150
ecology, 5, 7, 23, 24, 77–84, 145, 146, 147, 149, 150, 152, 160
ecophilosophy, 5
education, 6, 55–56, 58, 59, 60, 61, 62, 64, 93, 159, 180, 181, 182, 184
 value-free, 143–52
Egeria, 148
Egypt, 4, 52–64, 65, 68, 69–70, 201
Egyptian Feminist Union (EFU), 52, 60, 62
Elders, Joycelyn, 182
empiricism, 119, 143, 144–45, 152
epistemology, 112, 122, 157, 164, 165
equity, 24
erotophobia, 179, 182–83, 184, 191
Euro-centrism, 16
existentialism, 112, 115

fana, 92
al-Farabi, 94, 95
al-Faruqi, Lois Lamya', 53
Feminine, Divine, 3, 16–17, 19
'feminist, divine', 3–4, 15–16, 19, 22
Femininity, 34, 41, 42, 78, 82

feminism, 3–4, 7, 8, 20, 22–23, 24, 77–79, 82, 147, 149, 150–51, 173, 190
 Arab, 52, 54, 55, 58, 61, 63
 Black, 22, 161
 intersectional, 162, 163
 Islamic, 4, 1, 52–70
 Islamist, 4, 62–63, 64, 65, 68–69, 70
 Jewish, 1, 33
 multiracial, 161, 162
 secular, 4, 63, 64, 70
 see also 'feminist, divine'; ecofeminism; theology, feminist
Femme (identity), 47
First Nations people, 25, 26, 177, 178, 188, 191, see also Indigenous people; Native Americans
flourishing, 6, 57, 157, 158, 165
Foo, Lora Jo, 20
Foucault, Michel, 180, 182
Four Directions, the, 18, 177
Freedman, Maurice, 117
fundamentalism, 20, 62–64, 65

Gandhi, M. K., 136
gardens, 13, 22, 97
gay bars, 6–7, 170–75
gender, 1, 4, 5, 6, 16, 20, 22, 24, 25, 33, 34, 37, 38–39, 41, 42, 46, 47, 61, 63, 64, 78, 80, 159, 160, 162, 164, 177, 178, 179, 181, 184
genderqueer, 17, 185
genocide, 3, 79, 127, 130, 134
Germany, 8, 127
Gevurah, 34, 38, 40, 41, 42, 43, 47, 48
al-Ghazali, Abu Hamid, 5, 97–102
al-Ghazali, Zeinab, 62–63, 65, 68, 69
Gikatilla, Joseph, 36–37, 38, 39–40, 41, 42
Goddess, the, 15, 16, 17, 24
Godhead, 33, 36
grammar, 113–14, 122
Gregory of Nyssa, 148
Grim, John, 80
Gutkind, Eric, 117

Hadith, 65–68
al-Hallaj, Mansur Ibn, 5, 91–92, 98, 99, 100, 101

Hammond, Jon Paul, 7, 186, 190–91
Haraway, Donna, 80, 81, 82
Harb, Tal'at, 56, 59
Harjo, Joy, 17
Harris, Craig Gerard Joachim, 190
Hassidism, 118
hate crimes, 2
healers, 14, 18, 19–20, 22, 25, 94, 180, 182, 184, 192
Hechler, William, 118
Heidegger, Martin, 124, 127
Herzl, Theodor, 118
Hesed, 34, 39–41, 43
heterosexism, 179, 180, 184
hijab, 56–57, see also veiling
Hinduism, 20, 147
HIV/AIDS, 177–93
    HIV-in-intersection, 7, 179, 182, 185–86
Hokmah, 34, 38, 40
Holocaust (Shoah), 8, 127, 134, 135, 136
hooks, bell, 162
Husserl, Edmund, 112, 124

Ibn Ahmed, Ruwaym, 97
Ibn Anas, Malik, 67
Ibn Sina, 94, 95
Ibo people, 23
Idemili (goddess), 24
identity politics, 159
IDF (Israeli Defence Force), 135, 136
iman, 93
immanence, 111, 118, 120, 127, 132
inclusivity, 5, 15, 16, 22, 163
Indigenous people, 2, 4, 13, 15, 16, 17–18, 19, 22, 25–26, 56, 59, 69, 78, 81, 161, 180
industrialization, 53, 180
infanticide, female, 52
inter-faith dialogue, 1, 117, 151, 157
intersectionality, 6, 78, 157, 158, 178–79, 182, 185, 186
    application to religious studies, 160–65
Irigaray, Luce, 82
Islam, 1, 4, 24, 93, 95, 102, 147
    feminism in, 52–70, 151

Shi'ite, 93
Sunni, 91, 92, 102
Israel, State of, 135, 136, 137, 138, 146, 147, 164

Jahiliyya, 68, 69
Jainism, 83, 151
Jaspers, Karl, 127
Jerome, 148–49
Jonas, Regina, 1
Judaism, 1, 119, 136, 147
Julian of Norwich, 149
al-Junayd, Abdul Qasim, 92, 96, 97, 99

Kabbalah, 4, 33–47
Kader, Soha 'Abdel, 53, 57
al-Kalabadhi, Abu Bakr, 96
Kalam, 94
Kant, Emmanuel, 112, 144
Khalilullah, Ibrahim, 189
Khuri, Richard, 93, 94

Lady Gaga, 170
Landauer, Gustav, 117
language, 6, 18, 61, 81, 109, 113, 118, 123
lesbians, 20, 47, 172, 174, 178, 179, 182, 183, 185
Levinas, Emmanuel, 5, 77, 83, 108, 109, 110, 111–12, 114, 123, 124–27, 129, 130–31, 134, 137
LGBTQIA+ people, 2, 6–7, 159, 170, 172, 173, 174
liberation, 17
    gay, 173
    women's, 22, 25, 54–55, 59, 59, 60, 63, 66, 69
Liberation Theology, 146, 147, 163
Lithuania, 124

Macrina, 148
Malchut, 4, 33, 41, 42
Marxism, 63, 161
masculinity, 33–34, 38, 39, 41, 42, 46, 47
Matristics, 148, 150
medicine, 62, 182
Meir, Golda, 136
Mernissi, Fatima, 65–68, 70

mestiza, 15, 16
#MeToo movement, 160
misogyny, 52, 59, 62, 65, 66
mitzvoth, 35, 40
modernity, 52, 53
Montanists, 148
Morton, Timothy, 5, 77, 80, 81, 82, 84
Moses de Leon, 35
mothers, Yoruba, 23
Muhammed, Prophet, 61, 65, 66
Musa, Moayyad Ibrahim Mohammad, 195–96
Muslim Brotherhood (Egypt), 63, 64, 68
mysticism, 35, 91–94, 98, 99, 102, 118, 119, 120, 122

Nahda, 54, 63
nakedness, 23, 129
Nassef, Hifni Bey, 62
Nassef, Malak Hifni, 60, 61–62, 65
Nasser, Gamal Abdel, 64
natality, 128–29, 130, 132, 134
Native Americans, 79, 188, 191
al-Nawawi, 101
Nazism, 127, 129, 130, 134
Neo-Platonism, 95
nepantlera, 15
Nicaragua, 164
Nnobi people, 24
nonhuman others, 77, 78, 79, 80, 82
Norlind, Theodor Gustav, 117

Obama, Barack, 172
ontology, 112, 122, 124, 129
Orlando massacre (Pulse nightclub massacre) (2016), 6–7, 170–75

Paganism, 24, 79, 176
Palestine, 63, 127, 134–38, 146, 147, 164
patriarchy, 16, 23, 24, 54, 78, 79, 80, 82, 148
  internalized, 78
phenomenology, 77, 83, see also eco-phenomenology
Plato, 94
Plumwood, Val, 5, 79
polygamy, 58, 61

postcolonial theory, 77, 161
postsecular, the, 84
prisoners, 178, 180, 181–82, 185, 188, 191, 192
privilege, 6, 93, 148, 157, 159, 163, 179, 180
privilege blindness, 157

Qazim, Safinaz, 65, 68–69
queer theory, 81
queerness, 4, 7, 47, 172, 173–74, 178, 182, 183, 185
quilts, 13
Qur'an, the (Koran), 4, 20, 52, 56, 57, 61, 63, 65, 66, 67, 68, 98, 101

racism, 3, 78, 150, 159, 162, 179, 180, 182, 183, 188, 191
Rahel-Freund, Else, 114
Rahman, Fazlur, 92, 102
Rang, Florens Christian, 117, 118
rape, 3, 20, 173, 183
reciprocity, 18, 114, 124
Reformation, 149
reproductive rights, 180
Rosenstock-Huessy, Eugen, 112, 117
Rosenzweig, Franz, 5, 108–17, 118–21, 119, 122–23, 124–27, 129, 131–34, 137
Ruether, Rosemary Radford, 3, 6, 163–64

Sa'id, Edward, 58
sacredness, 7, 15, 17, 18–19, 21, 25, 35, 68, 77, 84, 172, 173, 187, 192
sacrifice, 44–45, 121
Sadat, Anwar, 64
al-Sarraj, Abu Nasr, 96–97
Saucedo-Martinez, Concha, 18
Saudi Arabia, 2
Scholem, Gershom, 129, 130
scientific method, 143, 145
Second World War, see World War II
secularism, 1, 4, 35, 52, 61, 64
sefirot, 34–35, 36, 38, 39–41, 43–44, 45, 46, 47
segregation, 54, 58, 162
semen, 38

sexism, 21, 22, 24, 61, 78, 146, 147, 151, 159, 162, 179, 180, 191
sexuality, 6, 63, 78, 160, 174, 178–79, 182–84, 196
Sha'are Orah (Gates of Light), 4, 33, 35, 36–37, 38, 39, 41, 42, 43, 44, 46, 47
Shafiq, Doria, 61
Sha'rawi, Huda, 52, 60, 61–62, 65
Shari'a, 55–56, 57, 61, 92, 102
Sharon, Ariel, 135, 136
Shatahat, 5, 91, 98, 99, 100, 102
Shekhinah, 4, 33–47
Shibli, 97
Sikhism, 151
sitra ahara, 34
slavery, 20, 61, 80, 159, 178, 180
  sexual, 20
Smith, Barbara, 161
social media, 6, 7, 159, 170, 174
social justice, 3, 4, 25, 26, 169
Socrates, 115
solidarity, 3, 6, 7, 157–58, 160, 162, 163–65, 172, 173, 174
song, 13, 24, 189, 196
South Africa, 164
speciesism, 78
'speech-thinking', 110, 111, 112–13, 114, 115–17, 118, 121, 122, 124, 125, 132
spirits, 13, 22
spirituality, 3, 4, 16, 20, 25, 26, 179
Sprachendenken, 110, 112, 124
Standing Deer, 192
'star-seeing', 120
Stein, Edith, 1
Stonewall riots, 170, 172, 173, 175
Sudan, 1, 2–3, 7, 195–96
Sufism, 1, 5, 91–102
Sunnah, 56, 57
surprise, 5, 6, 109, 110–11, 116, 121, 126, 130–31, 133–34, 138
sustainability, 150, 152
Swimme, Brian Thomas, 80
symbolism, 34, 38, 46, 64, 119, 120

al-Tahtawi, Rifa'ah Ra', 58
Teilhard de Chardin, Pierre, 80
Teish, Luisah, 14–15

testosterone, 79
Tetragrammaton, 36
Thanksgiving, 7, 186, 187, 190
'Thanxgrieving', 7, 186–92
the@ologies, 7, 177–78, 183, 186
theology, feminist, 4, 7, 33, 147, 149, 150–51
theism, 95
Thornton Dill, Bonnie, 162
Tif'eret, 34, 35–36, 38, 39, 41, 43, 44, 45, 46
tikkun olam, 25
Torah, 34, 35, 36–37
totalitarianism, 127, 130
totality, 56, 110
transcendence, 110, 111
transdisciplinarity, 16
transgender people, 39, 42, 44, 182, 183, 185
transphobia, 182, 191
transvestism, 34, 42, 44
tribalism, 22
Trump administration, 2, 158
Truth, Sojourner, 161, 178–79
Tucker, Mary Evelyn, 80

Ukraine, 124
'Umar Ibn al-Khattab, Caliph, 67
uterus, 37–38, 41, 46
value-free education, see under education
Van Eeden, Frederik, 117
Vasconcelos, Jose, 15
veiling, 54, 56, 58, 59, 60, 62, 64, see also hijab
Viet Nam War, 25

Wadud, Amina, 20, 70
Walker, Alice, 13, 22, 26
Warren, Karen, 5, 78, 79
Watt, W. Montgomery, 92, 99–100, 101–102
Westernization, 52, 57, 62, 64
Wolfskehl, Karl, 5, 108, 109–10, 117, 120, 131, 134
womanism, 7, 22, 161, 162, 163, 178, 190
Women's Caucus of the American Academy of Religion, 157–60
World War I, 5, 108, 117, 126

World War II, 5, 63, 108, 124, 126

Yemen, 2
Yesod, 34, 38, 39, 40, 41, 43, 48
Yoruba religion, 20–23

al-Zayat, Latifa, 64
Zionism, 63
Zohar (Book of Splendor), 4, 33, 34, 35–36, 37, 38, 39, 42–45, 46–47

www.ingramcontent.com/pod-product-compliance
Lightning Source LLC
Chambersburg PA
CBHW062037220426
43662CB00010B/1541